Modern Web Performance Optimization

Methods, Tools, and Patterns to Speed Up Digital Platforms

Shailesh Kumar Shivakumar

Apress®

Modern Web Performance Optimization: Methods, Tools, and Patterns to Speed Up Digital Platforms

Shailesh Kumar Shivakumar
Bengaluru, India

ISBN-13 (pbk): 978-1-4842-6527-7   ISBN-13 (electronic): 978-1-4842-6528-4
https://doi.org/10.1007/978-1-4842-6528-4

Copyright © 2020 by Shailesh Kumar Shivakumar

This work is subject to copyright. All rights are reserved by the Publisher, whether the whole or part of the material is concerned, specifically the rights of translation, reprinting, reuse of illustrations, recitation, broadcasting, reproduction on microfilms or in any other physical way, and transmission or information storage and retrieval, electronic adaptation, computer software, or by similar or dissimilar methodology now known or hereafter developed.

Trademarked names, logos, and images may appear in this book. Rather than use a trademark symbol with every occurrence of a trademarked name, logo, or image we use the names, logos, and images only in an editorial fashion and to the benefit of the trademark owner, with no intention of infringement of the trademark.

The use in this publication of trade names, trademarks, service marks, and similar terms, even if they are not identified as such, is not to be taken as an expression of opinion as to whether or not they are subject to proprietary rights.

While the advice and information in this book are believed to be true and accurate at the date of publication, neither the authors nor the editors nor the publisher can accept any legal responsibility for any errors or omissions that may be made. The publisher makes no warranty, express or implied, with respect to the material contained herein.

Managing Director, Apress Media LLC: Welmoed Spahr
Acquisitions Editor: Shiva Ramachandran
Development Editor: Rita Fernando
Coordinating Editor: Rita Fernando

Cover designed by eStudioCalamar

Cover image designed by Freepik (www.freepik.com)

Distributed to the book trade worldwide by Springer Science+Business Media New York, 1 New York Plaza, New York, NY 10004. Phone 1-800-SPRINGER, fax (201) 348-4505, e-mail orders-ny@springer-sbm.com, or visit www.springeronline.com. Apress Media, LLC is a California LLC and the sole member (owner) is Springer Science + Business Media Finance Inc (SSBM Finance Inc). SSBM Finance Inc is a **Delaware** corporation.

For information on translations, please e-mail booktranslations@springernature.com; for reprint, paperback, or audio rights, please e-mail bookpermissions@springernature.com.

Apress titles may be purchased in bulk for academic, corporate, or promotional use. eBook versions and licenses are also available for most titles. For more information, reference our Print and eBook Bulk Sales web page at http://www.apress.com/bulk-sales.

Any source code or other supplementary material referenced by the author in this book is available to readers on GitHub via the book's product page, located at www.apress.com/9781484265277. For more detailed information, please visit http://www.apress.com/source-code.

Printed on acid-free paper

I would like to dedicate this book to whom I owe more than I can ever repay and those who have immensely blessed me.

My parents, Shivakumara Setty V and Anasuya T M, for their unending love and strength

My wife, Chaitra Prabhudeva, and my son, Shishir, for their unwavering patience and time.

My in-laws, Prabhudeva T M and Krishnaveni B, from for their unconditional warmth and support.

All my school teachers, who bestowed lots of love and knowledge upon me.

Table of Contents

About the Author xix

Acknowledgments xxi

Introduction xxiii

Part I: Introduction to Web Performance Optimization 1

Chapter 1: Getting Started with Web Performance Optimization 3

Web Performance Optimization (WPO) 3

Web Performance Optimization Dimensions 6

Web Performance Optimizations at Various Lifecycle Stages 8

    Web Performance During Project Architecture Phase 8

    Web Performance-Based Project Design Phase 10

    Performance-Based Development 12

    Performance Testing 13

    Performance Maintenance 13

Web Performance Governance Concepts 13

    Definition of Performance SLAs 13

    Performance Metrics and KPIs 13

    Web Page Metrics 14

    Performance Monitoring 16

Web Performance Optimizations at Various Layers 16

    Web Performance Optimization End-To-End Flow 16

    Performance Optimization at the User-Agent Layer 18

    Performance Optimization at the Content Delivery Network (CDN) Layer 18

    Taxonomy of Performance Optimization at the Web Server and Proxy Server Layer 18

    Taxonomy of Performance Optimization at the Application Server Layer 20

TABLE OF CONTENTS

    Performance Optimization at the Database Server Layer 21

    Performance Optimization at the Enterprise Interface Layer 21

    Performance Optimization at the File Storage Server Layer 22

    Taxonomy of Performance Optimization at the Content Management
    Server (CMS) Layer 22

    Taxonomy of Performance Optimization at the Infrastructure Layer 23

  Summary 25

Chapter 2: General Web Performance Optimization Methods 27

  Survey of Tools and Methods for Performance Optimization of Web Components 28

    Survey of Tools Used in the Web Performance Optimization of Various
    Web Components 28

    Survey of Web Performance Optimization Methods 34

  Performance Bottlenecks and Web Performance Patterns at Various Layers 37

  Survey of Predominant Web Performance Optimization Techniques 38

    Caching and Prefetching 39

    Cache Architecture 39

    Performance Optimization of Content and Assets Through Prefetching 41

  Content Chunking 43

  Network and Request Processing Pipeline Optimization 44

    DNS Lookup Time and Connection Time Optimization 44

    Time to First Byte (TTFB) Optimization 44

  Web Performance Optimization Considerations 44

    Mobile Web Performance Optimization 44

    End-to-End Performance Monitoring Methods and Tools 45

    Cloud-Based Performance Optimizations 45

    Analyzing and Debugging End-to-End Performance Issues 45

    Performance Metrics and Measurement 45

  Design for Performance 45

  Summary 46

TABLE OF CONTENTS

Part II: Modern Web Optimization 47

Chapter 3: Web Performance Optimization Framework 49

Web Performance Reference Architecture 50

Web Performance Optimization Framework 52

    Performance-Based Design 54

    Performance-Based Development 59

    Web Performance Bottlenecks and Web Performance Antipatterns 62

    Web Performance Testing 69

    Web Performance Monitoring 71

    Web Performance Governance 73

Proposed Web Performance Maturity Model 76

Summary 78

Chapter 4: Mobile Web Performance Optimization 79

Mobile Web Framework 80

Performance Optimization of Angular Framework 81

    Design-Related Performance Optimizations 81

    Network-level Performance Optimizations 83

    Runtime Performance Optimizations 84

Performance Optimization of the React Framework 86

    Design-Related Performance Optimizations 86

    Network-Level Performance Optimizations 90

    Runtime Performance Optimizations 90

Common Performance Optimizations for JavaScript Frameworks 91

    Content Compression 91

    Leverage CDN for Resources 92

    Web Worker 92

    Server-Side Rendering 92

    Progressive Web App (PWA) 93

    Caching 93

    Image Optimization 93

vii

TABLE OF CONTENTS

    Video Optimization...94

    Leverage Resource Hints..94

    Font Optimization..94

    Content Streaming..95

    Migration to HTTP/2..95

    Search Engine Optimization (SEO)..95

    Profiling 96

    Optimizing the Critical Rendering Path..96

    Static Site Generators...97

    Network-Level Performance Optimizations...97

  HTML5 Performance Optimizations 100

    Hardware Acceleration 101

    Native Multimedia Support...101

    Offline Storage..101

    Lazy Initialization..101

    Element Attributes 101

  Summary..102

Chapter 5: Modern Web Platform Performance Principles.......................105

  Overview 105

  Traditional Web vs. Modern Web..106

  Modern Web Design..107

    Drivers for Modern Web Design..107

    The Key Capabilities of a Modern Web Platform 110

    The Building Blocks of a Modern Web Platform 112

    The Business Imperatives of a Modern Web Platform..............................113

  Reference Architecture: React-based Modern Web Application.....................116

  Reference Architecture: Angular-based Modern Web Application..................118

    The Flow of Angular Solution Components...119

  Realization of Modern Web Solution Tenets 121

  Modern Web Platform Governance 125

    Modern Web Platform Development Tools..125

viii

DevOps for Modern Web Platforms	127
Governance Metrics	132
Progressive Web Apps (PWA)	134
Performance Optimization of Modern Web Apps	134
Design Best Practices for Modern Web Applications	134
Modern Web Key Design Principles	136
Modern Web Integration Design Principles	138
Summary	142

Part III: Performance Validation and Infrastructure 145

Chapter 6: Web Performance Validation 147

What Is Web Performance Validation?	147
Trends in Web Performance Testing	149
Types of Web Performance Testing	150
Key Performance Testing Metrics	151
Common Performance Issues Across Tiers	152
Approach to Web Performance Validation	153
Prerequisites for Web Performance Testing	153
Web Performance Testing Phases	156
Web Performance Prediction Model	159
Web Performance Testing Tools	160
Mobile App Performance Validation	161
Workload Modeling	164
Prerequisites for Workload Modeling	164
Process of Workload Modeling	164
Sample Workload Model Template	167
Web Performance Test Methodology	167
Continuous Performance Testing	169
Performance Testing Maturity Model	171
Summary	173

TABLE OF CONTENTS

Chapter 7: Web Performance Monitoring and Infrastructure Planning 175

Performance Monitoring Metrics 176

Service Metrics 176

System Metrics 179

Server Metrics 180

Business Metrics 181

Web Application Performance Metrics 183

Building Performance Monitoring Ecosystem 183

Performance Monitoring Tools and Frameworks 183

Performance Monitoring Best Practices 186

Application Performance Monitoring (APM) 192

Server Health Check Monitoring Setup 193

Real-Time Performance Monitoring Setup 194

Real User Monitoring (RUM) 195

Infrastructure Planning for Performance 196

Non-Functional Requirements (NFR) 196

Infrastructure Planning Process 201

Initial Infrastructure Sizing Process 202

Disaster Recovery (DR) Strategy 204

Proactive Robust Monitoring and Alerting Setup 205

Container Pod Monitoring 208

Log Monitoring 209

Database Monitoring 209

Application Monitoring 209

Alerts and Notification 209

CICD Setup 209

Summary 210

Part IV: Performance Case Studies 213

Chapter 8: Web Performance Optimization Case Study 215

Case Study Background 215

High-Level Architecture 216

Key Solution Components	218
Core Performance Challenges	218
Web Performance Assessment Approach	219
Performance Assessment Scope	219
Performance Assessment Exercise Approach	220
Performance Assessment Checklist	221
Web Performance Assessment Exercise	223
Performance Tools for Performance Assessment	223
Performance Assessment of Presentation Layer	225
Performance Assessment of Server Layer	226
Web Performance Optimization Recommendations	226
Performance Improvement Recommendations for the Presentation Layer	226
Server-Layer Performance Improvement Recommendations	231
Recommended Tools for Performance Optimization	234
Performance-related Design Recommendations	234
Proposal for Early Warning System (EWS)	234
Design recommendations for Server-side Components	238
Architecture and Design Recommendations	238
Summary	242

Chapter 9: Performance Engineering Case Study 243

Performance Engineering Overview	243
Performance Engineering Process	244
Requirements and KPI Definition	244
Performance Test Strategy and Design	244
Iterative Performance Test Execution	245
Performance Analysis and Recommendation	245
Performance Engineering Report	245
A Brief Overview of the Application	246
High-Level Flow	246
Technology Ecosystem	246

TABLE OF CONTENTS

Web Performance Analysis 247
    Web Frameworks and JavaScript Framework 247
    Page Load Times and Page Size Analysis for Key Pages 247
    Presentation Component Analysis 248
    Web Analytics Report Analysis 248
    Business Components Performance Analysis 249
    Service Performance Analysis 249
    Database Performance Analysis 250

Infrastructure Analysis 250
    AS-IS Capacity and Network Analysis 250
    Server Configuration Analysis 251
    Cache Configuration Analysis 251
    Infrastructure Recommendations 251

Performance Testing 252
    Performance Testing Tools 252
    Performance Test Setup and Execution 252

Performance Bottleneck Analysis and Problem Patterns 256
    Bottleneck Analysis 257
    Availability Analysis 257
    Common Performance Problem Pattern 257

Performance Optimization Recommendations 259
    Web Performance Optimization Recommendations 259
    Server-side Performance Optimization (Services and Database) 260

Performance Roadmap 263
    Short-Term Plan (30 Days) 263
    Medium-Term Plan (60 Days) 264
    Long-Term Plan (>60 Days) 264

Summary 269

TABLE OF CONTENTS

Part V: Performance Patterns 271

Chapter 10: Modern Web Performance Patterns 273

Presentation Patterns and Best Practices.. 274

    Common Performance Antipatterns 274

    Common Presentation Patterns... 275

    Presentation Layer Best Practices... 277

Progressive Web Architecture (PWA) Patterns 278

    Context 279

    Drivers 279

    Core Patterns.. 279

    High-Level Flow.. 282

    Considerations.. 283

    Variations.. 284

    Advantages... 284

    Relevant Use Cases 286

    Tools and Technologies.. 286

Cache-Aside Pattern 286

    Context 286

    Drivers 286

    Solution 287

    Considerations.. 288

    Variations.. 289

    Advantages... 290

    Relevant Use Cases 290

    Tools and Technologies.. 290

PRPL Pattern 290

    Context 291

    Drivers 291

    Solution 291

xiii

TABLE OF CONTENTS

    Considerations 293

    Variations 293

    Advantages 293

        Relevant Use Cases 294

        Tools and Technologies 294

  Isomorphic Pattern 294

    Context 294

    Drivers 295

    Solution 295

    Considerations 296

    Advantages 297

    Relevant Use Cases 297

    Tools and Technologies 297

  Modern Web Scenarios 298

  Summary 299

Chapter 11: Modern Web Data Patterns 301

  Common Data-related Antipatterns and Best Practices 302

    Data-related Antipatterns 302

    Data-related Best Practices 302

    Common Data Patterns 303

  Saga Pattern 305

    Drivers 305

    Solution 306

    Variations 306

    Considerations 307

    Advantages 307

    Relevant Use Cases 308

    Tools and Frameworks 308

  CQRS Pattern and Event Sourcing Pattern 308

    Drivers 308

    Solution 309

TABLE OF CONTENTS

    Solution Description 310

    Considerations 312

    Variations 312

    Advantages 313

    Relevant Use Cases 313

    Tools and Frameworks 314

Data Lake Design Pattern 314

    Drivers 314

    Solution 315

    Considerations 316

    Advantages 317

    Relevant Use Cases 317

    Tools and Technologies 318

NoSQL Pattern 318

    Drivers 319

    Solution 319

    Considerations 321

    Advantages 321

    Relevant Use Cases 321

    Tools and Frameworks 322

Modern Web Scenarios 322

Summary 324

Chapter 12: Modern Web Integration Patterns 327

Common Integration Antipatterns and Best Practices 328

    Network-related Antipatterns 328

    Integration-related Antipatterns 328

    Integration-related Best Practices and Common Patterns 329

Microservice Patterns 332

    Context 333

    Drivers 334

    Core Patterns 334

xv

TABLE OF CONTENTS

    Solution 339

    Considerations 342

    Variations 343

    Advantages 343

    Relevant Use Cases 344

    Tools and Frameworks 344

    Technology Choices 344

  Event-Driven Architecture 347

    Context 347

    Solution 348

    Considerations 350

    Advantages 351

    Relevant Use Cases 351

    Tools and Frameworks 352

  GraphQL 352

    Drivers 352

    Solution 352

    Considerations 353

    Advantages 353

    Relevant Use Cases 353

    Tools and Frameworks 353

  Modern Web Scenarios 354

  Summary 355

Appendix A: Performance Optimization Checklist 359

  Performance Testing Checklist 359

  Java Performance Checklist 363

  JDBC Performance Checklist 366

  Memory Leak Analysis Checklist 366

  Application Server Configuration Checklist 367

Appendix B: Database Performance Optimization 369
Oracle Performance-Tuning Checklist 369
DB2 Performance Tuning Checklist 375

Appendix C: Performance Test Report Template 379
Executive Summary 379
Introduction 379
Objective 380
Performance Testing Scope 380
Performance Testing Environment 380
Performance Testing Dependencies\Assumptions 381
Architectural Model 381
Approach to Performance Testing 382
Performance Test Results and Observations 382
Tuning Implementation Between Execution Cycles 382
Recommendations 383
Open Items 383
Conclusion 383
Other Information 384

Appendix D: Performance Test Strategy Template 385
Introduction 385
Performance Testing Dependencies and Execution Support 389
Performance Testing Steps/Activities 390
Test Execution Contingency Planning 397
Deliverables 397
Performance Testing Risks 397
Glossary of Performance Terms 398

Bibliography 399

Index 421

xvii

About the Author

Dr. Shailesh Kumar Shivakumar is an inventor, author, researcher, and enterprise architect. He is an award-winning, digital technology practitioner with skills in technology, practice management, and a wide spectrum of digital technologies, including enterprise portals, content systems, enterprise search, and performance engineering. Dr. Shailesh has a distinctive record for the "maximum [number of] books on digital technologies published internationally by a single author," awarded by the India Book of Records. He was featured in national daily newspapers for this achievement. He has received a Grandmaster honor from the Asia Book of Records. He is a Guinness World Records holder for successfully developing a mobile application in a coding marathon. Google's knowledge graph on Dr. Shailesh can be accessed at https://g.co/kgs/8hz565.

Dr. Shailesh has a PhD in computer science and completed an executive program in business management. He is the author of seven technical books published by the world's top academic publishers. He has published a dozen technical white papers, blogs, and technical magazine articles and has authored eight textbook chapters for undergraduate programs. He has published more than twenty research papers in reputed international journals and is a member of the editorial boards for three leading international journals. Dr. Shailesh has presented multiple papers at IEEE conferences and a JavaOne conference. Dr. Shailesh's work is quoted and mentioned in world's reputed knowledge sources such as Wikipedia and Quora.

Dr. Shailesh has inventions related to web security and personalization and holds two US patents. He also has ten patent applications. He has given talks and participated in panel discussions at international conferences. He has been twice interviewed by *InfoQ* magazine, an international magazine on software topics. He was on the Conference Advisory Committee of the International Conference on Computational Intelligence and Communication (ICCIC-19).

ABOUT THE AUTHOR

Dr. Shailesh has more than 19 years of industry experience and was the chief architect in building a digital platform, which won a Best Web Support Site 2013 global award. He is a seasoned architect who is deeply focused on enterprise architecture, building alliance partnerships with product vendors. He has a proven track record of executing complex, large-scale programs. He has successfully architected and led many engagements for Fortune 500 clients. He has built globally deployed enterprise applications. He also has headed up a center of excellence for digital practices and developed several digital solutions as well as intellectual property to accelerate digital solution development. He has led multiple thought leadership and productivity improvement initiatives and has been part of special interest groups related to emerging web technologies at his organization.

Dr. Shailesh was awarded the prestigious Albert Nelson Marquis Lifetime Achievement Award 2018 for technology leadership and has won multiple other awards, including a listing in *Marquis Who's Who 2018* and the prestigious Infosys Award for Excellence 2013–14 for multitalented thought leader. He has been awarded multiple awards at his organization for his exemplary performance and contributions, including the Pinnacle Award, Brand Ambassador Award 2013, Unit Champion Award, Best Project Team Award, and Best Employee Award 2015. He is featured as an "Infy star" in the Infosys Hall of Fame. He was honored as the chief guest of honor at Presidency College's IT Fest COMPUTANTRA-2018 and was a guest of honor at ISTE student chapters at BNMIT, Bangalore.

Dr. Shailesh holds numerous professional certifications, including TOGAF 9, Deep Learning Nanodegree certification from Udacity, AWS Certified Solutions Architect, Oracle Certified Master (OCM) in Java EE5 Enterprise Architect, IBM Certified SOA Solution Designer, and IBM Certified Solution Architect Cloud Computing Infrastructure. He can be reached at https://drshailesh.in/.

Acknowledgments

I am deeply indebted to my wife, Chaitra, and son, Shishir, for their immense and unconditional support for all my initiatives. I would like to convey my sincere and heartfelt thanks to TP Vasanth, my brother-in-law, for his constant stream of support and inspiration. I would also like to recognize and thank Dr. P. V. Suresh for his constant encouragement and immense support.

My special thanks to the A team at Apress, including Rita Fernando and Shivangi Ramachandran, for all their timely support and review help. The team is highly proactive and super-responsive in planning and execution. I would also like to thank the editorial team and design team at Apress for the beautiful book design. I owe much of the book's success to the Apress team.

Introduction

Modern web platforms are popular user-engagement tools. They are important vehicles for enterprises to realize their digital strategies. The optimal performance of the modern web is a key success factor to drive user traffic and keep web users engaged by providing useful information. Web architects and performance engineers need to design for optimal performance in the modern web for the long-term success of web systems. Performance is a critical success factor for modern web platforms. It leads to high user satisfaction, increased user engagement, increased user traffic, and more. Web performance optimization (WPO) deals with various aspects of modern web performance.

WPO Dimensions Explored in This Book

Performance optimization is a journey spanning various life cycle stages of a project. To achieve optimal performance, you should look at end-to-end layers, solution components, performance testing, monitoring, and infrastructure.

This book adopts a multifaceted approach to WPO. The core WPO dimensions discussed in the book are depicted in Figure I-1.

INTRODUCTION

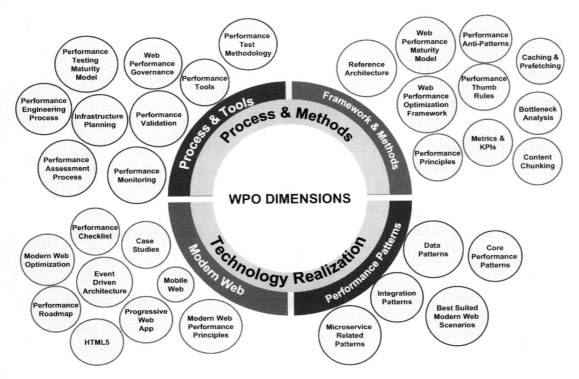

Figure I-1. *WPO dimensions*

Broadly we can categorize the WPO dimensions into "Process and Methods" and "Technology Realization" categories. The "Process and Methods" category covers the process and tools and framework and methods dimensions; The "Technology Realization" category covers modern web and performance patterns dimensions. The **Process and Tools** dimension discusses performance optimization processes, tools, and governance. Various performance testing tools, the web performance test methodology, performance governance, and the performance testing maturity model are in this dimension. Performance monitoring methods, tools, and best practices are examined. Infrastructure-related optimizations are also a part of this dimension. I cover this dimension in Chapter 2, Chapter 3 and Chapter 6.

The **Framework and Methods** dimension explains methods and best practices in performance optimization. In this context, proven performance best practices, methods, tools, KPIs (key performance indicators), and metrics and principles for modern web platforms are covered. Performance optimizations across various layers, reference architecture, performance metrics, and KPIs, network-related performance optimizations, and caching methods and are covered. The web performance

INTRODUCTION

optimization framework provides comprehensive coverage of performance optimizations at various SDLC phases and various application layers. Performance antipatterns, the web performance maturity model, and bottleneck analyses are also in this dimension. I cover various topics of this dimension in Chapter 3, Chapter 4 and Chapter 5.

The **Performance Patterns** dimension covers patterns related to performance, data, and integration used in various modern web platforms. You learn various details about each of the patterns, including solution, drivers, flow, advantages and disadvantages, and applicable scenarios. I describe applicable real-world scenarios for core performance-related patterns (such as progressive web architecture patterns, Cache aside pattern, the PRPL pattern, and the isomorphic pattern), data-related patterns (such as SAGA, CQRS, data lakes, and NoSQL), and integration-related patterns (such as microservices, event-driven architecture, and GraphQL). For each of the patterns I cover the applicable modern web scenarios. I also discuss common best practices and variants in each of the patterns. I cover various topics of this dimension in Chapter 10, Chapter 11 and Chapter 12.

The **Modern Web** dimension explains the tenets of modern web technologies, such as PWA, HTML5, and event-driven architecture. I describe core performance optimizations principles for modern web platforms, and you look at real-world case studies on performance engineering and legacy modernization and modern web development. The case studies cover layer-wise performance assessments, web performance assessment approach, web performance assessment exercise, web performance optimization recommendations, and performance-related design recommendations. I cover this dimension in Chapter 4, Chapter 8 and Chapter 9.

How This Book Is Organized

The book is organized into five parts based on logically related performance topics.

- **Part 1** focuses on performance challenges, scenarios, and commonly adopted performance best practices. This part mainly covers the performance optimization of traditional web applications. It surveys existing performance optimization methods and lists the most common performance optimization methods.

INTRODUCTION

- **Part 2** dives into modern web platforms and describes design guidelines, performance principles, performance optimization methods, tools, and principles. There is a discussion on mobile web applications and progressive web applications. This part also elaborates on the "web performance optimization framework," which covers performance optimization dimensions.

- **Part 3** covers various aspects of performance testing, including key performance testing metrics, workload modeling, web performance test methodology, and performance testing maturity model. This part also discusses performance monitoring to maintain optimal performance. A discussion on performance monitoring includes monitoring metrics, application performance monitoring (APM), building performance monitoring ecosystem, and infrastructure planning for performance.

- **Part 4** looks closely at two real-world performance optimization case studies. A performance engineering case study covers layer-wise challenges, solution components, performance optimization, infrastructure analysis, recommendations, and performance roadmaps. A legacy web optimization case study covers the web performance assessment approach, a web performance assessment exercise, web performance optimization recommendations, and performance-related design recommendations.

- **Part 5** covers the main patterns that impact the performance of modern web platforms. It discusses the context, drivers, solution, advantages, and applicable modern web scenarios for core performance patterns, data-related patterns, and integration-related pattern. For each of the patterns, there are applicable real-world scenarios.

- The Appendix four include checklists and templates. The checklists and templates compliment the methods and frameworks discussed in the chapters. This includes a web performance checklist, database performance checklist, performance test report template, performance test strategy template, and security assessment checklist. You can use the templates and checklists as reference for code reviews and performance testing.

Key Takeaways of This Book

After reading this book, you should understand the following performance optimization methods and frameworks.

- The comprehensive web performance optimization framework covering performance optimization methods for all SDLC phases and the performance maturity model
- Web performance taxonomy at various layers of the modern web application
- Performance optimizations methods, design principles, tools, and frameworks for modern web platforms
- Performance optimization processes, such as bottleneck analysis, performance assessment, performance testing, performance monitoring, workload modeling, and infrastructure planning
- Various performance metrics and KPIs for performance monitoring and testing
- Real-world performance engineering case studies for end-to-end performance optimization across all layers
- Modern web optimization principles, methods, and tools
- Performance patterns to optimize the performance, data, and integration of the modern web
- Usable templates, checklists such as web performance checklist, database performance checklist, performance test report template, performance test strategy template, modern web application security assessment checklist from the appendix sections

INTRODUCTION

Intended Audience

The book is intended for digital enthusiasts, performance engineers, web developers, front-end engineers, integration architects, data architects, full stack developers, enterprise architects, project managers, program managers, and CIOs.

> **Note** Examples of various tools, technologies, and frameworks are provided in discussing WPO concepts. All the examples are for pedagogical purposes, and as such, the book does not recommend any particular tool or technology.

PART I

Introduction to Web Performance Optimization

CHAPTER 1

Getting Started with Web Performance Optimization

A faster web page positively impacts the user experience and ultimately leads to increased user satisfaction. It influences online revenue and search engine rankings. User traffic and repeat visits are also dependent on web page performance. Web performance optimization (WPO) plays a crucial role in optimizing the performance of public web pages.

This chapter looks at the key impact factors of WPO. It describes WPO dimensions, WPO lifecycle stages, WPO governance concepts, and layer-wise WPO optimization methods.

Web Performance Optimization (WPO)

Web performance optimization covers methods, tools, and best practices to improve the end-to-end performance of a web page. The main WPO topics—such as impact, dimensions, and gaps, are covered in this section.

Web performance optimization (WPO) involves all methods to improve the performance of a web page. WPO includes optimizing the performance of page components, such as HTML content, web components, page elements, and page assets. End-to-end WPO provides techniques, best practices, rules of thumb, and methodologies. The key components used in WPO are web content, images, videos, CSS/JS files, XML/JSON files, and other presentation components.

CHAPTER 1　GETTING STARTED WITH WEB PERFORMANCE OPTIMIZATION

WPO has an impact on the following aspects.

- **Customer churn**: Research indicates that customers tend to abandon slower web pages.

- **User impact**: The page performance impacts usability. The performance of landing/gateway pages and key processes is directly co-related to the overall user experience.

- **Site traffic**: User engagement and user traffic increases for fast loading pages. The high performance pages also increase the conversion rate and reduces the abandonment rate.

- **Revenue**: Online revenue is directly correlated to the performance of key pages and transactions for e-commerce sites.

- **Multi-device optimization**: The web page performance plays a crucial role in usability on mobile devices

- **Search engine ranking**: Search engines use page performance as one of the ranking criteria.

- **Omnichannel advantage**: Mobile devices can easily access a page that performs well.

The impact of WPO on page performance is depicted in Figure 1-1.

CHAPTER 1 ■ GETTING STARTED WITH WEB PERFORMANCE OPTIMIZATION

Figure 1-1. *Impact of WPO*

The high-level impact WPO categories are depicted in Figure 1-2.

Figure 1-2. *WPO impact categories*

CHAPTER 1　GETTING STARTED WITH WEB PERFORMANCE OPTIMIZATION

WPO impacts the end-user experience, influences expectations, and enables the online platform. In the subsequent sections of this chapter, we shall look at basics of WPO dimensions and the taxonomy of WPO dimensions. We shall also briefly look at the Web Performance Patterns and best practices. We also cover the high level performance testing, performance optimization at various layers, performance optimization at various project lifecycle stages and performance governance.

Web Performance Optimization Dimensions

Web performance is a function of many different factors. The key factors that influence web performance are web components (HTML content, images/assets, scripts, style sheets), project lifecycle activities, request processing pipelines, and performance governance. Each of these factors has second-level elements that impact performance; for instance, a request processing pipeline includes all systems involved in processing a web request across all layers. Performance governance includes performance metrics, performance processes, and SLAs. Each of these factors is part of overall web performance optimization. Exploring WPO dimensions helps you to holistically understand the web performance.

A master taxonomy of WPO dimensions is depicted in Figure 1-3. Each of the layers in the WPO taxonomy is discussed in the next section. The high-level categories in the WPO dimensions taxonomy are as follows.

- **Web performance optimization in different phases of the project**: This category explores web performance optimization methods in different phases of the project. Performance architecture, performance-based design, performance-based development, and performance testing and performance maintenance are in this dimension, which is covered in Chapter 2.

CHAPTER 1 ■ GETTING STARTED WITH WEB PERFORMANCE OPTIMIZATION

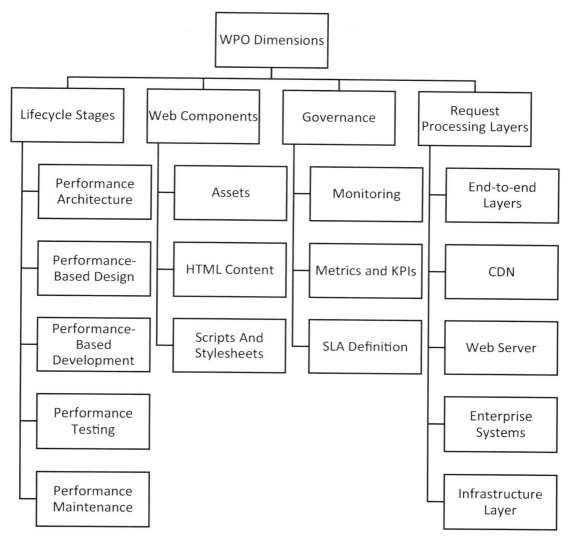

Figure 1-3. *Taxonomy of WPO dimensions*

- **Web performance optimization of various web components**: State-of-the-art methods and tools used in performance optimization of various web components are presented in Chapter 2. The tools and methods used for optimizing the performance of static assets (JavaScript, CSS, and images) and HTML content are also covered.

- **Governance**: Various governance aspects, such as performance monitoring, performance metrics, and KPIs and SLAs are discussed in Chapter 2.

7

CHAPTER 1   GETTING STARTED WITH WEB PERFORMANCE OPTIMIZATION

- **Request processing layers**: Performance optimization methods at all layers involved in the end-to-end web request processing pipeline are covered in Chapter 2. The chapter also discusses web performance optimization methods across the client layer, content delivery layer, web server layer, application server layer, database layer, integration layer, file storage layer, content layer, and infrastructure layer.

Web Performance Optimizations at Various Lifecycle Stages

This section looks at web performance optimization techniques implemented at different stages of a development lifecycle.

Web Performance During Project Architecture Phase

This phase defines the architecture principles from a performance standpoint. These principles can be used in later stages to develop a performance design checklist and for performance-based development. Web performance best practices and rules of thumb are categorized in this phase. Web performance patterns, web architecture patterns, and scalable web architecture principles are defined in this stage.

Web Performance Patterns

The following are some of the key web performance patterns for optimal performance.

- **Make web components lighter**. Move them closer to the layer used, cache them longer, and load them more intelligently.
- **Layer-wise caching** at all layers in the request processing pipeline for optimal performance.
- The **progressive enhancement technique** uses open standards such as XHTML, CSS, and JavaScript to overlay dynamic content with CSS, JavaScript to provide cross-browser, accessible content. The technique consists of the behavior layer (implemented through unobtrusive JavaScript), presentation layer (implemented through CSS), structure layer (implemented through HTML standards), and core content layer.

These layers are selectively added based on the device's capability to maximize usability and accessibility.

- **Use minimal round trips**. A web page should avoid chatty server calls. Wherever possible, the calls should be batched to minimize them.

- **In an asynchronous loading pattern**, all page assets are loaded asynchronously, and resource requests should adopt asynchronous communication.

- **In a lazy loading pattern**, the page assets are loaded when required and on-demand.

- **In lightweight design**, the page adopts a lean model using web-oriented architecture and a lightweight integration technique.

- **In a device-specific rendition**, the page content and assets are optimized for the rendition device.

- **In responsive page content**, responsive design for HTML elements and adaptive design for content are followed.

Web Architecture Patterns

Architecture patterns define the proven solution design principles for recurring problems. The core performance patterns are covered in Chapter 10, data patterns are covered in Chapter 11, and integration patterns are covered in Chapter 12. This section discusses core architecture patterns for optimal performance.

- **The model-view-controller (MVC) architecture** is the widely used architecture pattern that creates a loosely coupled flexible web applications with modular components. From a performance viewpoint, interactional styles such as event observation and notification, publish/subscribe, and asynchronous communication can be added as features for MVC applications. Most modern web applications heavily use Representational State Transfer (REST) architecture style, which provides lightweight and asynchronous methods for requesting and updating web resources.

CHAPTER 1   GETTING STARTED WITH WEB PERFORMANCE OPTIMIZATION

- **Microservices architecture** allows you to build a web application as a composition of multiple independently scalable services. The architecture uses a lightweight communication mechanism and functional model for building services. Since each of the microservices are individually scalable, you could build a highly scalable system using microservices. Microservices-based patterns are discussed in Chapter 12.

- **Web-oriented architecture (WOA)** involves lightweight pluggable client-side widgets. WOA architecture is lightweight in design, and you can easily implement web performance best practices. AJAX-based client-side MVC and model–view–view model (MVVM) architectures to build rich, interactive, and responsive web applications. Web architecture principles are discussed in Chapter 10 and Chapter 12.

Distributed computing, grid computing, parallel computing, and cloud computing are other considerations for performance optimization based on the scenarios.

Web Performance-Based Project Design Phase

This lifecycle stage features the performance best practices and guidelines for web performance optimization. It defines the performance checklists and best practices that would be used for performance-based development and testing. Web developers and architects can use this as a reference while developing web applications. Some of these optimizations are also available as filters, including Apache's mode_pagespeed module for minification, merging, and externalizing inline JS/CSS through filters. Performance antipatterns and performance best practices to address them are covered in the next section.

Performance Antipatterns, Performance Patterns, and Design Best Practices

Antipatterns are grouped into logical categories, such as page design, server call design, and web assets design. Antipatterns related to performance, data, and integration are discussed in Chapter 10, Chapter 11, and Chapter 12.

10

Page Design Patterns and Best practices

The following are performance best practices and performance design patterns that apply to the design phase of the project.

- **Avoiding extraneous content**, such as advertisements, can improve the number of objects per page on an average by 25% and improves latency on an average by 30%.

- **Adopting a user-centric design approach** addresses challenges related to usability, information discovery, accessibility, task completion.

- **Conducting iterative performance testing** assesses the page performance across geography and omnichannel testing for all pages.

- **Adopting user-friendly and intuitive information architecture** and minimizing pages/links needed to find the information or reach the correct page. Create information architecture and page flows based on user goals and user personas to reach the information quickly and complete the intended task.

- **Use simple page design**. The home pages and complex pages should have a simple User Interface (UI) design consisting of minimal UI components. Complex page design and page cluttering should be avoided. Optimize the landing page through techniques such as eyeball tracking, uncluttering, targeted, and useful information, and A/B (a.k.a. split) testing/multivariate testing analysis. The right pane elements can load late as its performance is less critical.

- **Use responsive design**. You can leverage responsive web design methods to flexible UI for various mobile devices. Users perceive instantaneous response if the page load time is between 0.1 second and 0.2 second. Hence it is important to adopt responsive design to create interactive and highly performing UI elements.

- **Use the minimize page weight**. The overall page size should be between 100 KB and 400 KB for home pages and landing pages. Minimizing session size and cookie size reduces the overall page weight.

- **Business-critical processes** should be optimized. This includes business process optimization, page design optimization, search optimization, check out/shopping process optimization, and user registration optimization.

- **Remove known performance blockers** such as numerous unnecessary links, iframes, numerous pages, and non-intuitive information architecture.

- **AJAX-enable** web applications to fetch resources and load page data. It results in more responsive and shorter inter-request times and lower traffic.

Design of Server Calls

Let's discuss the main best practices for server calls and back-end services invocation.

Use the asynchronous AJAX calls to get the dynamic data from service APIs. Load the data only on demand lazily to reduce the initial page load time. Specify design goals for external and third-party scripts. The main design goals for the external scripts are small size scripts, readable scripts, unobtrusive loading, and easy to copy-paste to the host page and asynchronous support.

Performance-Based Development

During the implementation and build phase, the development team uses the architecture principles and performance design checklist. We have discussed the performance based development in Chapter 3. In addition to this, other key activities include the following.

- Conduct performance code reviews and automated performance analysis after completing each delivery milestone.

- Carry out load testing and stress testing based on the specified NFRs to identify any performance and scalability issues.

- Conduct performance testing on all supported browsers and mobile devices.

- Use continuous integration (CI) and continuous development (CD) methodology to iteratively deploy business capabilities.

Performance Testing

During the performance testing stage, you test the conformance of the application to the specified performance SLAs under various load conditions. A performance testing tool loads the application, and various performance metrics and system resources (e.g., the server response time, throughput, and resource utilization) are monitored. Performance testing methods and tools are discussed in Chapter 6.

Performance Maintenance

Post-production, web performance SLAs are maintained. This includes establishing a robust performance monitoring setup to provide real-time performance metrics reports and performance SLA violation alerts. Robust monitoring setup is discussed in Chapter 7.

Web Performance Governance Concepts

Performance governance is a key aspect of web performance reference architecture depicted. Well-established performance governance is key to achieve optimal web performance and sustain it in the long run. This section looks at various aspects of web performance governance.

Definition of Performance SLAs

During the requirements elaboration phase, various performance SLAs need to be defined. During the same phase, all applicable performance metrics should be defined. These metrics and SLAs are further used for performance testing, monitoring, and reporting purposes.

Performance Metrics and KPIs

Performance metrics are used to measure, track, monitor, and report the performance of the application against the defined performance SLAs.

CHAPTER 1 GETTING STARTED WITH WEB PERFORMANCE OPTIMIZATION

Web Page Metrics

This category provides the main timing and size metrics used for measuring the web page performance. The following are the main metrics used in measuring the WPO.

- **Page response time (PRT) or page load time (PLT)** is the overall time taken for rendering the page Document Object Model (DOM). It is the total time between initial request and the time when all page objects are downloaded. PLT includes the DNS resolution time, TCP connection time, time to first byte (TTFB), and DOM rendition time. PLT is measured using window.onload event. PLT is also defined by the time elapsed between the page request and when the DOMLoad event is fired. Normally, the response times are measured at various user loads, such as average load and peak load, to measure web site behavior. At the end of the DOM load time, page DOM is loaded, and at the end of render time, the page is fully functional with all page behavior available to the user. The page is fully interactive after render time.

    Page response time = DNS lookup time + TCP Connect time+ server response time (time needed for sending, waiting, and receiving) + Object download time.

- **Time to first byte (TTFB)** is the time it takes for the server to send the first-byte response to the client. TTFB is the measure of the total wait time until the browser receives the response from the server.

- **Above-the-fold-time (AFT)** is the time it takes for the pixels above the fold (user view) to be painted and when the content stops changing. It is a visual indicator of the page performance.

- **User ready time (URT)** measures when the page's essential elements are ready for the user.

- A **speed index** represents the average time taken to render the visible parts of the web page.

- **Perceived response time**, also known as *perceived load time*, is the page load time perceived by the end user. The perceived response time can also be measured with AFT and URT. In most scenarios, it is equivalent to the DOM load time because the user can see the key information on the page. You can optimize perceived load time by loading the key content in the beginning (critical resources) and injecting the JavaScript-based behavior during the render phase. Partial page refresh and on-demand loading, lazy loading, and asynchronous loading are other techniques to optimize perceived load time. We have discussed PRPL pattern and other patterns to optimize the perceived response time in Chapter 10.

- **Overall page size or page weight** is the total page size, which includes the size of all constituent HTML content, assets, JavaScript (JS), Cascading Style Sheet (CSS), images, and other elements. Naturally, a larger page size would negatively impact the overall page performance.

- **Asset size** is the total size of all static assets on the page. This includes the size of all images, multimedia files, JavaScript files, CSS files, JSON files, XML files, and so forth. Since assets contribute heavily to the overall page size, thereby affecting the performance, this metric is closely watched for optimization.

- **Asset load time** presents the total time taken by all assets on a web page. You can also check the individual load time and size for each of the assets to analyze the performance of assets.

- **Resource requests** measure several resource requests that are required for complete page rendition. It is the total of image requests, file requests, asynchronous requests, and so forth. A high number of synchronous resource requests blocks the page and impacts the page size and page load times.

- **Round-trip time (RTT)** is the total time needed for establishing a connection between client and server. It impacts resource download time and page load time.

- **Time to first result** is the time when the first result shows up on the page (e.g., the first result in a search results page).

Various page load times are depicted in Figure 1-4.

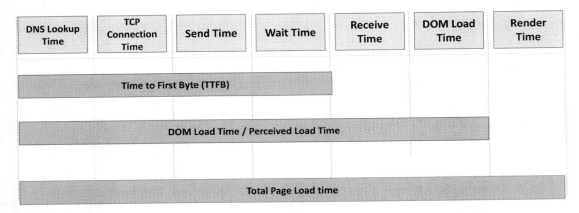

Figure 1-4. Page load times

Performance Monitoring

Performance monitoring involves monitoring key parameters such as memory consumption rate, CPU utilization, possible memory leaks, disk I/O, and application response time. We have discussed the performance monitoring in detail in Chapter 7.

Web Performance Optimizations at Various Layers

The performance perceived by the end-user is impacted by all the layers involved in the web request processing pipeline. For optimal web performance, you should optimize the performance at each layer. This section takes a closer look at each of the core layers involved in a typical web request processing pipeline.

In many systems, the web server, application server, database server, CMS, infrastructure, services, and file storage servers are processing a web request. This section looks at the performance optimizations done at each of these layers for optimal web performance perceived by the end user. It discusses the performance bottlenecks and the performance patterns that address those bottlenecks. We have also included the multi-layer performance performance optimization as part of performance optimization framework in Chapter 3.

Web Performance Optimization End-To-End Flow

Figure 1-5 depicts performance optimizations done at various layers and the systems involved in a typical web request processing.

CHAPTER 1   GETTING STARTED WITH WEB PERFORMANCE OPTIMIZATION

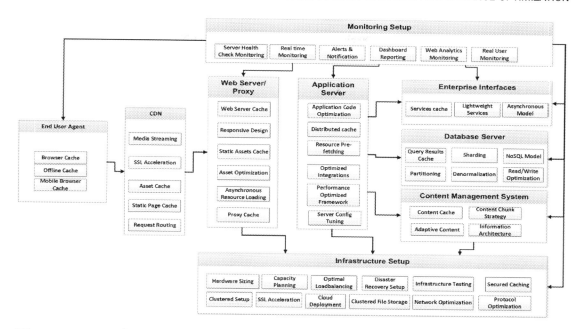

Figure 1-5. *End-to-end performance processing pipeline*

Figure 1-5 identifies layer-wise performance optimization methods for the end-to-end web request processing pipeline. Web request originates from user agents (browsers) or user devices (mobile devices, tablets, etc.). In this layer, the browser cache is often used for page performance optimization. The request then goes to the content delivery network (CDN) where JS/CSS, videos, images, JSON, and other static assets are cached. CDN also forward caches the static page content and can be used for caching static web pages.

The next layer of systems is web servers and proxy servers that cache static page assets. At the web server layer, you can set cache header rules. Asynchronous asset loading and responsive web page design are other performance optimization techniques adopted in this layer. At the application server layer, you can leverage server-side caching frameworks, application code optimization, distributed caching model, parallel computing, and use continuous and iterative performance testing.

At the upstream system layer (enterprise interfaces, database server, content management system), you can leverage services cache to cache service responses, query result cache for caching query results, content cache to cache content and fragments, and adaptive content design.

A properly sized infrastructure setup is needed for all the servers to ensure that all the systems in the web request processing pipeline properly scale for the user load.

Infrastructure sizing is discussed in Chapter 7. Monitoring infrastructure constantly monitors the hardware components and provides monitoring reports and real-time notifications. Upcoming sections explore the layer-wise performance optimizations detail.

Performance Optimization at the User-Agent Layer

This layer consists of various kinds of desktop browsers, mobile devices, such as smartphones, PDAs, and other end-user-experience devices. Many users (40%–60%) come with an empty cache, which provides a big opportunity to cache static assets. When the expiry date or maximum age or cache-control (using cache-control: max-age) HTTP headers are added to static assets such as images, JS/CSS files, JSON files, browsers would cache it. For HTML5 applications, the cache manifest and application cache features can be used. Other features such as localStorage for storing client-side data used across sessions to reduce HTTP requests can be used for HTML5 scenarios. We have discussed various caching methods for modern web applications in Chapter 4.

Performance Optimization at the Content Delivery Network (CDN) Layer

CDN is a distributed network of servers that can forward-cache content and assets and serve them to the client from the nearest node in the network. CDN can effectively address main Internet delivery challenges such as peering point congestion, inefficient communication protocols, scalability, inefficient routing protocols, unreliable networks, application limitations, and slow rate of change adoption. CDNs forward cache the static assets (images, CSS, JS, videos, etc.) to the globally distributed edge servers. Web sites that are heavy in image and multimedia content and static content can leverage CDNs for video scalability and accelerate live streaming.

Taxonomy of Performance Optimization at the Web Server and Proxy Server Layer

Taxonomy defines the categorized group of topics in a hierarchy. The taxonomy of web component category and web components optimized at the web server layer is shown in Figure 1-6.

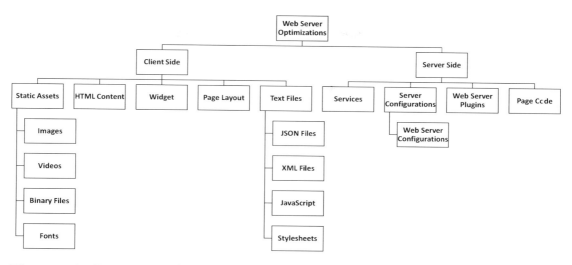

Figure 1-6. *Taxonomy of web server performance optimizations*

The taxonomy of optimized web components (as shown in Figure 1-6) falls under two categories: client-side and server-side components. Client-side components include the web components that are optimized for a user agent/browser. Web components such as static assets, HTML content, widgets, page layout, and text-based files fall into this category. Further static assets include web components such as images, videos, and binary assets, and text files include JS/CSS, JSON/XML, and font files. Processing and rendering page layout also play a role in page performance. The main bottlenecks for CPU during page rendition are CSS selectors, processing layout elements (which consumes about 50% of CPU time), and text processing.

Server-side components include web components hosted in a web server such as web server plugins, page back-end code, services, and server configuration files. Web server plugins such as mod_backhand can be used for load balancing for Apache web servers. Plugins mod_proxy and mod_cache can be used for content caching for Apache servers; mod_SPDY provides SPDY support for Apache servers and mod_pagespeed for optimizing performance. Apache web server uses mod_expiry module for cache expiry setting and mod_gzip for compression. Web servers can be configured to optimize the web request handling.

CHAPTER 1   GETTING STARTED WITH WEB PERFORMANCE OPTIMIZATION

Taxonomy of Performance Optimization at the Application Server Layer

A good back-end processing time is less than 100 milliseconds because it directly impacts TTFB. The performance optimizations at the application server end play a key role in end-to-end performance optimization. The taxonomy of application server layer optimizations is shown in the following Figure 1-7.

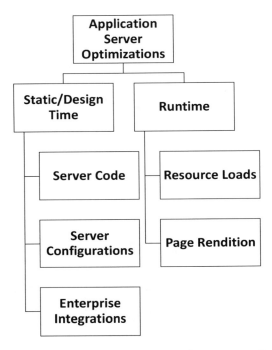

Figure 1-7. *Taxonomy of Application Server Performance Optimizations*

The performance optimizations at the application server end can be categorized into static or design time and runtime. Static/design time performance optimization includes components optimized during development time in offline mode. This category includes application code, server configurations, and enterprise integrations. The performance optimization of application code includes using a performance tuning of code, adhering to performance checklists and guidelines, profiling code, and conducting regular performance-related code reviews.

Server configurations optimizations include configuration of the heap memory, turning off unnecessary modules, fine-tuning the thread settings, fine-tuning the garbage collector settings, adjusting the JVM settings, configuring connection pool

CHAPTER 1   GETTING STARTED WITH WEB PERFORMANCE OPTIMIZATION

settings, configuring cache and expiry headers. Each product vendor provides a set of recommended settings and configurations for their servers that can be leveraged for fine-tuning the settings.

Performance optimization for enterprise integration includes using optimal integration methodology, using services-based integration, leveraging asynchronous model of service invocation.

Runtime components include resource loading modules that predict resource needs and uses prefetching techniques to optimally prefetch the needed resources. Page rendition components use performance optimization techniques such as responsive and adaptive design techniques for optimal performance for a given user agent/browser at the runtime.

Performance Optimization at the Database Server Layer

The performance optimizations on the database server end include clustered design, leveraging database level caching, horizontal and vertical partitioning, sharding based on a logical grouping of data, denormalization for faster read access, read/write optimization, data replication, data snapshots, and adopting a NoSQL model for applicable scenarios. The upstream layers (e.g., application layer, data services layer) could adopt other performance optimization measures such as batch queries, the result set size restriction, connection pooling, caching query results. Some of the other performance optimization measures done at the database layer are to keep the read-write ratio to 80/20, vertical partitioning of logically independent tables, sharding/horizontal partitioning based on a logical grouping of the primary key, usage of database caching (write-through cache, write-back cache). Data-related patterns to improve performance is discussed in Chapter 11.

Performance Optimization at the Enterprise Interface Layer

The key performance optimization measures for enterprise interfaces is to enable service access for the interfaces. After enabling the service access, you could adopt other performance best practices such as asynchronous access, lightweight service access, services cache, and service response prefetching. Data-related patterns that improve performance are discussed in Chapter 12.

Performance Optimization at the File Storage Server Layer

Application files should be stored in network file storage devices for optimal performance. Distributed fault-tolerant file systems such as MogileFS and Amazon S3 should be leveraged to provide robust replication and scalability and performance. The file storage should provide high availability and failure recovery service.

Taxonomy of Performance Optimization at the Content Management Server (CMS) Layer

A web page content comes from HTML content fragment (from the web server) or web content stored in the CMS. The high-level taxonomy of various performance optimizations at the CMS is depicted in Figure 1-8.

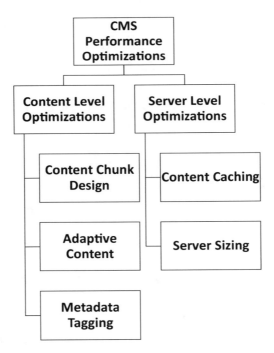

Figure 1-8. Taxonomy of CMS performance optimization

The first-level categories of CMS performance optimizations are content-level optimizations related to core content and server-level optimizations that include performance optimizations done at the CMS server end.

CHAPTER 1 GETTING STARTED WITH WEB PERFORMANCE OPTIMIZATION

A key content-level optimization is content chunking. Content chunking and content-based caching is an effective strategy to enhance content performance and reusability. Modular content is more reusable and easily cacheable. Content chunk reduces the network traffic and optimizes performance in mobile devices. Chunked data is widely used in CDN for performance optimization, and the chunking concept can also be used for device-specific rendering.

Taxonomy of Performance Optimization at the Infrastructure Layer

You need to properly plan for infrastructure components for optimal web performance. This involves optimal sizing and capacity planning, network planning, load balancer setup, infrastructure testing, clustered setup, cloud deployment, protocol optimization, and disaster recovery (DR) setup. More about infrastructure planning is discussed in Chapter 7. The taxonomy of performance optimizations at the infrastructure level is depicted in Figure 1-9.

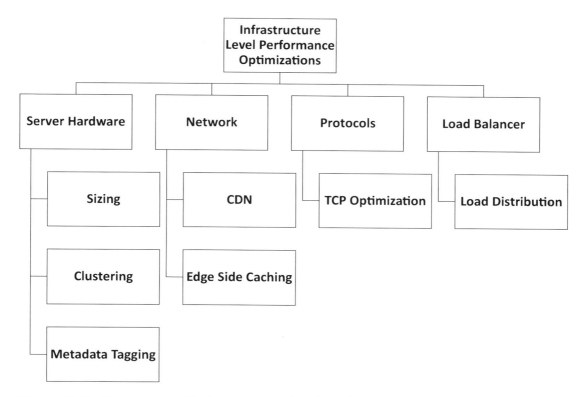

Figure 1-9. *Taxonomy of infrastructure-level performance optimizations*

The main categories of infrastructure components are hardware servers, networks, protocols, and load balancers.

Hardware Servers

The infrastructure planning exercise involves expected user load, transaction rate, expected growth rate, data volume, content volume, and other non-functional SLAs (e.g., performance, scalability, availability, and security), and then planning for suitable sizing. A proper capacity planning of resources such as CPU, memory should be done for all the servers.

Network Optimization

Like hardware sizing, the network should also be rightly sized based on the content volume, expected throughput, and expected response times.

Protocol Optimization

TCP modifications and enabling HTTP pipelining improves the page load time, and the initial congestion window (ICW) increase reduces the page load times by hundreds of milliseconds. Congestion control in TCP and high-speed TCP are other TCP optimization techniques. SPDY is another protocol that can be used for performance optimization. SPDY uses request multiplexing (multiplexes multiple HTTP transactions into a single TCP connection reducing TCP connection setup time) and hence receives concurrent content and provides content and HTTP header compression. HTTP/2 protocol provides many improvements for performance optimization.

Load Balancer

At the load balancer level, it is possible to use DNS load balancing (using a round-robin algorithm or network proximity-based address resolution) and adaptive Time to Live (TTL), where TTL is assigned based on the client's request rate. Another technique for load balancing is to use a dispatcher and DNS routing to route the request to one of the back-end servers for optimal workload distribution transparently to the client.

Summary

- Web performance optimization (WPO) involves all methods to improve the performance of a web page.

- WPO has an impact on customer churn, user impact, site traffic, revenue, multi-device optimization, search engine ranking, and omnichannel advantage.

- The key WPO dimensions are web performance optimization in different phases of the project, web performance optimization of various web components, and governance and request processing layers.

- The key web architecture patterns are model-view-controller architecture, microservices architecture, and web-oriented architecture (WOA).

- The key web page design antipatterns are the bad design of key pages, cluttered and heavy landing pages, the absence of real-time performance monitoring, using uncompressed images and scripts, and having front-end single point of failure (SPOF).

- Performance-based development includes performing iterative and phase-wise performance review, testing the pages at average and high user loads, testing the page for all supported browsers, continuous integration, and testing, performing regular and iterative performance testing, and using a lightweight service-based integration model.

- The key web performance governance concepts are the definition of performance SLAs, performance metrics and KPIs, web page metrics, and performance monitoring.

CHAPTER 2

General Web Performance Optimization Methods

End-to-end web performance optimization (WPO) involves optimizing various systems, components, and layers involved in the web request processing pipeline through techniques, best practices, rules of thumb, and methodologies. This chapter surveys state-of-art research methods, tools, techniques, and performance characteristics of various aspects of end-to-end web performance optimization. It adopts a multidimensional approach to exploring web performance optimization from various angles, such as the project lifecycle, the request processing pipeline, performance governance, and key web components. This first-of-a-kind approach provides vital insights into the performance impact factors needed for comprehensive performance optimization.

This chapter looks at various methods, tools, and design elements related to web performance aspects at all the layers in the web request processing pipeline (the web server layer, application server layer, integration layer, etc.). The main topics covered in this chapter are as follows.

- Surveying the existing tools, methods, best practices, and antipatterns in WPO from the following dimensions
    - Survey of tools used in web performance optimization
    - Survey of existing methods used in web performance optimization
- We shall also look at Web Performance Optimization considerations, Network and Request Processing Pipeline Optimization

CHAPTER 2   GENERAL WEB PERFORMANCE OPTIMIZATION METHODS

Survey of Tools and Methods for Performance Optimization of Web Components

This section discusses various tools and methods used in web component performance optimization.

Survey of Tools Used in the Web Performance Optimization of Various Web Components

This section provides a list of commonly used tools for implementing web performance optimizations. Table 2-1 lists the tools for performance optimization.

CHAPTER 2　GENERAL WEB PERFORMANCE OPTIMIZATION METHODS

Table 2-1. Web Performance Optimization Tools

Tool Category	Open Source/ Commercial Tool(s)	Web Performance Utility/Advantage								
		Page Analysis	Caching Optimization	Network Asset Analysis	Non-blocked loading	Page Validation Testing	Load Testing	Performance testing	Web Analytics	Monitoring	Bottleneck Analysis
Web Page Analysis tools (HTML analysis, performance benchmarking, improvement guidelines)	Yahoo YSlow, Google PageSpeed, HTTPWatch, Dynatrace AJAX Edition	✓			✓				✓		

(continued)

CHAPTER 2 GENERAL WEB PERFORMANCE OPTIMIZATION METHODS

Table 2-1. (*continued*)

Tool Category	Open Source/ Commercial Tool(s)	Page Analysis	Caching Analysis	Network Optimization	Asset Optimization	Non-blocked loading	Page Validation	Load Testing	Performance testing	Web Analytics	Monitoring	Bottleneck Analysis
Page development tools (analysis of page load times, asset size, asset load times, etc.)	Firebug, Google Chrome Developer toolbar, Fiddler, HTTP Archive, CSSLint, JSLint, W3 CSS Validator, W3 HTML validator	✓		✓		✓						✓
Asset merging and minification (JS/CSS minification)	Yahoo UI (YUI) minifier, JavaScript Minifier, JSCompress				✓							

30

CHAPTER 2 GENERAL WEB PERFORMANCE OPTIMIZATION METHODS

Page Performance Testing tools (load simulation)	JMeter, LoadUI, Grinder, Selenium		✓	✓		✓
Image compression tools	PNGCrush, Smush It, Imgmini, JPEG Mini	✓				
Web Server Plugins (for automatic compression, minification, merging, placement, caching, etc.)	Mod_pageSpeed, mod_cache, mod_SPDY, mod_expiry, mod_gzip	✓	✓	✓	✓	
Website Performance Testing	GTMetrix, Pingdom	✓	✓		✓	✓

(continued)

31

CHAPTER 2 GENERAL WEB PERFORMANCE OPTIMIZATION METHODS

Table 2-1. (*continued*)

Tool Category	Open Source/ Commercial Tool(s)	Page Analysis	Caching Analysis	Network Analysis	Asset Optimization	Non-blocked loading	Page Validation	Load Testing	Performance testing	Web Analytics	Monitoring	Bottleneck Analysis
Synthetic monitoring (transactions simulation and performance statistics)	Web Page test, DynaTrace Synthetic monitoring	✓		✓							✓	✓
CDN	Akamai, CloudFlare, KeyCDN,		✓			✓						
Web Analytics (track user behavior, performance reporting)	Google Web Analytics, Omniture, Piwik									✓	✓	✓
CSS Optimization tools	CSS Sprites, SpriteMe, SpritePad				✓							

CHAPTER 2 GENERAL WEB PERFORMANCE OPTIMIZATION METHODS

Category	Tools				
Bottleneck Analysis (dependency and bottleneck analysis)	WebProphet, WProf			✓	
Real User Monitoring (RUM) (monitoring and bottleneck analysis)	New Relic, Dynatrace, Gomez	✓	✓		
Network analysis (network traffic, HTTP headers, request/responses, protocol analysis)	Wireshark, Charles Proxy	✓		✓	
Application Performance Monitoring (APM) (Layer wise monitoring of application code)	New Relic, Dyna Trace Monitoring, Nagios		✓		✓

33

Survey of Web Performance Optimization Methods

Table 2-2 summarizes high-level WPO methods. It provides a two-dimensional analysis of WPO techniques and their impact on web performance.

CHAPTER 2 GENERAL WEB PERFORMANCE OPTIMIZATION METHODS

Table 2-2. WPO Techniques Summary

WPO Technique	Performance Optimization Impact			Optimization Layer			Optimization Time		Request Processing Pipeline Layer (Browser/CDN/Web Server/Application Server/DB Server/CMS/Infrastructure)	Candidate Web Component
	Request Optimization	Page Size Optimization	Page Load Time Optimization	Asset Optimization	Client Side	Server side	Design Time	Run Time		
Asset caching	✓	✘✘	✓	✓	✓	✘✘	✓	✓	Browser/CDN/Web Server	Images, CSS/JS, Video
Infrastructure Sizing	✘✘	✘✘	✓	✘✘	✘✘	✓	✓	✘✘	Infrastructure, network	
Prefetching	✓	✘✘	✓	✓	✓	✘✘	✘✘	✓	Browser/CDN/Web Server	Images, content CSS/JS, Video, files
Performance Monitoring	✘✘	✘✘	✘✘	✘✘	✓	✓	✓✘	✓	Web Server/Application Server/DB Server/CMS/Infrastructure	Pages, widgets, download times
Performance Testing	✘✘	✘✘	✘✘	✘✘	✓	✓	✓	✓	Web Server/Application Server/DB Server/CMS/Infrastructure	Pages, widgets, download times

(continued)

35

CHAPTER 2 GENERAL WEB PERFORMANCE OPTIMIZATION METHODS

Table 2-2. (*continued*)

WPO Technique	Performance Optimization Impact			Optimization Layer			Optimization Time		Request Processing Pipeline Layer (Browser/CDN/Web Server/Application Server/DB Server/CMS/ Infrastructure)	Candidate Web Component
	Request Optimization	Page Size Optimization	Page Load Time Optimization	Asset Optimization	Client Side	Server side	Design Time	Run Time		
Asynchronous loading	✓	✓	✓	✗✗	✓	✗✗	✗✗	✓	Browser/Web Server/ Infrastructure	Images, CSS/JS, video
Multi-layer caching	✓	✓	✓	✓	✓	✓	✓	✓	Web Server/ Application Server/ DB Server/CMS/ Infrastructure	Images, CSS/JS, services, object, content

Performance Bottlenecks and Web Performance Patterns at Various Layers

Table 2-3 highlights the key performance bottleneck-causing components at various layers in the web request processing pipeline and identifies the main performance patterns that address those bottlenecks.

Table 2-3. *Web Performance Bottlenecks and Performance Patterns*

Component Causing Bottleneck	Bottleneck Scenario at High Load	Web Performance Optimization Pattern
User-Agent Layer		
Page-level web objects	> 100 objects per page impact page size and page load times.	Minimize objects per page and load resources asynchronously
Resource requests	>20 synchronous resource requests per page impact the page load time	Minimize HTTP requests Avoid long-running scripts Use asynchronous calls Minify and merge resources to minimize resource requests
Inline image and inline script	Inline images and inline scripts increase page load time.	Externalize images and scripts. Avoid inline scripts and images.
Web objects in the critical path	HTML parsing and JS execution form 35% of the critical path and creates a bottleneck.	Avoid long-running scripts. Use asynchronous scripts.

(*continued*)

CHAPTER 2 GENERAL WEB PERFORMANCE OPTIMIZATION METHODS

Table 2-3. (*continued*)

Component Causing Bottleneck	Bottleneck Scenario at High Load	Web Performance Optimization Pattern
Web Server Layer		
Third-party script/external object	Creates front-end SPOF for long-running scripts.	Use async scripts and test third-party objects. Use time out to avoid blocking.
Scripts	A synchronous request of long-running scripts/files blocks the page and creates a single point of failure.	Asynchronous resource requests and on-demand loading Use the iframe of the third-party scripts. Real user monitoring of performance metrics
Application Server Layer		
Server response	Impacts TTFB and latency and page load time by 10%	CDN usage, connection caching
Server configuration	Improper connection pool size, connection pool setting, threads, and pool size impact performance of heavy loads	Fine-tune and test the application server settings.
Network Layer		
DNS lookup	DNS Lookup impacts the initial connection setup	DNS caching and connection caching

Survey of Predominant Web Performance Optimization Techniques

This section looks at the major web performance optimization techniques that have maximum impact on web performance. Techniques such as caching, asset optimization, prefetching, request pipeline optimization, and performance optimization tools are explained. The latest trends on the Web, including AJAX and mobile web performance, are also discussed.

CHAPTER 2   GENERAL WEB PERFORMANCE OPTIMIZATION METHODS

Caching and Prefetching

Caching is a key enabler for improving the performance of the Web. Caching has a multifold impact on web performance. Essentially, caching fetches the required pre-processed data from the nearest location, making easier and faster access to the required data. Caching improves page load times, service completion times, and perceived page response time. It also reduces latency and consumed bandwidth. And, it minimizes the load on source systems to improve scalability, performance, and availability. Caching also enhances system scalability and uses optimal network bandwidth. Caching is done at multiple layers: the application layer, infrastructure layer and integration layer (services and resource invocation).

Cache Architecture

Based on the cached data type and nature of caching, you can broadly classify caching into two categories: static caching and dynamic caching. Static caching globally stores fixed/static data common to all users, sessions, contexts, and scenarios in its cache. Dynamic caching stores dynamic data specific for a given session/user in its cache. Figure 2-1 provides various subcategories of static caching and dynamic caching.

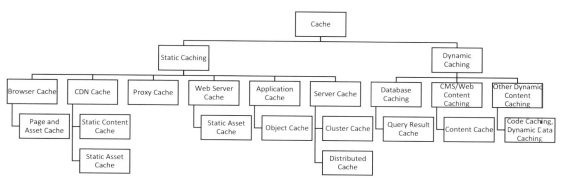

Figure 2-1. *Cache categories*

Static caching is used for in-memory lookups and immutable reference values. Hence static caching is ideally used to cache the lookup values from a system of records (SOR).

A browser-layer cache is the nearest cache location for the end user. Browsers use HTTP headers to decide the caching details.

CHAPTER 2　GENERAL WEB PERFORMANCE OPTIMIZATION METHODS

A CDN-layer cache provides caching for static global assets such as images, videos, static web content, static pages, multimedia files, JS/CSS files, and related content.

A proxy-layer cache provides caching at reverse proxies to enhance the throughput and response times of the web servers. A proxy server caches the resources (e.g., page content, assets, documents, data, and content) fetched from source systems and improves the overall response performance.

A web server–layer cache provides caching for HTML fragments, images, and static content.

An application-layer cache caches objects. Data and content retrieved from database calls, service calls, lookup lists, and controlled values, which are frequently used and updated across pages and user sessions.

Server-layer caching includes built-in caching support for caching pages, content, and data.

Dynamic caching consists of database-driven data, CMS-driven content, personalized content, services-driven information, and so forth. Database caching includes query result caching to cache query results.

CMS caching includes caching web content retrieved from content management systems.

Caching is essential in maintaining optimal performance. The following are various caching opportunities to improve web performance.

- Browser caching
  - Leverage cache-control and expiry header for static assets
  - Set the expiry value based on the frequency of change
- Asset caching
  - Static assets like images, JS/CSS stored in a web server
  - Leverage web server cache settings
- CDN caching
  - CDN servers can be leveraged to serve assets to diversified geographies
- Page caching
  - Leverage web page caching for custom tags getting data from a remote data source

- Create custom caching tags/variables for frequently accessed content on a web page.
  - Static drop-down values
  - Controlled list displaying reference values such as country list, language list.
  - The cached list is stored in JSON

Performance Optimization of Content and Assets Through Prefetching

A prefetching process anticipates the future needs for the content and keeps the content ready before the actual request happens. Prefetching naturally reduces costly real-time resource calls, reduces latency, and improves performance. Often the prefetched content is stored in the cache for efficient access. A combination of efficient caching along with prefetching is a very effective method for performance optimization. Most effective prefetching algorithms predict the objects that will be accessed in the future and prefetches them.

Prefetching is done at various layers in the request processing pipeline: browsers prefetch from a web server or proxy server, and the proxy server prefetches from the web server. CDNs also prefetch embedded application content/associated content and follow embedded links and keep it ready in memory. For prefetch between browser and web server, models such as the *prediction by partial matching* (PPM) data compressor, resource reference patterns, and a user's historical access pattern can be used to predict future access. Between the web proxy and web server, most of the techniques propose pushing of content from the web server to the proxy server.

Another technique is to understand common users' interests and access patterns through the proxy logs and then prefetch the most popular content. Similarly, browsers can also prefetch content from proxy servers, and a few proxies use PPM to push content to browser clients.

The origin servers (e.g., application servers) can also prefetch the content and assets using the access logs and content popularity. OpenWrt module does a popularity-based prefetch of DNS records, and it keeps TCP connections to frequently used web sites active. There are other prefetching techniques, such as the following.

CHAPTER 2 GENERAL WEB PERFORMANCE OPTIMIZATION METHODS

- **Association rules-based prefetching** involves pages that are grouped based on the likelihood of intragroup resources being accessed together. Association rules consider the order of page access in a user session, the adjacency of pages, and recency of pages to group the pages and prefetch them.

- **Markov prediction model** uses the history of users' access sequences for predicting future access probability. The technique uses the Markov model in a web application context using the application access pattern.

- **Use prediction by partial match (PPM)** to predict the content that will likely be accessed by the user using the historical access data. PB-PPM is a variant of PPM, which uses the subset of historical access data by using popularity (frequency of access) as the filter.

- **A dependency graph (DG)** is constructed using the web pages as nodes and a weighted edge between nodes indicating the next access probability. A dependency graph can prefetch using a probability threshold.

- **Predictive prefetching** can be done using server hints.

- **Cost functions** include popularity functions (uses object popularity for prefetching), object lifetime-based prefetch (prefetches the object with the longest lifetime, and good fetch (uses a combination of popularity and update rate for prefetching).

- **Clustering techniques** that group pages based on content similarity, web navigation graphs, cube models, and page ranking. Page content belonging to the cluster is prefetched. The clustering technique prefetches based on the clusters of web pages using the web user's access patterns.

- **Stochastic Petri nets (SPN)** prefetching considers metrics such as hit ratio, byte hit ratio, latency, and throughput for prefetching.

- **Other prefetching techniques** include intelligent prefetching, which prefetches the content to the user's nearest location; weblog analysis to predict a web user's future requests; semantic prefetching, which uses document semantics for predicting future requests; and location-aware prefetching that prefetches relevant data based on access location.

File-based prefetching algorithms use references, the correlation between file accesses for automatic prefetching. For prefetching in web scenarios, resource prefetching happens using the users' browsing behavior to predict future accesses, access history, and weblog mining; the prefetching method fetches using the objects' lifetime and popularity. Weighted graph and partial match prediction and semantic techniques are other prefetching techniques.

Content Chunking

The content chunking method decomposes the web page into multiple smaller content sections. Each of the content sections discusses a logical topic that is potentially reusable in other pages. For instance, on a product information page, the description chunk can be reused on the product list page to provide a brief summary. Content chunks are normally managed in the content management system (CMS). This includes taxonomy and the hierarchy of the content and its associated metadata. Content chunks with appropriate metadata are tagged and categorized so that they are easily discovered and retrieved. Chunks reduce network traffic and to reduce download time in mobile devices. Chunked data is also widely used in CDN for performance optimization. Content chunks are used in device-specific rendering and for handling dynamic data.

To summarize, existing techniques use content fragments to handle dynamic content using the following methods.

- Identifying reusable chunks and segregating static chunks from dynamic chunks

- Using dynamic fragments to automatically push the updated content to page through dynamic fragments

- Designing the cache differently for static and dynamic chunks

CHAPTER 2   GENERAL WEB PERFORMANCE OPTIMIZATION METHODS

Network and Request Processing Pipeline Optimization

Optimizing the network and web request pipeline is an effective web performance optimization technique. Network and request processing optimization are discussed in this section.

DNS Lookup Time and Connection Time Optimization

Network devices can cache DNS records and prefetch DNS records and TCP connections to speed up the time needed for DNS lookup and TCP connection, reducing the latency. The connection caching and DNS caching improves the load times by 35% and 10%, respectively. DNS lookup time is optimized through caching and minimizing DNS records.

Time to First Byte (TTFB) Optimization

An average of 10% to 20% of page load time is consumed by DNS lookup; 20% to 30% of page load is consumed by connection setup time; TTFB takes 40% to 60% of page load time; and content downloading takes about 10% to 20% of the total page load time. TTFB forms the biggest contributor to the total web page latency. Time to first byte is improved by using CDN and server-side application code optimization and connection caching.

DNS record caching improves DNS lookup time, connection caching for optimizing connection time, connection caching, CDNs optimizing TTFB and DNS caching, and content caching for optimizing object download time.

Web Performance Optimization Considerations

This section looks at considerations related to web performance optimization.

Mobile Web Performance Optimization

Mobile is becoming the primary target platform. Optimization of the Web for mobile devices is increasingly important. Asset optimization, content rendition, user experience enhancement, progressive/adaptive enhancement, communication protocols, automatic page layout structuring, and data exchange formats are some of the key trends in this category.

End-to-End Performance Monitoring Methods and Tools

Existing monitoring tools monitor a portion of the performance processing pipeline. As a result, performance engineers and system administrators need to employ multiple tools and technologies to get the complete picture of performance. The granularity of monitoring also varies across tools and technologies. Hence, an end-to-end tool that can monitor all the systems and components involved in the performance processing pipeline is needed.

Cloud-Based Performance Optimizations

Methods and techniques for optimizing cloud-based web applications is another important research area. As more and more web applications embrace the cloud phenomenon, a cloud-ready web application with optimal web performance is highly desirable. This area includes research topics such as automatic performance detection in the cloud, accurate performance monitoring, and reporting for cloud-based applications.

Analyzing and Debugging End-to-End Performance Issues

Troubleshooting and analyzing end-to-end performance issues is challenging due to various layers, systems, and components. There is scope for identifying methods to efficiently identify and analyze performance bottleneck scenarios, which helps with troubleshooting. Tools that could proactively indicate potential performance bottlenecks or leading indicators/markers of performance issues are highly desirable.

Performance Metrics and Measurement

It is necessary to identify various performance metrics that impact the end-user experience and measure them efficiently.

Design for Performance

This section looks at the key design aspects of performance-based design. The common problems with web performance are discussed next.

CHAPTER 2 GENERAL WEB PERFORMANCE OPTIMIZATION METHODS

Summary

- Common web performance optimization tools include the following: web page analysis tools (HTML analysis, performance benchmarking, improvement guidelines), page development tools (analysis of page load times, asset size, asset load times, etc.), asset merging and minification tools (JS/CSS minification), page performance testing tools (load simulation), image compression tools, web server plugins (for automatic compression, minification, merging, placement, caching, etc.), CSS optimization tools, bottleneck analysis (dependency and bottleneck analysis), real user monitoring (RUM) (monitoring and bottleneck analysis), network analysis (network traffic, HTTP headers, request/responses, protocol analysis), and application performance monitoring (APM) (layer-wise monitoring of application code).

- The key performance bottleneck areas are page-level web objects, resource requests, inline image and inline script, web objects in the critical path, web server layer, third-party script/external object, scripts, application server layer, server response, server configuration, network layer, and DNS lookup.

- The key web performance antipatterns are heavy landing/gateway pages, bad integration design, and the absence of key process testing, an omnichannel strategy, and early and iterative performance testing.

- Common performance best practices include lightweight design, search-centered experiences, asynchronous alternatives, omnichannel optimization, layered architecture, iterative testing, and monitoring.

PART II

Modern Web Optimization

CHAPTER 3

Web Performance Optimization Framework

To achieve optimal performance, you need a performance optimization framework that defines the performance optimization methods and tools for end-to-end performance optimization. A web performance optimization (WPO) framework addresses various concerns of web performance optimizations and provides a blueprint for the web community to achieve performance goals. This chapter proposes a web reference architecture that identifies all the systems, layers, and components involved in end-to-end performance optimization. A web performance optimization framework looks at web performance holistically and elaborates on the performance optimization methods for each layer.

A performance maturity model defines various stages of performance maturity for an organization. An organization can assess its current maturity level using this model.

This chapter looks at the web performance optimization framework and web performance maturity model. It also discusses various steps in end-to-end performance-based development.

To develop a performance-optimized web application, you need to ensure that you follow the performance guidelines and best practices in all phases of the project. A performance-driven development approach is needed to ensure that the web application meets the performance service-level agreement (SLA). A web performance optimization framework covers the end-to-end phases of project stages.

A web performance optimization framework provides guidelines and methods for adopting a performance-driven development framework for web applications. The web performance optimization framework is designed with the following objectives.

- Provides steps and checklists from a performance standpoint at all project lifecycle stages.

CHAPTER 3   WEB PERFORMANCE OPTIMIZATION FRAMEWORK

- Provides the multi-layer WPO methods across the complete web request processing pipeline. Elaborates performance-based design, performance-focused development, performance testing, and performance monitoring.
- Optimizes performance for the entire web request processing pipeline.
- Provides performance governance describing the roles, responsibilities, and process steps in web performance optimization.

The web performance optimization framework is used in the development of an optimized and personalized web site. Let's look at the web performance reference architecture that explains all the layers covering various dimensions of web performance optimization. The next section proposes a web performance optimization framework that describes various activities that need to be carried out at various project lifecycle phases from a performance standpoint.

Web Performance Reference Architecture

This section discusses a comprehensive web performance reference architecture that covers various dimensions of web performance optimization.

A web performance reference architecture is depicted in Figure 3-1. It consists of various categories of web performance. The web performance reference architecture covers the core dimensions of the web performance: performance at project lifecycle stages, web request processing pipeline at various layers, the performance of key web components, and performance governance. The proposed web performance optimization framework covers all the layers and components depicted in the web performance reference architecture.

The reference architecture depicted in Figure 3-1 serves as a guide for the structured organization of various aspects of web performance optimization.

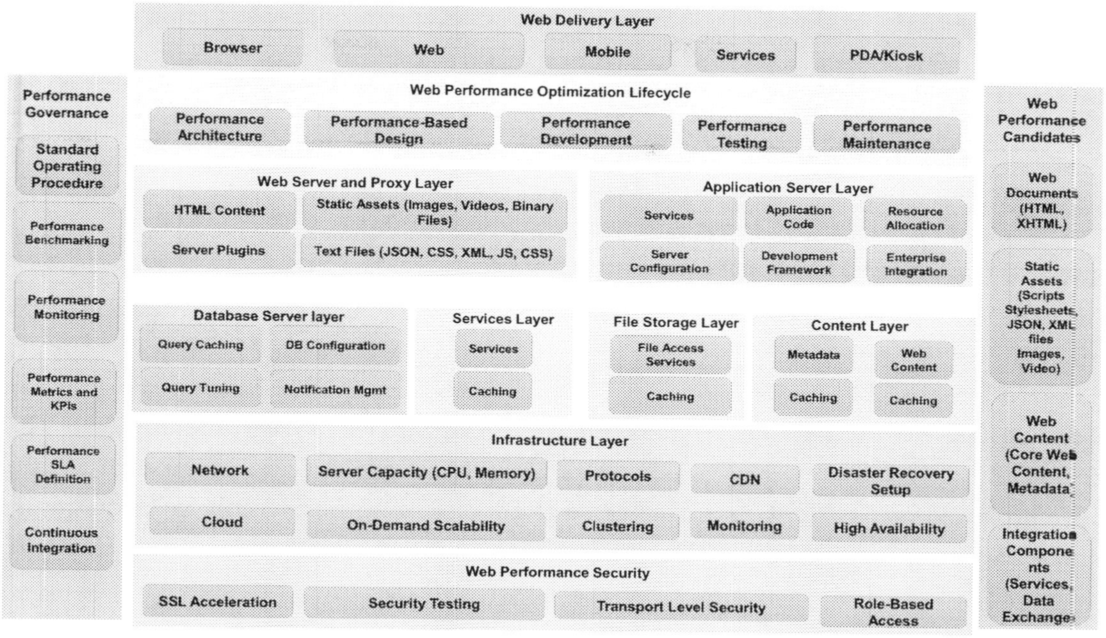

CHAPTER 3 WEB PERFORMANCE OPTIMIZATION FRAMEWORK

Figure 3-1. *Web performance reference architecture*

The web performance reference architecture depicted in Figure 3-1 groups the web performance concerns into various categories. The first category is the *web delivery layer*, consisting of end-user devices and user agents. The second category, the *web performance optimization lifecycle*, defines the performance optimizations in project lifecycle stages. The third category, the *web performance optimization layers*, elaborates various layers involved in the web request processing pipeline. The *web performance candidates* category explores key web components that need to be optimized. *Performance governance* describes various governance-related elements.

The web delivery layer consists of various channels, such as browsers, mobile devices, web services, tablets, PDAs, smartphones, and kiosks through which the end user experiences the information and perceives the web performance. End-user performance is measured in this layer.

The web performance optimization lifecycle encompasses various performance optimization measures undertaken at different stages of the development lifecycle. Architecture principles and performance guidelines/SLAs are defined in the architecture definition stage. Performance modeling, performance benchmarking, and performance-based design are conducted during the design phase. The performance guidelines

51

are implemented and tested in the development phase as part of performance-based development. The performance SLAs are monitored and maintained on production environment as a part of performance maintenance.

The core portion of the web performance reference architecture are the web performance optimization layers. To achieve an optimal end-to-end web performance, it is necessary to optimize the performance at all the layers involved in the web request processing pipeline. In the web server and proxy layer, web components such as HTML content, static assets, JS/CSS files must be optimized. At the application server layer, the application code, server configuration, services should be fine-tuned. Queries, the result cache, and configuration need to be optimized at the database layer. Data-related patterns are discussed in Chapter 11. Service optimization and service caching are done at the services layer. Integration-related patterns to optimize the performance are covered in Chapter 12. At the infrastructure layer, it is important to optimize the network, hardware sizing, protocols, disaster recovery setup, and use a CDN. The security layer involves SSL acceleration, transport-level security, and security-related elements. Infrastructure sizing is discussed in Chapter 7.

Performance governance is a continuously ongoing activity throughout all performance lifecycle phases and at all layers. It involves performance SLA monitoring, performance reporting, and notification, defining performance metrics, KPIs, and continuous integration. Performance governance covers the standard operation procedures (SOP) and performance optimization–related processes.

The reference architecture also lists key web performance candidate components that are optimized as part of the web performance optimization exercise. This includes web documents such as images, scripts such as JavaScript, CSS files, videos, HTML, JSON, XML, web content, and integration components.

Next, let's discuss a web performance optimization framework covering all layers and components discussed in the web performance reference architecture.

Web Performance Optimization Framework

A web performance optimization framework addresses various performance optimizations, as depicted in the reference architecture in Figure 3-1. The web performance optimization framework covers various WPO dimensions, such as performance optimizations at various lifecycle stages, performance optimizations

CHAPTER 3 WEB PERFORMANCE OPTIMIZATION FRAMEWORK

at various layers, and performance governance. The web performance optimization framework is used in all phases of the project lifecycle. This section discusses the web performance optimization framework and the reference implementation of the framework.

The performance optimization framework is depicted in Figure 3-2. The framework covers various components and activities in four stages of web development.

The web performance optimization framework specifies the main performance optimization methods at various phases.

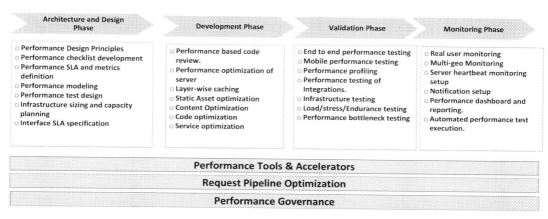

Figure 3-2. *Web performance optimization framework*

During the design and architecture phase, you can adopt a performance-based design. This includes defining performance design principles and developing a performance checklist and performance patterns used during development and testing phases. You also finalize the performance SLAs related to the response time, throughput, resource utilization, and so forth. You design performance test cases and setup an optimally sized infrastructure. Performance modeling and user load modeling of the application are done using peak user loads, peak usage hours, application usage patterns, and identifying key performance scenarios and performance objectives and metrics.

During the development phase, a performance-based development methodology is adopted using iterative performance code reviews. Application code, server configurations, and web pages are fine-tuned from a performance standpoint. The development team uses the performance design checklist and architecture principles

CHAPTER 3　WEB PERFORMANCE OPTIMIZATION FRAMEWORK

defined in the design and architecture phase. We have provided a Performance Optimization Checklist in Appendix A that can be used as reference. The multi-layer caching system is also developed in this phase. Asset, service, and content optimization techniques are implemented for page modules.

The performance validation phase involves iterative performance testing and measuring all the identified performance metrics and SLAs for end-to-end performance scenarios. You conduct various types of performance testing, such as peak load testing, infrastructure testing, endurance testing, infrastructure, and content volume testing. During the performance testing and analysis phase, you identify performance bottlenecks and fine-tune components and systems to address the bottleneck. Performance testing is also conducted on all supported browsers and mobile devices.

In the monitoring phase, you mainly conduct performance monitoring activities such as server health check monitoring, real-time application monitoring, automated performance testing. SLA violations are reported and notified proactively to system administrators to take corrective actions.

Horizontal components such as performance tools and accelerators are used in all project phases for enhanced productivity. Web performance governance spans all phases of web performance optimization. Web performance is optimized at various phases in the web request processing pipeline.

Let's now have a deeper discussion on each of the stages in the web performance optimization framework covering the performance-based design, performance-focused development, performance testing, and performance monitoring.

Performance-Based Design

This section looks at performance rules, design checklists, and tools used during the design phase. The main performance rules and their performance impact are defined in Table 3-1.

Table 3-1. *Categorized Performance Rules*

Category	Performance Rule	Impact on web performance
Request Optimization	Minimize HTTP requests.	Reduces bandwidth consumed
	Concatenate all scripts and stylesheets into a single master file.	Merging reduces the network calls
	Eliminate all duplicate files and unnecessary files.	Eliminates unnecessary server calls
	Remove HTTP 404 causing links.	Eliminates unnecessary resource calls
	Asynchronously load the JavaScript.	Improves the perceived page load time
	Eliminate iframes.	Reduces the blocking of the parent window
	Remove redirects.	Avoids additional calls
	Cache DNS records.	Minimizes the DNS lookup time
Web Object Size Optimization	Minify JS and CSS files.	Reduces the overall page size
	Enable image compression.	Reduces the overall page size
	Compress the HTML content using gzip compression.	Reduces the overall page size
	Remove HTML whitespace.	Reduces the overall page size
Http Header Optimization	Use cache-control headers for static assets such as images, CSS, JSON, and so forth.	Reduces the load time for static assets
	Serve the static assets with appropriate expire cache header.	Reduces the load time for static assets
Asset Placement	Place CSS files in the head tag at the top of the page.	Improves the initial page load time

(*continued*)

Table 3-1. (*continued*)

Category	Performance Rule	Impact on web performance
	Place JS files at the bottom.	Improves the perceived page load time by eliminating the blocking of critical render resources
	Externalize inline JS or CSS.	Enables browser caching and parallel downloads
Image Optimization	Load images asynchronously on-demand.	Improves page render time
	Optimize the image size based on the requesting device.	Improves page rendering time for various devices
	Use web-friendly image format	Reduces overall page size
	Scale images with exact width and height	Optimizes the overall image size
	Use image maps and CSS sprites wherein multiples images are combined and rendered using style rules.	Eliminate unnecessary image requests
Network Optimization	Use CDN to serve static images.	Reduces the load time for images
	Host the images and multimedia files in different servers.	Improves the page load time as browsers can download the multimedia files in parallel
External Dependency Optimization	Optimize the external and third-party scripts and dependencies.	Improves the overall page load time
Web Application Design Optimization	Conduct iterative performance testing.	Uncovers the performance issues early and fix them
	Use a lightweight service-based integration model and load the data asynchronously on-demand.	Improves service response time

Performance Design Principles

The key page performance design principles are as follows.

Lightweight design (web components such as pages, UI components, etc.)

- Include only core functionality and required UI components on landing/gateway pages.
- Use optimized/compressed marquee image and other media on the landing pages.
- Use lightweight integration mode such as REST with JSON.

Search-centered experience

- Position highly optimized search as a key tool for information discovery.
- Provide intuitive information architecture.
- Leverage metadata tagging for content for efficient information discovery.

Asynchronous service invocation

- Use AJAX calls on web pages to optimize the perceived page load time
- Use the lazy loading data model for web page components.
- Leverage stateless REST services for integration.

Omnichannel optimization

- Design web page components for mobile devices.
- Develop UI components supported for all browsers.

Layered architecture

- Design a multi-layered system architecture based on the "separation of concerns" architecture principle; each layer handles distinct responsibility.
- Use loosely coupled layers and solution components.

CHAPTER 3   WEB PERFORMANCE OPTIMIZATION FRAMEWORK

Iterative testing and monitoring

- Test early and test often for each iteration and all milestones.
- Use layer-wise testing for all layers.
- Continuous real-time monitoring and notification

The key design principles are summarized in Figure 3-3.

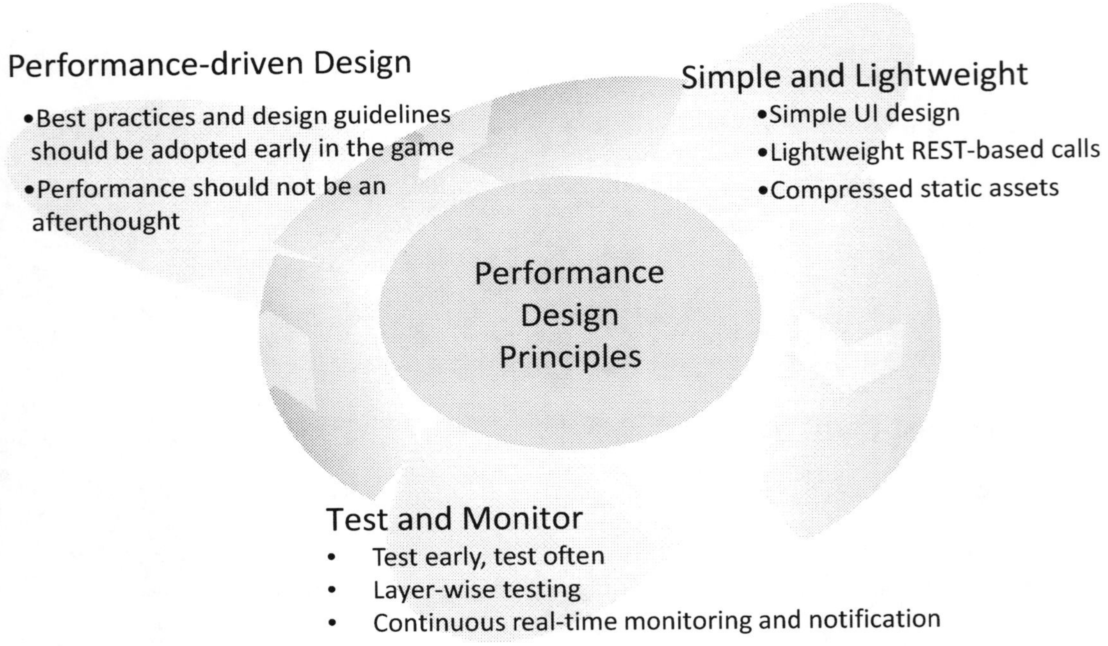

Performance-driven Design
- Best practices and design guidelines should be adopted early in the game
- Performance should not be an afterthought

Simple and Lightweight
- Simple UI design
- Lightweight REST-based calls
- Compressed static assets

Performance Design Principles

Test and Monitor
- Test early, test often
- Layer-wise testing
- Continuous real-time monitoring and notification

Figure 3-3. Performance design principles

Tools for Web Performance Optimization

Table 3-2 lists various web performance optimization tools that are used for testing.

CHAPTER 3 WEB PERFORMANCE OPTIMIZATION FRAMEWORK

Table 3-2. *Performance Optimization Tools*

Testing Type	Open Source Tool(s)
Web testing	• Selenium • Crawljax • Cucumber • HtmlUnit
HTML Compliance Testing	• W3C validator
Web Performance Analysis	• Yahoo Yslow • Google PageSpeed
Performance Testing	• JMeter • LoadUI
Static Code Analysis Tools	• FindBugs • Eclipse • Checkstyle • SonarSource • PMD
Profiling Tool	• JProfiler
Service Testing	• SOAPUI

Performance-Based Development

Performance-based development is the key step in the performance-driven development framework. In this phase, performance bottlenecks and performance antipatterns are identified, and then all the performance optimization rules and best practices are applied. This section also looks at optimizing performance on existing web applications.

During the build stage, developers need to follow the performance best practices and performance guidelines defined in the design phase. The main web performance optimization methods that are followed during the implementation phase are provided.

The key UI optimizations and its impact on the page response time are shown in Table 3-3.

CHAPTER 3   WEB PERFORMANCE OPTIMIZATION FRAMEWORK

Table 3-3. *UI-Level Performance Optimization*

UI Optimizations	Impact on Page Response Time
Static asset optimization (JS, CSS, JSON, XML) Merge into minimal sets • Minify the merged files • CSS at the top and JS files at the bottom	• Merging reduces the number of HTTP requests • Minification reduces the overall page size speeding the page load • Merging and minification improves perceived page load by approximately 25% • Appropriate positioning improves the perceived page load time
Binary assets (image, media, Flash) • Use the compressed format and CSS Sprites • Use CDN for edge side caching	• Optimizes the overall page size • Improves performance on mobile devices • CDN provides optimized performance for multi-geographies. CDN approximately improves the page response times by 10%
Web page–related • Remove any duplicate/unnecessary calls • Reduce the white spaces	• Reduces the number of HTTP requests • Optimized DOM size for the end web page

The key performance-related guidelines are depicted in Figure 3-4.

CHAPTER 3 WEB PERFORMANCE OPTIMIZATION FRAMEWORK

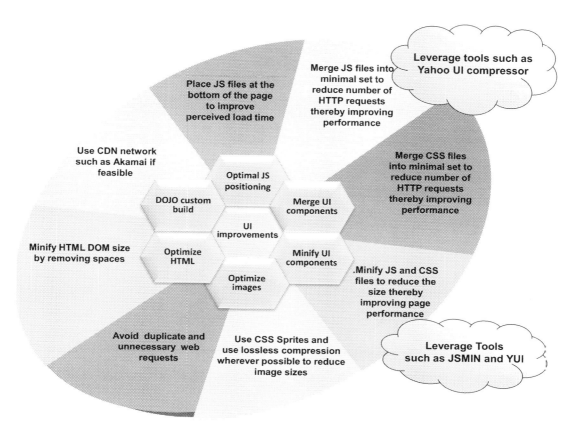

Figure 3-4. Performance best practice guidelines

Top-Down Performance Optimization for Improving Performance of Existing Applications

For existing applications and legacy applications, you adopt the top-down analysis to identify the existing performance bottlenecks. We have used the top down performance optimization in the case study discussed in Chapter 8.

The following are the steps for top-down performance optimization.

1. Apply the 80-20 rule to analyze the performance by identifying the top 20% of the popular pages/processes that are most frequently used.

2. Root cause analysis by leveraging tools to identify the component-wise, layer-wise, and asset-wise size and load times. Analyze the

CHAPTER 3 WEB PERFORMANCE OPTIMIZATION FRAMEWORK

components in each of the layers to identify the performance bottleneck. Address the identified performance bottleneck with the best practices and solution patterns.

3. Iteratively cover the remaining pages and transactions.

4. Continuously monitor the performance of the pages.

The key activities in top-down performance optimization are depicted in Figure 3-5.

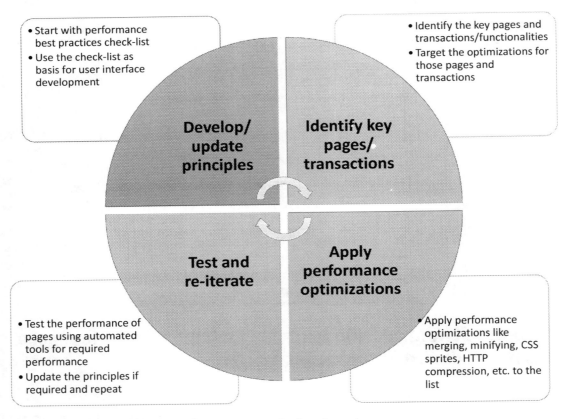

Figure 3-5. *Top-down performance optimization steps*

Web Performance Bottlenecks and Web Performance Antipatterns

Let's look at common performance bottlenecks and antipatterns, which impact web performance. Table 3-4 provides a list of commonly occurring performance bottlenecks.

CHAPTER 3　WEB PERFORMANCE OPTIMIZATION FRAMEWORK

Table 3-4. Performance Bottleneck and Antipatterns

Bottleneck Area	Performance Antipatterns
Web Page Design	• Heavy landing/gateway pages • UI design with many components and functionality • Pages designed with huge images
Third-Party Components	Third-party scripts and widgets could block page load and impact overall page performance.
Network Bandwidth	Usage of suboptimal network bandwidth across internal systems
Server Configuration	Not adopting optimal server settings for parameters such as heap memory, thread pool size, connection pool size, and so forth
Infrastructure Capacity	• Usage of suboptimal memory, CPU, disk capacity for servers • Not conducting load testing, stress testing, endurance testing, and related performance tests
Performance Testing	• Not conducting all necessary performance tests (e.g., load test, stress test, endurance test) for a web application. • Conducting performance testing at the end of the application development. • Not conducting omnichannel testing to test performance on mobile platforms.
Application Code	• Not conducting a performance code review. • Not performing iterative performance testing.
Service Calls	• Non-validated frequent service calls. • Heavy usage of synchronous service calls.
Integration Design	• Third-party component integration without a proper SLA framework.
Process Validation	• Lack of performance testing of overall steps and/or for process/transaction.
Omnichannel Strategy	• The absence of mobility-enabled sites or lack of multi-device testing.

Chapter 3   Web Performance Optimization Framework

Figure 3-6 provides the performance effort matrix, which provides the effort needed for implementing each of the performance rules and its impact on the overall page performance.

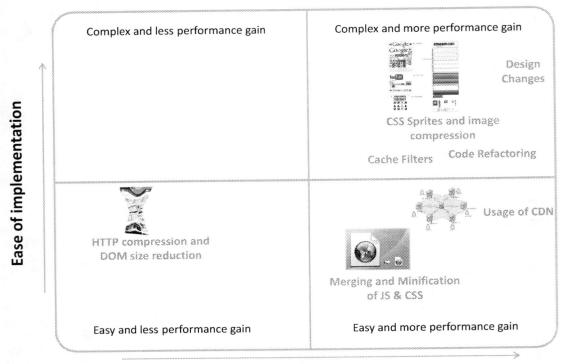

Figure 3-6. *Performance effort matrix*

Merging and minification of JS/CSS files and asset placement and usage of CDN (e.g., Akamai) are relatively easier to implement and provides maximum performance benefits. Hence, these need to be implemented first. In the next step, you need to implement other performance optimization measures, such as CSS sprites, image compression, cache filters, and so forth. In the last step, you look at HTTP compression and DOM size/page size reduction.

Content Optimization

A web page consists of multiple content sections. The page content comes from HTML fragments or web content stored in CMS. Let's look at ways to optimize the web content retrieved from CMS.

- While designing the content strategy, think of content in chunks instead of a monolithic content. Modular content chunk makes the content reusable and enhances the caching optimization.

- Use adaptive techniques (e.g., progressive enhancement/ degradation) while creating the content. This automatically makes the content optimal for all devices.

- Cache the content at the chunk level. Fine-tune the caching period based on the content update frequency. Perform on-demand chunk cache invalidation when new content is published.

- Adopt user-friendly information architecture for easier and faster discovery of relevant content.

- Tag the content chunks with relevant metadata and tags that help achieve accurate information discovery.

Asset Optimization

Non-HTML resources, such as images, scripts, and JSON, consume the bulk of the page size.

Figure 3-7 is a pictorial representation of the impact of assets on page load time and page size.

CHAPTER 3 WEB PERFORMANCE OPTIMIZATION FRAMEWORK

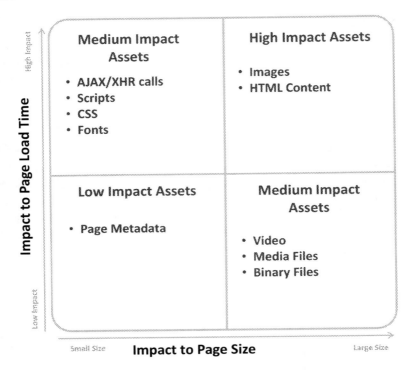

Figure 3-7. Impact of assets on page load time and page size

Since 80% of load time is spent making HTTP requests for non-HTML content, you should look at design optimization of these web components. Table 3-6 covers the optimization techniques of high-impact assets (e.g., images) and medium-impact assets (e.g., scripts and video).

Table 3-6. *Asset Optimization Techniques*

Asset Optimization Technique	Candidate Asset Types				Impact on Page Performance			
	Images	JS/CSS	JSON/XML	Videos	Non-blocked loading	Optimize Page Load time	Minimize Resource Requests	Reduce Page Size
Merging multiple assets into a master asset/object inlining	✓	✓	✓			✓	✓	
Asset Minification	✓	✓	✓	✓		✓		✓
Asset Resize	✓			✓		✓		✓
Asynchronous resource invocation	✓	✓	✓		✓	✓	✓	
On-demand/lazy loading	✓	✓	✓	✓	✓	✓	✓	✓
Adaptive resizing	✓			✓				✓
CSS Sprites	✓					✓	✓	✓
Lightweight/Web-friendly Data Exchange format		✓				✓	✓	✓
Right Asset Positioning (CSS at top and JS at the bottom)		✓			✓	✓		
Domain sharding and parallelize downloads	✓	✓	✓		✓	✓		

(*continued*)

67

CHAPTER 3 WEB PERFORMANCE OPTIMIZATION FRAMEWORK

Table 3-6. (*continued*)

Asset Optimization Technique	Candidate Asset Types					Impact on Page Performance		
	Images	JS/CSS	JSON/XML	Videos	Non-blocked loading	Optimize Page Load time	Minimize Resource Requests	Reduce Page Size
Leverage cache control headers and expires tag	✓	✓	✓	✓	✓	✓		
Defer parsing		✓			✓	✓		
gzip compression	✓	✓		✓		✓		✓
Leverage browser and proxy caching	✓	✓	✓	✓		✓	✓	
Cacheable favicon	✓					✓		
Minimal HTTP requests	✓	✓	✓			✓	✓	
Externalize resources	✓	✓	✓	✓	✓	✓		
Minimize request size	✓	✓	✓	✓		✓		✓
Remove unused, invalid, duplicate links, resources	✓	✓	✓			✓	✓	
Use exact dimensions	✓			✓		✓		✓
Unblocked loading		✓			✓			
Avoid inline	✓	✓				✓		✓

(*continued*)

CHAPTER 3　WEB PERFORMANCE OPTIMIZATION FRAMEWORK

Table 3-6. (*continued*)

Asset Optimization Technique	Candidate Asset Types				Impact on Page Performance			
	Images	JS/ CSS	JSON/ XML	Videos	Non-blocked loading	Optimize Page Load time	Minimize Resource Requests	Reduce Page Size
Avoid CSS expression		✓				✓		
Minimize redirects	✓	✓	✓	✓				
Avoid long-running Scripts		✓			✓	✓		
Minimize cookie size								✓
Optimize external scripts		✓			✓	✓		
Group CSS selectors and CSS declarations		✓				✓		

Adopting asset optimization techniques, on average, decreases 35% of resource requests and reduces the overall page size by 35%. A combination of gzip and minification reduces the average page size by up to 78%

Web Performance Testing

Multidimensional web performance testing is essential for validating and maintaining performance SLAs. Figure 3-8 shows the four dimensions of performance testing.

69

CHAPTER 3   WEB PERFORMANCE OPTIMIZATION FRAMEWORK

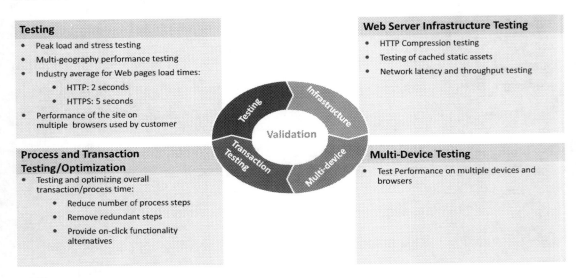

Figure 3-8. Dimensions of performance testing

End-to-end performance testing is needed to ensure optimal page performance. The following are various validations needed for end-to-end testing. We have covered the details of performance testing in Chapter 6.

Load Testing

In this category, a web application is subjected to peak load and stress load testing. The testing should be conducted for applications distributed across various geographies and on all supported browsers and user devices. The industry standard for page load time is 2 seconds for HTTP pages and 5 seconds for HTTPS pages. The testing should be conducted to validate the performance SLA at various loads. The following are key performance tests.

- **Load testing:** In this scenario, the normal load is used while varying the concurrent users to test the behavior of the web application. The application's response time and system resources are monitored.

- **Stress testing:** The application is subjected to an above-peak load condition to check the behavior of the application. The test is conducted to understand the breaking point of the application.

- **Endurance testing**: Normal load testing is conducted for an extended duration (normally up to 72 hours) to check for resource utilization and memory leaks.

- **Spike testing**: It tests application behavior during a sudden increase in user load.

Infrastructure Testing

Various infrastructure components (e.g., web servers, database servers, application servers) need to be tested and monitored at various loads. Server resources (e.g., CPU memory) should be monitored along with network latency and throughput during the testing process.

Process and Transaction Testing

In this phase, the key business transactions and processes are tested end to end. Processes like product checkout, user registration, and other crucial business activities are ideal candidates for testing. You explore optimization alternatives such as a process step reduction, process automation, removal of redundant process steps, and one-click alternatives (e.g., one-click checkout) in this phase.

Web Performance Monitoring

The last step in performance-based design is continuous performance monitoring. The various steps and activities in this process are depicted in Figure 3-9. We have covered the details of performance monitoring in Chapter 7.

CHAPTER 3 WEB PERFORMANCE OPTIMIZATION FRAMEWORK

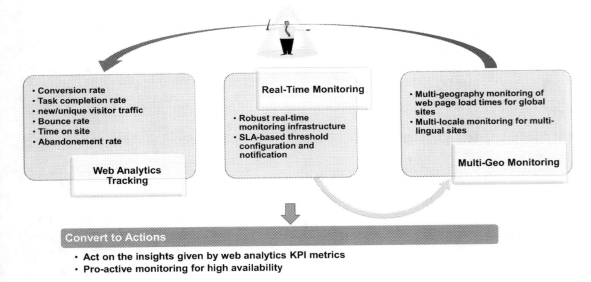

Figure 3-9. Performance monitoring process

Performance Tracking

In this phase, you use analytics tools (e.g., Omniture, Google Web Analytics) to track and monitor page performance metrics such as visitor traffic, page load time (PLT), conversion rate, and time on site, bounce rate, and abandonment rate. You use a web analytics dashboard to analyze the popular pages, user traffic, bounce rate, and so forth.

Real-Time Monitoring

A monitoring infrastructure includes real-time monitoring software and configuration setup to continuously check performance SLAs. The performance metrics and SLAs are tracked in real time, and reports/notifications are sent to site administrators who are in SLA violation.

Multi-Geo Monitoring

For a globally distributed web site, real-time monitoring is done from different geographies to test the performance of various languages and geo-specific sites.

All the insights gathered through monitoring are converted into actions, and proactive monitoring is an essential component of high availability.

CHAPTER 3 WEB PERFORMANCE OPTIMIZATION FRAMEWORK

End-to-end monitoring is needed to sustain optimal performance. The following are various aspects of monitoring.

- **Monitoring metrics: Define and track the following monitoring metrics for the application.**
  - Conversion rate
  - Task completion rate
  - New/unique visitor traffic
  - Bounce rate
  - Time on site
  - Abandonment rate
- **Monitoring infrastructure: Establish a real-time monitoring infrastructure to check the performance of the application.**
  - Robust real-time monitoring infrastructure
  - SLA-based threshold configuration and notification
  - Define governance processes for monitoring and notification
- **Enable multi-geo monitoring for global web platforms.**
  - Multi-geography monitoring of web page load times for global sites
  - Multi-locale monitoring for multilingual sites

Performance monitoring is discussed further in Chapter 7.

Web Performance Governance

Web performance governance defines performance elements that are governed and the methods and processes for performance governance. Performance governance identifies the roles and responsibilities for the methods. Figure 3-10 shows various aspects of performance governance.

CHAPTER 3 WEB PERFORMANCE OPTIMIZATION FRAMEWORK

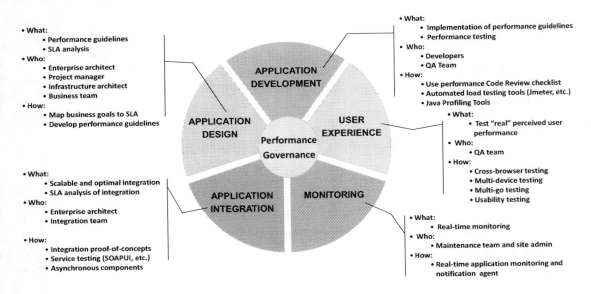

Figure 3-10. *Performance governance*

As depicted in Figure 3-10, the five dimensions of web performance are as follows.

- **Application design**: In the application design phase, the performance guidelines and performance SLAs need to be governed. Enterprise architects define various performance guidelines, performance patterns, and best practices. Business analysts define performance SLAs.

- **Application development**: During the application development phase, adherence to performance guidelines should be governed. Additionally, performance testing needs to be carried out to validate the performance SLAs. Application developers and quality assurance (QA) teams perform these activities. To validate the adherence to performance guidelines, application developers can use various performance checklists. QA team can leverage performance testing tools and profiling tools to conduct performance testing.

CHAPTER 3 WEB PERFORMANCE OPTIMIZATION FRAMEWORK

- **User experience**: In this category, the "perceived performance" of the end user should be governed. The quality assurance team governs this by conducting cross-browser testing, multi-device testing, multi-geo testing, and usability testing. Real user monitoring (RUM) tools can also be leveraged to conduct end-user performance testing.

- **Monitoring**: In this category, application monitoring and system monitoring need to be governed by the maintenance team. Robust monitoring needs real-time application monitoring and notification infrastructure.

- **Application integration**: In this category, enterprise architects and integration teams govern the performance of the enterprise integrations. The integration governance involves performance testing of the integration and service testing.

Figure 3-11 depicts the logical architecture of the reference solution implementing the framework.

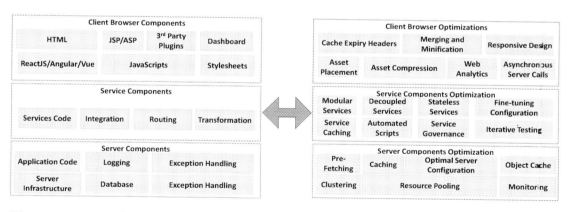

Figure 3-11. *Reference solution implementation*

Figure 3-11 also shows the optimization done at each of the layers.

75

CHAPTER 3   WEB PERFORMANCE OPTIMIZATION FRAMEWORK

Proposed Web Performance Maturity Model

A web performance maturity model features performance maturity stages and the web performance optimization methods adopted in each stage. A web performance maturity model is used for the following.

- Identifying the current performance maturity level of the web application.
- Identifying any performance gaps within existing web applications.
- Defining a performance roadmap for the web application.
- Planning for future web performance improvements.
- Identifying the performance optimization methods and the components at various project lifecycle stages.

The high-level stages of a web performance maturity model are featured in Figure 3-12.

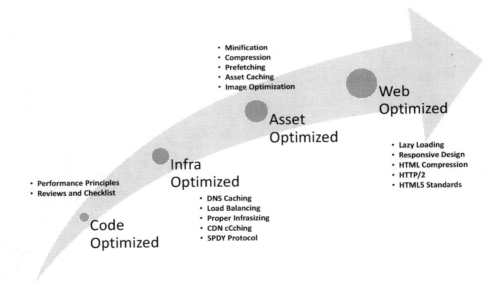

Figure 3-12. *Proposed web performance optimization maturity model*

This identifies four stages of the web performance maturity model: code optimized, infra-optimized, asset optimized, and web optimized. Figure 3-12 depicts the four stages of the maturity model.

The code-optimized maturity stage involves performance optimization principles, code reviews, and performance checklists. The impact on overall performance is below 10% on average. WPO techniques are used in application code and modules in the architecture and design and code development lifecycle stages.

The infra-optimized maturity stage includes infrasizing, load balancing, DNS caching, and asset minification. The impact of these WPO techniques on web performance is in the range of 10% to 30%. Infrastructure sizing and load balancing impacts page load time; DNS caching optimize the page load time by approximately 10%, and the asset minification technique optimizes the page size by approximately 16%. In the web server layer and network layer, you can use these WPO techniques on components such as assets and networks.

The asset-optimized maturity stage has a performance impact in the approximate range of 31% to 60%. Layer-wise caching and prefetching optimizes the page load time. Connection caching improves page load time by approximately 35%. Merging assets reduces page size by approximately 38%. *Time to first byte* (TTFB) optimizes the page load time by approximately 40%. The usage of the SPDY protocol improves the page load time by approximately 55%. WPO techniques are applied to assets, protocols, and connection in all layers.

In the web-optimized stage, WPO techniques impact web performance in the range of 61% to 100%. Mobile web optimization improves page size. AJAX optimization improves page load time. Browser caching reduces the overall page size by approximately 65%. HTML compression reduces the page size by approximately 70%. On-demand loading improves page load time by approximately 77%. A combination of gzip compression and minification reduces overall page size by approximately 78%. CDN caching improves page load time up to 100%. You can apply these techniques to JS/CSS files, multimedia files, web content, and services at the end-user layer, CDN layer, and web server layer.

CHAPTER 3 WEB PERFORMANCE OPTIMIZATION FRAMEWORK

Summary

- A web performance optimization framework provides guidelines and methods for developing a performance-driven development framework for web applications.

- Web performance reference architecture covers optimizations related to the web delivery layer, web performance optimization lifecycle, web performance optimization layers, performance governance.

- The web delivery layer consists of various channels such as a browser, mobile devices, web services, PDAs, smartphones, and kiosks through which the end user experiences the information and perceives the web performance.

- Web performance optimization lifecycle encompasses various performance optimization measures undertaken at different stages of the development lifecycle.

- Web performance optimization layers aim to optimize end-to-end web performance and performance at all the layers involved in the web request processing pipeline.

- The key performance best practices are lightweight design, search-centered experience, asynchronous service invocation, omnichannel optimization, layered architecture, iterative testing, and monitoring.

- Web optimization framework specifies the main performance optimization methods at various phases, such as the design phase, development phase, validation phase, and monitoring phase.

- The web performance maturity model depicts various performance maturity stages and the web performance optimization methods adopted in each stage.

- The web performance maturity model consists of the "Code Optimized" stage, "Infra Optimized" stage, "Asset Optimized" and "Web Optimized" stage.

CHAPTER 4

Mobile Web Performance Optimization

The mobile web is a widely popular digital delivery platform as mobile phones are fast becoming the primary gateways for Internet users. The mobile web provides an optimal user experience on various browsers and mobile devices. Mobile web users expect fast-loading mobile web platforms, especially on mobile devices. Mobile web performance highly influences user traffic, bounce rates, site abandonment rates, average session time, conversion rates, page views, user satisfaction, user retention rates, and ad revenue rates. In a nutshell, a high-performing mobile web platform is crucial to the success of an organization's digital strategy.

The mobile web provides the flexibility of a single code base for desktop browsers and mobile browsers. The single code base makes the mobile web a popular option among enterprises delivering user-engagement platforms.

Today's web platforms handle a lot of data and render an engaging user interface. Page size, page data, and scripts are increasing by the day. Mobile web users expect a faster response time on mobile browsers. To manage users' expectations, you need to holistically look at design factors, network parameters, and runtime parameters to fully optimize modern web applications.

This chapter discusses performance best practices on a mobile web platform. It looks at Angular and React, the two most popular JavaScript frameworks, diving into design-related, network-related, and runtime performance optimizations.

HTML5 apps offer a wide variety of web performance optimization features, which are discussed at the end of the chapter.

Performance engineers, web developers, digital architects, project managers, and program managers should find this chapter useful.

CHAPTER 4　MOBILE WEB PERFORMANCE OPTIMIZATION

Mobile Web Framework

JavaScript frameworks are the most popular choice for developing mobile web applications. Angular, React, and Vue are the most widely used JavaScript frameworks. Table 4-1 compares the key characteristics of these three frameworks and includes applicable scenarios.

Table 4-1. Comparison of popular JavaScript frameworks

Criteria	Angular	React	Vue
General	An end-to-end framework, TypeScript, and component-based, HTML-based template, two-way data binding, Ahead of Time (AOT) support	JavaScript libraries for building user interfaces, JSX-based templates, one-way data binding, use virtual DOM	A progressive framework, HTML-based templates, two-way data binding
Applicable Use Cases	Single-page applications (SPA), large scale enterprise applications	Data-intensive applications, SPA with multiple views, headless CMS, and e-commerce platform	Single-page applications (SPA)
Architecture Pattern	Model-view-view-model (MVVM)	MVC, Atomic design pattern	MVVM
Language	TypeScript	JavaScript (ES6)	JavaScript
Dependency Injection	Supported	Supported through HOC	Supported
Server-Side Rendering And SEO	Supported through Angular Universal	SSR Supported through NextJS and SEO supported through React Helmet	Supported through NUXT.js
Security Support	JWT-based authentication, CSRF and XSSI support by HTTPClient library, Dynamic Forms, DOM sanitizer, computed properties	Dynamic forms, computed properties	X-CSRF-TOKEN support for CSRF vulnerability, Dynamic Forms, DOM sanitizer, computed properties, Google Caja

(continued)

Table 4-1. (*continued*)

Criteria	Angular	React	Vue
Progressive Web App Support	Yes, through the Ionic 2 library	Supported	Yes, through Vue CLI
Cross-Platform Support	Ionic 2 provides a single code base for all mobile platforms	React Native for building the native mobile apps	Vue native support, Cordova support
Unit Testing Support	Jasmine test framework, Karma test runner	ZEST, Enzyme	Karma test runner
Hosting Options	Firebase, AWS, Docker	Firebase, AWS, Docker	Firebase
GraphQL	Supported	Supported	Supported

Performance Optimization of Angular Framework

Angular is one of the most popular open source web frameworks for building client-side single-page applications (SPA). Angular uses TypeScript for core development. Angular uses component-based architecture for building client-side applications.

Angular applications are optimized in three dimensions from performance standpoint: design, network, and runtime. Design performance optimizations discuss optimizing the Angular code during the design phase. Network performance optimizations discuss the performance improvement of the load time of the applications (such as latency improvement, response time improvement, and reducing bandwidth consumption). Runtime performance optimizations improve the performance of the angular application during runtime. Runtime optimizations improve the optimizations related to page rendering and change detection.

Design-Related Performance Optimizations

This section discusses common design-related performance optimizations. As a basic hygiene factor, you should adhere to Angular's recommended naming conventions, comments, and folder structure.

Some the key naming conventions use dashed case for element selectors; *upper camel case* for class names, module names, interface, pipes, and services; lower camel case for property names, method names, and variable names; a *module suffix* for module names; and dots and dashes to separate words in a descriptive name. *Linting* is used for validating coding standards.

You need to document appropriate comments at the beginning of the file and for service calls, complex logic, and on other required places.

Leveraging Service Workers

Service workers play the role of HTTP proxy on the client browser end. A service worker intercepts client requests and handles them appropriately. Based on network availability, a service worker can load data from the application cache. We have discussed the server worker based pattern in Chapter 10.

You can use the Angular mobile toolkit or an offline plugin for a webpack to implement this design.

Ahead-of-Time (AoT) Compilation

Use ahead-of-time (AoT) compilation for production build to ensure the code is optimized for production. AoT compiles most of the code during build time and minimizes the processing overhead at the browser level. AoT checks should also be done when integrating a third-party library, at code check-in and integration, with package.json files, and during a webpack change.

Unit Testing

Ensure that unit testing is part of the development process. You can use the built-in `ng test` command to run a unit test as part of the build process.

Removal of Unused Code

Once development is complete, developers should make sure that they remove unused references, code blocks, and files (images, CSS, JS, fonts, dependencies, etc.) so that bundles are optimized for production deployment. Evaluate all third-party libraries to check if it is possible to include a smaller version of the files. Remove all the unused fonts on the application.

Multiple Threads Using Web Workers

Leverage web workers to run the computationally intensive code in a separate thread. This avoids blocking the main UI thread.

Leveraging the defer and async Attributes

Add the `defer` attribute to the script tag to defer the loading of a synchronous scripts until the document is parsed. Similarly, the `async` attribute delays the script load until the document is parsed. The `defer` and `async` attributes improve a page's interactivity. You can use the `async` attribute for web analytics scripts.

Network-level Performance Optimizations

Network performance optimizations optimize network-related parameters, such as the number of requests, bandwidth consumption, and so forth.

Bundling and Code Splitting

Bundling reduces the total number of HTTP requests a browser makes to get an application. Reducing the total number of HTTP requests minimizes performance issues caused by network latency. Code splitting is done at the component level and at the route level to optimize bundle size. Code splitting creates chunks of the code base (including the JavaScript code) that are lazily loaded; only the needed chunks are loaded on demand. Chunks are progressively loaded when the user accesses the corresponding code modules. Code splitting reduces the first meaningful paint (FMP) time and time to interactive (TTI), especially for mobile browsers.

You can use tools such as Webpack, Webpack Code Splitting, SplitChunksPlugin, HTTP/2, Rollup, SystemJS Builder, and Browserify for bundling.

Minification

The process of minification eliminates white space, delimiters, comments, dead code, and mangled variables to reduce the overall size of the payload. The reduced payload size consumes less bandwidth, thereby improving the page load performance. Page download and execution times are also improved.

You can use tools such as Uglify or Google Closure Compiler for minification. These tools reduce bundle size through mangling, removing white space, removing comments, and so forth.

Removal of Unnecessary Code

To reduce the overall bundle size of the application, you can trim the white space in the templates by setting preserveWhitespaces in ComponentMetadata as false.

In the final version of the application, you can use the *tree-shaking method* to remove unnecessary methods and imports that are not used or referenced. You can use tools such as Webpack, Rollup, and the Google Closure compiler for tree-shaking. Angular's AoT compilation converts Angular HTML-like templates to JavaScript for efficient tree-shaking and removes all unnecessary directives to reduce the bundle size.

Lazy Loading

For large pages, you can lazily load application modules and resources (images, videos, pages, etc.) on-demand when users access corresponding functionality. Lazy loading reduces the bundle size and improves the initial page load time. It is recommended to lazily load the below-the-fold content (the content that is not currently visible to the user) and lazily load it only on user access. Lazy loading is enabled for components and routes.

For instance, on a typical e-commerce application's search page, you can load the search module and the search results module; when the user selects the product and clicks the "Add to cart" button, you can load the shopping cart module.

You can use Webpack to load the module asynchronously.

Resource Prefetching

Based on the application requirements, you can prefetch application resources such as images, scripts, stylesheets, JSON files, and so forth. Prefetching improves the user experience by optimizing the first meaningful paint. You can leverage the `PreloadingStrategy` class to implement the prefetching.

Runtime Performance Optimizations

The performance optimizations done during page rendition at runtime are described next.

CHAPTER 4 MOBILE WEB PERFORMANCE OPTIMIZATION

Leveraging Application Shell

The application shell improves the user's perceived load time. The application shell renders a minimized user interface on the initial load.

You can use the Angular mobile toolkit or Angular Universal to implement the application shell architecture.

Enable Production Mode

Angular has a default debug mode that runs change detection twice. You can disable the extra check happening in development mode by turning on enableProdMode. For production code, you can also use the buildoptimizer flag with Angular CLI.

Ahead of Time (AoT) Compilation

AoT compilation improves runtime performance by reducing the compilation-related computations. AoT performs compilation as part of the build process.

You can use Compiler CLI, Angular2-seed, or Angular CLI for using AoT.

Change Detection Optimizations

The Angular framework triggers change detection for all the component hierarchies at all asynchronous events. Change detection leads to heavy computation, which impacts the performance. One way to optimize this is to skip change detection on the component subtrees that are not impacted by the asynchronous event.

The following methods optimize change detection.

- Disable change detection for selected subtrees using the OnPush change detection strategy.

- Detach the change detector for a specific component tree so that the change detection is skipped for the subtree. You can use local change detection to run change detection only for the required component.

- Based on the use case, execute the code outside the Angular zone.

CHAPTER 4　MOBILE WEB PERFORMANCE OPTIMIZATION

Leveraging Pure Pipes

The `@Pipe` decorator sets the `Pure` attribute as true so that Angular can cache the output for a given input. The pure pipes do not cause any side effects and make the behavior predictable so that it is easily cached and avoids recomputation.

Performance Optimization of the React Framework

React is widely used for building single-page applications. The React framework is very useful for dynamic applications and data-intensive applications that need frequent and real-time data updates. React uses virtual DOM to efficiently manage data-intensive applications.

Design-Related Performance Optimizations

Folder structure and naming conventions are the basic design guidelines you need to handle while designing a React solution.

Some of the key naming conventions for React solution components are as follows.

- Follow upper camel case for filenames and React components.
- Follow lower camel case for property names.
- Use the filename for the component name.

To improve code readability, use the comments at the beginning of the file, during interaction with components, while using async services, and wherever complex logic is written.

This section covers key design optimizations from a performance standpoint.

React UI Framework

There are multiple React UI frameworks for handling UI development and for styling. The most popular React UI frameworks are React Bootstrap, Material-UI, Ant Design, and Semantic UI. You should do a thorough fitment analysis of the React UI frameworks based on the application requirements. The following describes the key strengths of each of the UI frameworks.

- React Bootstrap fits well with simple UI requirements. It provides support for components such as overlays, tooltips, alerts, and pagination.

- Ant Design is used for complex UI consisting of internationalization, table views, hierarchical tree views, data display components, calendars, and so forth.

- Material-UI is used for UI needs such as autocomplete, selection controls, expansion panels, and so forth.

Atomic Design Pattern

You build the higher-order views as the composition of modular lower-level modules. In the atomic design pattern, the lowest building block is called an *atom*. Buttons, links, input fields, and drop-down fields are examples of atoms. You compose atoms into *molecules*, such as panels, forms, and so forth. You build *layouts* using the molecules. Finally, you build the page using layouts.

The atomic design pattern enables you to develop modular, reusable, configurable, and extensible components. The atomic design pattern enables the plug-and-play model by providing ready-to-use components.

In solution design, you develop a library or catalog (also known as playbook) of the atomic design components. The development team can refer to the catalog to explore reusability while building new pages.

Higher-Order Component (HOC)

Develop higher-order components (HOCs) for crosscutting components that share functionality. A HOC wraps the original component in a container component. The following are HOC best practices.

- Use composition instead of mutation to create HOC.

- Use a wrapped component to pass the unrelated props.

- Use HOCs outside as variables.

Separating Container and Presentation Components

Separate container components from presentation components. A clean separation aligns with the separation of concerns (SoC) principle and neatly decouples responsibilities. Container components such as pages and user lists have the following features.

- Stateful and state management
- No DOM elements (except wrapper div); no styles
- HOC to create other components
- Provide and retrieve data from other components

Presentation components like List and UserInfo have these key features.

- DOM markup and their own styles
- Functional components
- Props to receive data and callbacks

Production Build

Check production builds iteratively by using the `npm run build` command. Check a production build while integrating with third-party libraries, code integration, and during code check-in.

Linting Check

Linting validates coding standards. Check coding standards by using the `npm run lint` command iteratively.

Removing Unused Code and Dependencies

Once development is complete, manually remove the unused code, blocks, modules, and references to ensure that the production bundle is optimal.

Analyze the unused dependencies and remove the unused features or files from all the dependencies.

Using React Fragments

Logically group the data to corresponding React fragments on pages. React fragments remove unnecessary DOM elements and optimize them to load the page faster. Using React fragment, you can group children without adding nodes.

Immutable Objects

Immutable objects are easily created, tested, and tracked. In a React component model, use an immutable data structure for handling *props* and *state*. You can use the `concat` and `assign` functions to create immutable objects. Libraries such as immutable.js, immutable-helper, seamless-immutable, and React-copy-write create an immutable data structure. Immutable objects reduce temporal coupling.

Throttling and Debouncing

Leverage *throttling* to delay the execution of event handlers wherever needed to optimize the performance. For instance, you can use throttling to handle infinite scroll events to inject the delay in event handling so that you can stack multiple events at once. Throttling ensures that an event handling function only runs at a fixed interval.

The debouncing feature ignores event handler calls until the event handler calls have stopped for a specified time. For instance, you can use debouncing for the type-ahead feature, where each keypress event triggers an event handler function; instead of handling every keypress event, you can wait until the user stops typing for a second, and then get the matching records from the database to improve performance.

Code Chunking

You can use plugins such as CommonsChunkPlugins to identify and group the commonly used scripts, and split them to create common.js. You can create a common library based on the external libraries and create a separate chunk. This reduces the size of the overall bundle. Similarly, you can use ExtractTextWebpackPlugin to extract the CSS into a separate CSS file.

Browsers can cache the chunks, thereby improving page performance.

CHAPTER 4 MOBILE WEB PERFORMANCE OPTIMIZATION

Handling Large List Data

If the UI has a large set of data in a list, fast scrolling provides a sluggish UI response. This happens due to the huge rendering between components. In such cases, you can use a React virtualized list to handle the UI lag, which is due to large amounts of data.

Network-Level Performance Optimizations

The following are network-level performance optimizations for the React framework.

Middleware

Use middleware for handling interaction between services and views and handling all the business logic. Middleware intercepts the API calls for authorization, transformation, and caching.

Lazy Loading

You can lazily load React components using React.Lazy on demand. Lazy loading reduces the initial load time and the perceived load time of the web page. You can use React.Suspense to show the fallback content while the lazy load is happening.

Runtime Performance Optimizations

This section discusses performance optimizations that are done during page rendition at runtime.

Optimize Component Rerendering with shouldComponentUpdate and PureComponent

Use the `shouldComponentUpdate()` method to indicate if the component and its subcomponents in the component tree must be rerendered when props or state change. By avoiding unnecessary component rerendering, you can optimize the page performance. If there are multiple components on the page, it is recommended to use `shouldComponentUpdate()` to optimize page refresh time.

CHAPTER 4   MOBILE WEB PERFORMANCE OPTIMIZATION

Alternatively, use React.PureComponent, which has a default implementation of shouldComponentUpdate. PureComponent provides an immutable component state and props.

You can leverage libraries (e.g., why-did-you-update) that detect potentially unnecessary component renderers.

Caching with React.Memo

For costly function calls, you can implement *memorization* (in which you cache the results of a costly function call and use the cache when the function is invoked the next time with the same parameters) using React.Memo.

Using Production Mode

When the production build is ready, set the mode option of the webpack module builder to *production*. The production mode optimizes the build.

Common Performance Optimizations for JavaScript Frameworks

You can use common performance optimization methods for various JavaScript frameworks, such as Angular, React, and Vue. The common performance optimizations are covered in this section.

Content Compression

Compression reduces the overall response size, thereby reducing the overall bandwidth consumed. The client browser sets the Accept-Encoding header to indicate the supported encoding formats. The server sets the Content-Encoding header to indicate the compression algorithm used for the response. You can enable the gzip compression for scripts, images, text files, and HTML content.

You can use tools like deflate, gzip compression, Brotli, and Zopfli for the compression. You can also enable the gzip compression at the web server layer.

Leverage CDN for Resources

You can leverage the content delivery network (CDN) to serve web resources such as images, videos, web pages, and binary files. CDN provides runtime network-level performance optimizations and resource caching to improve overall performance. Since CDNs serve the resources from a different domain; browsers can download the CDN resources concurrently along with resources from the main website. This technique is called *domain sharding*, where you can host the resources at various subdomains of the CDN and load them concurrently on the browser. CDNs have a massive worldwide infrastructure to serve content from edges. You can cache Angular or React bundles and resources in the CDN.

Web Worker

For large applications with a complex component tree, change detection can impact the responsiveness. In such cases, you can run the application and change detection in a web worker while the main UI thread can render the main application UI. You can use web workers for all CPU intensive operations or heavy JavaScript or long-running tasks to work in the background without interrupting the main thread.

You can use Webpack Web Worker Loader for implementing the web worker model.

Server-Side Rendering

Large single-page applications (SPA) must wait until all the JavaScript needed for the initial rendering is available. As a result, the end users need to wait longer with SPA applications.

The server prerenders the requested HTML on the server end and serves the ready-to-use HTML to the browser, leading to reduced initial page load time. Server-side rendering is discussed in Chapter 10.

You can use Angular Universal or Preboot for implementing server-side rendering.

Progressive Web App (PWA)

Progressive web apps (PWA) provide offline capabilities and a native mobile app–like user experience. You can implement a progressive web app using Angular or React frameworks for faster performance. PWAs help the application handle animations smoothly and make them more responsive and interactive. An in-depth discussion of PWAs occurs in Chapter 10.

Caching

You can leverage a browser's cache for caching static assets such as images, scripts, and stylesheets that rarely change. You can set the cache-control, expires, and max-age HTTP cache headers so that the browser can cache the resources accordingly. You can also use Angular storage workers with the CacheStorage API and cache template expressions.

Image Optimization

Images take up most of a page's size; hence, image optimizations play a crucial role in overall page optimization. The following describes a few image-related optimizations.

- Use lossless image compression to reduce the bundle size and bandwidth consumed by the application. You can use multiple tools, such as TinyPNG and Squoosh, for image compression.

- Use responsive images with client hints and WebP format for images.

- Lazy load images on demand. Asynchronously load the images when the user needs it.

- The server should properly scale the images based on the user interface (desktop browser, mobile browser, etc.). Accordingly, use the proper image sizes.

- Reduce image size. You can use tools such as MozJPEG (for JPEG images), Pingo (for PNG images), and SVGO (for SVG) images.

- Use SVG images that have a lower memory footprint than JPEG images. You can style SVGs with CSS.

- Serve all the images for the page with CSS sprites.

- Load the image progressively. You can load the LQIP (low-quality image placeholders) on the initial page load to improve the FMP metric.

- Remove all unused images and replace the large-sized images with light-weight alternatives.

- Leverage the CDN to cache the images at the edge locations.

- Set the appropriate cache headers for the images to enable the caching of the images at the browser end.

- Use `<picture>` tag to serve the most optimal image format based on screen size.

- Using client hints such as DPR, Width, and Viewport-Width headers to deliver the most optimal image (based on screen size) and other parameters.

Video Optimization

Use animated WebP or HTML5 videos for optimal video rendering. Use lossy compression for videos before production deployment. Cache and serve the videos from CDN.

Leverage Resource Hints

Use resource hints such as DNS lookup, preload, preload, and preconnect on resources such as links and images to optimize page rendering. Browsers use resource hints to fetch a needed resource early, improving the time to interact. The *preconnect* hint also decreases the latency to connect to the third-party domain.

For instance, if the site uses a resource for a third-party site, you can preconnect to that site as follows.

```
<link rel="preconnect" href="site.com">
```

Font Optimization

The following are some key font optimizations.

- Load fonts asynchronously.

- Leverage the font-display in the CSS for optimal page performance.

- Use font swapping to load the web fonts. In the @font-face declaration, you can leverage font-display: swap.

Content Streaming

Leverage data streams to read and write asynchronous data chunks. The data stream-based applications start rendering upon receiving the first data chunk. You can leverage this to progressively render the content.

Migration to HTTP/2

HTTP/2 provides a greater performance improvement over earlier versions of the HTTP/1.1 protocol. HTTP/2 also supports other features such as server push, parallel resource download, and so forth. Once HTTP/2 is enabled, the server can push the resources such as images, JavaScript, CSS, fonts before the browser requests for the resources, thereby reducing the round-trip time. Enable HPACK compression in the HTTP/2 ecosystem.

Search Engine Optimization (SEO)

SEO defines methods and techniques to improve content discoverability by web search engines. Search engines use the SEO attributes to rank the web page content. For a robust SEO, you need to configure meta tags, descriptions, keywords, friendly URLs to describe the page content.

As single-page applications (SPAs) heavily use the JavaScript to dynamically add the content on the page, it is challenging for the web search bots to index the content.

One solution is to use server-side rendering (SSR) that renders the complete HTML with the content to the browser. For static content pages, you can use a technique called *prerendering*, in which a fully rendered static HTML is created beforehand and served to the search engine bots during crawling. You can use tools like Prerender.io or prerender-spa-plugin to implement prerendering.

CHAPTER 4   MOBILE WEB PERFORMANCE OPTIMIZATION

Profiling

You can leverage profiling tools to analyze the size and performance of the application code.

- The Webpack bundle analyzer provides insights into modules.
- The Google Chrome browser provides the Lighthouse tool to analyze the performance, accessibility, and SEO for mobile and desktop browsers.
- Page-auditing tools like Firebug, HTTPWatch, the Fiddler proxy, and Chrome DevTools analyze page performance.

Optimizing the Critical Rendering Path

A critical rendering path includes the resources (JavaScript, CSS files, images, etc.) that block critical content (content in the above-the-fold view). These resources block the browser, which impacts the first meaningful paint (FMP). To optimize the critical rendering path, you should do the following.

- Identify the critical rendering path for the web application.
- Identify all the resources that block the critical rendering path.
- Remove all the unnecessary resources and assets (JavaScript, CSS, images, fonts, etc.) blocking the critical rendering path.
- Compress the HTML to reduce the overall DOM size.
- Remove and defer unnecessary scripts, stylesheets, JSON files, and fonts.
- Use inline CSS for critical CSS in the <head> section and load the remaining CSS asynchronously.
- Load the scripts asynchronously.
- Load the web fonts asynchronously.
- Reduce the number of resources blocking the critical rendering path and reduce their size.
- Wherever possible, load the critical rendering path blocking resources asynchronously.
- Preload the critical resources such as JavaScript and CSS files using `<link preload />` tag.

- Use inline critical CSS for small style fragments in the critical rendering path.

- Remove all synchronous scripts and fonts in the <head> tag.

- Don't sequence the requests involved in a critical rendering path.

Static Site Generators

For websites that predominantly deliver static content for information delivery purposes, you can use the static site generators (SSG) built on JAM (Client-side **J**avaScript, Reusable **A**PIs, Prebuilt **M**arkup) principle.

During build time, you can use data (such as file data, RDBMS data), content (such as web content from CMS), and page templates to build static web pages/HTML pages (consisting of CSS and JS). You can also leverage many SSG frameworks, such as Gatsby JS.

The developed HTML pages are deployed to a CDN or a web server. When the user requests the page, ready-to-render HTML is available for the browser, making the model highly optimized and highly scalable. The HTML retrieves the data using JavaScript-based APIs.

Network-Level Performance Optimizations

This section focuses on network performance issues in a modern web platform and the best practices to address them. To understand networking timing, you can audit the page timings using tools such as Chrome Lighthouse, Firebug, HTTPWatch and WebPageTest . The key metrics that need to be measured are *time to first byte* (TTFB), *first meaningful paint* (FMP), and *time to interactive* (TTI). TTFB should be less than 200 milliseconds.

Key Resources Impacting Network Timings

The following are resources that have a high impact on network timings.

- Synchronous JavaScript block DOM construction and DOM rendering

- Blocking scripts and fonts that impact the render time

- Heavy images that impact the initial page load time

- Chatty server calls leading to multiple increased roundtrip time (RTT)

CHAPTER 4 MOBILE WEB PERFORMANCE OPTIMIZATION

Optimization of Browser Rendering Sequence

Table 4-2 highlights the four key stages of browser rendering. Each stage features a description, blocking scenarios, and best practices.

Table 4-2. *Browser Rendering Stages*

Order	Rendering Stage	Description	Render Blocking Scenarios	Optimization Methods
1	Document Object Model (DOM)	Get the HTML data and build the DOM tree	Large DOM size slows down the process, Waits for CSSOM Blocked by synchronous JavaScript	Compress the HTML, Use inline JavaScript in the <head> element, Load the JavaScript asynchronously. Minimize DOM elements
2	CSS Object Model (CSSOM)	Convert CSS rules	CSS and JS in the critical impacts the FMP.	Provide inline CSS for above-the-fold content. Use inline JavaScript in the <head> element. Load the JavaScript asynchronously Compress and minify the critical CSS and JavaScript.
3	Render Tree	Combine DOM with CSSOM to rendering style details		
4	Layout	Calculate the size and position for each element	Repaint happens when the viewport changes or when the render tree is updated	Cache the layout. Leverage static site rendering.
5	Paint	Browser paints the pixels	Complex styles or combination of styles increase paint time	Use prerendered HTML. Use server-side rendering. Leverage static site rendering.

Leverage CDN

The CDN forward caches the content and stores it in multiple data centers distributed across the world. CDN caches content such as images, videos, JavaScript, stylesheets, JSON files, binary files, and so forth. On global web platforms, CDN improves the load time for static content.

Amazon CloudFront, Akamail, and Cloudflare are a few examples of CDN systems.

Static Resource Best Practices

Implement the following best practices for static assets.

- Check the links on the web page and avoid redirects.
- Place CSS at the top and JavaScript at the bottom.
- Remove unnecessary scripts and stylesheets.
- Minify and merge the HTML (using tools such as HTMLMinifier), scripts (using tools such as UglifyJS), and stylesheets (using tools such as CSSNano).
- Analyze CSS performance (using TestMyCSS).
- Use WOFF 2.0 Web Font for improved performance time.
- Compress the HTML and images. Use responsive images and lazily load the images.
- Cache static assets using browser caching.

Optimize Network Timings

You can identify network waterfall timings from various browser tools. Table 4-3 highlights the network-related steps involved in page rendering, including optimization methods.

Table 4-3. *Network Timing and Optimization Methods*

Order	Network timing	Optimization Method
1	DNS Lookup	Preresolve the DNS based on analysis of user input. <link rel="dns-prefetch" href="/example.com">
2	TCP Connection	Perform TCP preconnect to keep the connection ready. <link rel="preconnect" href="https://exmaple.com" crossorigin>
3	HTTP Request and Response	Prefetch resources such as images, scripts, stylesheets, and so forth. <link rel="prefetch" href="/js/app.js">
4	Server Response Time/ TTFB	Use server-side rendering. Use static site rendering method for static content delivery. Use the PRPL pattern discussed in Chapter 10. Optimize the resources on critical rendering path.
5	Client-side Rendering	Use small JavaScript and CSS for critical pages to minimize the overhead related to parsing and execution. Explore the prerendering of the page. <link rel="prerender" href="/faq.html">

HTML5 Performance Optimizations

HTML5 provides standards-based web applications that leverage the latest features, including rich media support, enhanced user interaction, easy animation support, and many built-in features, such as geolocation support. You can leverage HTML5 features when building mobile web platforms.

The core HTML5-related performance features are covered in this section. You can leverage these features for relevant scenarios in the mobile web platform.

Note Not all browsers support all HTML5 features, so you should consider browser support when implementing features.

Hardware Acceleration

You can leverage hardware acceleration to improve rendering performance. UI-related use cases such as CSS3 3D transformations, CSS3 transitions (like animations), CSS3 translate, WebGL 3D drawing can leverage the GPU instead of the regular CPU. GPU-based hardware acceleration improves UI performance and reduces consumed resources (i.e., consumed memory, consumed power) on mobile devices.

The key UI transitions (sliding, flipping, rotating, etc.) can leverage hardware acceleration. You can also leverage the canvas element to draw the graphics.

Native Multimedia Support

HTML5 provides a standardized way to embed multimedia files. You can also configure a fallback to a supported format when the multimedia format is not supported. You can leverage JavaScript APIs such as networkState and readyState to handle the events. HTML5 provides attributes such as autoplay, play, pause, seek, volume, and other display controls.

HTML5 supports video formats such as OGG, WEBM, MP4, AVI, and FLV; video codecs such as H264, Theora, and VP8; and audio codecs such as Vorbis and AAC.

Offline Storage

HTML5 provides localStorage and sessionStorage to store and share attributes. You can use this for caching user input values across browser sessions.

Lazy Initialization

You can initialize the code lazily to improve perceived performance. You can implement lazy loading for images using the `loading="lazy"` attribute.

Element Attributes

HTML5 supports many attributes, such as autofocus, pattern (that supports regular expression), and elements such as output and data that eliminate the need for additional JavaScript functions.

Summary

- Angular, React, and Vue are the most widely used JavaScript frameworks.

- The design-related performance optimizations for the Angular framework are leveraging service workers, AoT compilation, unit testing, removal of unused code, leverage defer and async attributes, leverage defer and async attributes.

- The network-level performance optimizations for Angular are bundling and code splitting, minification, removal of unnecessary code, lazy loading, and resource prefetching.

- The runtime performance optimizations for angular are leveraging application shell, enable production mode, ahead of time (AoT) compilation, change detection optimizations, and leverage pure pipes.

- The design-related performance optimizations for the React framework are atomic design pattern, higher-order components (HOC), separation of container and presentation, production build, linting check, removal of unused code and dependencies, immutable objects, throttling and debouncing, code chunking, and handling large list data.

- The network-level performance optimizations for the React framework are using middleware and lazy loading.

- The runtime performance optimizations for the React framework are optimized component rerendering with shouldComponentUpdate and PureComponent, caching with React.Memo, and using production mode.

CHAPTER 4 MOBILE WEB PERFORMANCE OPTIMIZATION

- The common performance optimizations for JavaScript frameworks are content compression, leverage CDN for resources, web workers, server-side rendering, progressive web app (PWA), caching, image optimization, video optimization, leverage resource hints, font optimization, content streaming, migration to HTTP/2, search engine optimization (SEO), profiling, critical rendering path optimization, and static site generators.

- The core network optimizations include optimization of browser rendering sequence, leverage CDN, critical rendering path optimization, and optimize network timing.

- You can leverage the HTML5 features such as hardware acceleration, native multimedia support, offline storage, lazy initialization, and element attributes to provide optimal performance.

CHAPTER 5

Modern Web Platform Performance Principles

Modern web platforms play the main role in user engagement. Modern platforms provide high responsiveness, high performance, and a seamless omnichannel user experience. Web response time greatly influences the user experience and user satisfaction. Enhanced user engagement leads to higher user satisfaction, driving user traffic and increasing revenue for web platforms. An optimally performing web page also improves the platform's usability and users' loyalty.

Modern web platforms come in multiple flavors, such as mobile web, hybrid web, progressive web app, and so forth. This chapter explores the characteristics of each of the modern web platforms and their performance best practices. The chapter also explains the reference architecture for two popular frameworks and the solution components and solution flow.

This chapter discusses the core performance principles for the modern web platform. Later sections cover the drivers and key capabilities of modern web design, layer-wise building blocks, and business imperatives. We discuss high-level design principles, best practices, and performance principles. Performance engineers, web developers, digital architects, project managers, and program managers find this chapter useful.

Overview

Modern web platforms are a popular digital delivery channel that provide an engaging user experience. Performance and responsiveness are crucial success factors for modern web platforms. The overall performance optimization strategy for the modern web involves web design principles and leverages modern web capabilities and building blocks. A reference architecture defines a best practices-based solution's components and building blocks.

CHAPTER 5 MODERN WEB PLATFORM PERFORMANCE PRINCIPLES

Traditional Web vs. Modern Web

Before looking at the various principles and design aspects of modern web platforms, let's briefly looks at the differences between traditional web and modern web platforms, as highlighted in Table 5-1. Knowing the differences between the traditional web and the modern web helps you use performance dimensions and relevant optimization methods and tools for the modern web.

Table 5-1. Traditional Web vs. Modern Web

Category	Traditional Web (JSP or ASP-based web)	Modern Web (SPA, RWD, and PWA-based web)
Core Use Cases	Static content, less client-side interactivity, server-based rendering	High client-side interactivity, rich user interface, high responsiveness
Web Content Characteristics	Static, read-only, full page refresh for server calls	Dynamic, read-write
Compatibility	Supported by desktop browsers	Supports various browsers and mobile devices
Rendering	Full page rendering	Partial page rendering
Integration Methods	Synchronous, full-page blocking server-side calls, XML-based payload, stateful APIs	Asynchronous calls, stateless APIs, microservices, event-driven architecture, GraphQL, REST-based calls, JSON-based payloads
Integration Technologies	Enterprise service bus (ESB), API gateway, orchestration	Event mesh, choreography
Core Technology	HTML and CSS with less JavaScript Server-side frameworks	Predominantly JavaScript with CSS
Database Technology	Traditional RDBMS, strict consistency	NoSQL, in-memory database, cache, and distributed database, eventual consistency, data lakes
Architecture Patterns	MVC (model-view-controller)	MVVM (model-view-view-model)

(continued)

CHAPTER 5   MODERN WEB PLATFORM PERFORMANCE PRINCIPLES

Table 5-1. (*continued*)

Category	Traditional Web (JSP or ASP-based web)	Modern Web (SPA, RWD, and PWA-based web)
UI Design	Layout-based and segregated into site pages	User-centric, omnichannel compatible
Development Methodology	Waterfall	Agile, sprint-based, DevOps
Security	Server-based authentication (Active Directory, identity management systems)	Token-based security
Deployment Methodology	On-premise deployment	Cloud-native and cloud-based
Data Ecosystem	Enterprise data	Big data, social data

Modern Web Design

Modern web platforms are built around the key principles of user experience, responsiveness, and performance. Most modern web platforms are based on B2C (business to consumer) model, where the end users are web users. Hence, end users expect a highly responsive user experience similar to popular e-commerce and social media platforms.

This section discusses the modern web platform principles, key capabilities, and building blocks of a modern web platform.

Drivers for Modern Web Design

Web platforms and user experience go through continuous disruptions such as UI technology changes, integration changes, and design changes. The following are the key drivers for modern web platforms.

Hyperconnectivity enabled and empowered users

- Increased user expectations for user experience, features, performance, and availability
- Increased digital engagement across various digital channels

CHAPTER 5 MODERN WEB PLATFORM PERFORMANCE PRINCIPLES

- Increased holistic and personalized solutions for enhanced information discovery
- Delivery of contextual content for better usability
- Engages users actively across all channels
- Seamless omnichannel delivery on various mobile devices and browsers

Collaboration

- New types of collaboration for better information sharing
- Social integration with external social and collaboration platforms

Business model transformation

- Automation of business processes for improved productivity
- DevOps adoption for source control, release management, and automation processes
- High adoption of gamification features to improve participation; for instance, a sales dashboard comparing the achieved sales targets and ranking the high performers motivates the sales community
- Advanced self-service features such as search, investment calculators, knowledge base, recommendation, chats, and virtual assistants to empower the users
- Continuous process improvement through automation

Artificial intelligence (AI) and automation

- Chatbots and virtual assistants to assist users and enable access to common inquiries and information (e.g., product downloads)
- Enhanced cognitive services, such as metadata auto-tagging, text translation, personalized recommendations, and so forth
- Advanced analytics to gain insights into user behavior and user actions

Information discoverability

- Enables easy application discoverability through search, intuitive UI design
- Provides intuitive information architecture with well-defined site hierarchy, context menus, and navigation elements
- Provides a channel-specific responsive user interface

Active user engagement

- Enables gamification features
- Provides personalized and contextual data
- Provides seamless omnichannel experience
- Increases application loyalty and usage

Quick time to market

- Provides continuous integration for faster onboarding.
- Integrates DevOps practices to streamline the release management process
- Implements automation to improve productivity

Performance

- Ensures the predictable performance of applications across the year
- Provides real-time performance monitoring and real-time notifications
- Provides elastic scalability for the increased load without compromising the performance
- Sets up robust monitoring infrastructure to monitor and notify the performance in real-time

Cost optimization

- Cost-effective solution to cater to both web and mobile channels
- Leverages open standards and open source tools wherever possible
- Uses automation as the key productivity lever

CHAPTER 5 MODERN WEB PLATFORM PERFORMANCE PRINCIPLES

- Rapid application development using the tools, libraries, and built-in framework components
- Platform agnostic (desktop, tablet, or mobile devices) applications that perform well on the web and mobile devices, including Android and iOS. Develop once and use across various browsers and devices

Maintenance

- Extensible solution components
- Easy to operate the solution
- Ease of developing the solution

The Key Capabilities of a Modern Web Platform

A modern web platform fulfills the demands, needs, and expectations of web users. Figure 5-1 captures the core capabilities of the modern web platform.

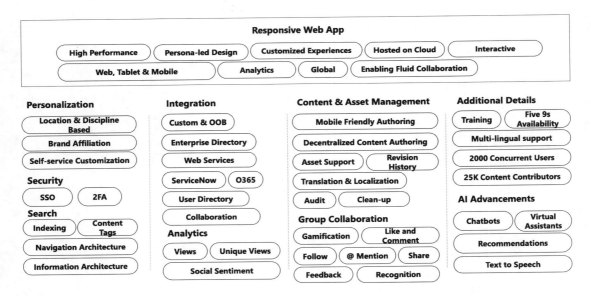

Figure 5-1. *Key capabilities of the modern web platform*

A **responsive web application** is designed based on user personas and provides personalized user experience (persona-based features and flow). Modern web applications are normally cloud-based (cloud-native or cloud supported) and is seamlessly delivered on various devices and browsers. Multilingual support, analytics, personalization, responsiveness, and collaboration are other key requirements for a responsive web application.

An enterprise web platform can provide other features such as personalization, security, search, integration, analytics, content, document, asset management, collaboration, and AI. A **personalization engine** allows the user to configure the preferences. The personalization engine also personalizes the user experience based on user location, brand affiliation, and self-service customization.

A **security module** manages responsibilities related to authentication, authorization, multifactor authentication. Single sign-on (SSO) is required for providing seamless access to authenticated systems.

An **enterprise search** capability enables crawling, indexing, and searching of various structured and unstructured data sources. Tagging and dynamic navigation architecture (tag-based navigation) are part of the search strategy.

An **enterprise integration module** is responsible for integrating with various systems such as user repository, a user directory, web services, collaboration, office 365, and ERP. Modern web platforms prefer lightweight, stateless, and microservice-based integration with token-based security. Modern web platforms use event-driven architecture (EDA) and use choreography using event mesh. The EDA is discussed in Chapter 12.

The **web analytics and page analytics module** capture user actions, user behavior, and user navigation pattern and provide the dashboard report capturing the analytics information.

The **content management and document/asset management** module provide mobile-friendly authoring, content tagging, translation, auditing, asset support, archiving, localization, and other content related needs.

The modern platform can effectively engage web users through **collaboration**. The collaboration module supports gamification, blogs, wikis, likes, at-mention, forums, calendar, feedback, follow, sharing, and reward and recognition.

Based on the application domain and non-functional requirements (NFR), the enterprise application can have **additional requirements** such as multilingual support, scalability requirements (concurrent users, content contributors), availability needs, and so forth.

CHAPTER 5 MODERN WEB PLATFORM PERFORMANCE PRINCIPLES

The **AI advancements module** supports AI-enabled chatbots, virtual assistants, smart recommendations, and text to speech.

The Building Blocks of a Modern Web Platform

A reference list of layer-wise building blocks as depicted in Figure 5-2. The building blocks are mainly for reference purposes. You need to identify additional building blocks based on the application domain needs.

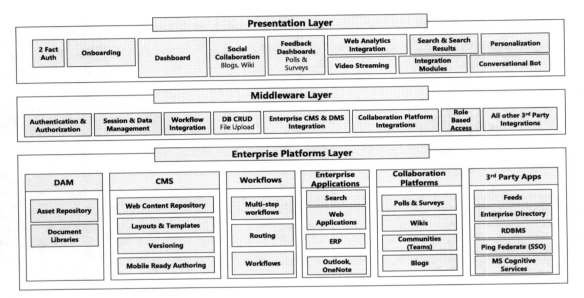

Figure 5-2. Modern web platform building blocks

Presentation Layer

The presentation layer is primarily the system of engagement for end users. The layer should support modules and capabilities such as social login, user onboarding, collaboration, analytics, streaming, search, and chatbots. The friendly dashboards personalize the information for the users.

End users view holistic and personalized information through intuitive dashboards. Modern web platforms provide responsive user interfaces (single-page applications) for seamless omnichannel user experience.

Middleware Layer

The middleware layer is responsible for orchestrating the integrations. The presentation layer components communicate with middleware components through stateless APIs to create a decoupled and extensible platform. The middleware is responsible for providing centralized integration and service orchestration capability. It integrates with authentication provider, workflow system, collaboration platform, CMS system, third-party systems, and other systems of records.

Enterprise Platforms Layer

The enterprise platforms layer consists of a system of record (SOR) that provides a source of truth for enterprise data. The core enterprise systems include a digital asset management system (DAM) that stores and manages digital assets such as documents, files, digital assets, and media; a content management system (CMS) that handles web content, metadata, content versioning, rich text editors, and content-authoring tools; a workflow system to handle business workflows; enterprise applications, such as web applications, web services, feeds, and ERPs; collaboration platforms, such as blogs, wikis, and communities; and third-party applications, such as feeds, enterprise directories, and cognitive services.

The Business Imperatives of a Modern Web Platform

The modern web platform addresses key business imperatives, as shown in Figure 5-3.

CHAPTER 5 MODERN WEB PLATFORM PERFORMANCE PRINCIPLES

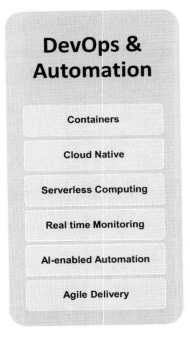

Figure 5-3. Business imperatives of the modern web platform

A **seamless omnichannel user experience** is the key business imperative for modern web platforms. The modern web platforms provide personalized user experience based on user preferences and implicit user attributes (location, transaction history, etc.). The user interface design is simple and minimalistic to provide an intuitive user experience on all digital channels and improve overall usability. Decision-making tools, self-service features, gamification, and AI-enabled chatbots enable and engage the end user.

Enterprise integrations provide enterprise data from the upstream systems. Modern web platforms use lightweight integration protocols (e.g., REST over HTTP) and lightweight data exchange formats (e.g., JSON). Modern web platforms use modular and stateless microservices. The modules across layers are loosely coupled. The presentation layer components use a headless mode of integration with back-end systems; for instance, the React-based UI uses headless APIs from a CMS to manage web content.

DevOps and automation are an integral part of the agile project delivery in which release management and deployment processes are streamlined and automated. Modern web applications are cloud-native, container-based, and use serverless functions, and hence the DevOps processes must support the code management and

CHAPTER 5   MODERN WEB PLATFORM PERFORMANCE PRINCIPLES

release management processes on the cloud. Real-time monitoring and notification infrastructure are enabled to improve system availability. You leverage the AI-based automation to improve the user experience.

The business objectives and technology realization methods for a modern digital platform are depicted in Figure 5-4.

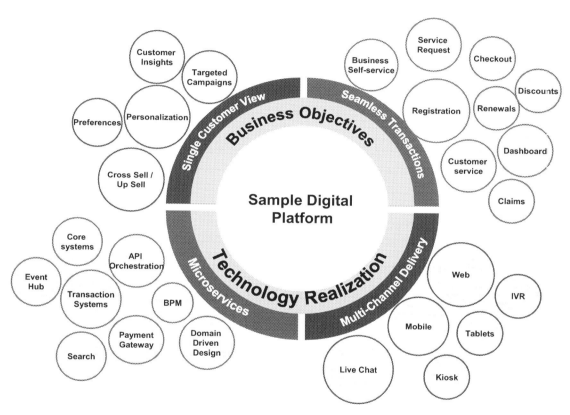

Figure 5-4. *Business objectives and technology realization of modern web platform*

The main success factor of a digital platform is to balance the business objective realization and technology realization. Figure 5-4 details two sample business objectives: single customer view and seamless transition. The single customer view enables the organizations to personalize the user experience, gain customer insights, and deliver targeted campaigns and use it for cross-selling and up-selling opportunities. Seamless transactions provide smoother and frictionless services such as registration, customer service, claims, dashboard, lead management, renewals, discounts, and business self-service.

CHAPTER 5　MODERN WEB PLATFORM PERFORMANCE PRINCIPLES

There are two core vehicles of technology realization: microservices and multichannel delivery. A microservices ecosystem forms the backbone of the modern application integration and services infrastructure, providing features such as API orchestration, domain-driven design (DDD), search, transaction management, and event-driven architecture (EDA). Multichannel delivery ensures that the solution provides a seamless user experience to various devices and browsers.

Reference Architecture: React-based Modern Web Application

Reference architecture defines the core solution components, integrations, and capabilities need to realize the solution. It is based on well-defined design guidelines and architectural principles. The core solution components provide various presentation capabilities, such as dashboard, forms, search, web analytics, and personalization. This section discusses reference architecture based on two popular modern web frameworks: React and Angular.

A React framework–based modern web application is depicted in Figure 5-5.

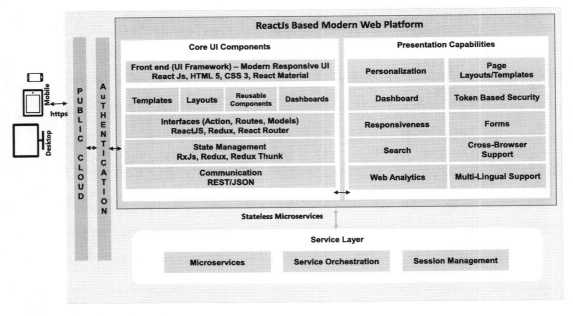

Figure 5-5. *React-based modern web architecture*

CHAPTER 5   MODERN WEB PLATFORM PERFORMANCE PRINCIPLES

The core UI framework consists of React JavaScript libraries, HTML5, CSS3, React Material, and templates, layouts, and components. The core UI components enable the presentation capabilities such as personalized dashboards, forms, and so forth.

Interfaces include action, routes, and models and act as a bridge between UI components and middleware. Middleware orchestrates the flow between views and services. The middleware also manages error handling, and invoking async action. Interfaces and components invoke services through middleware. Redux handles global state management.

The presentation components are integrated with other systems such as web services, third-party systems, and enterprise directories through REST-based endpoints. Integration is loosely coupled and lightweight and is based on proven methods and industry best practices. For communication, you can use Axios or Apollo.

Interaction and request processing of a React-based application is represented in Figure 5-6.

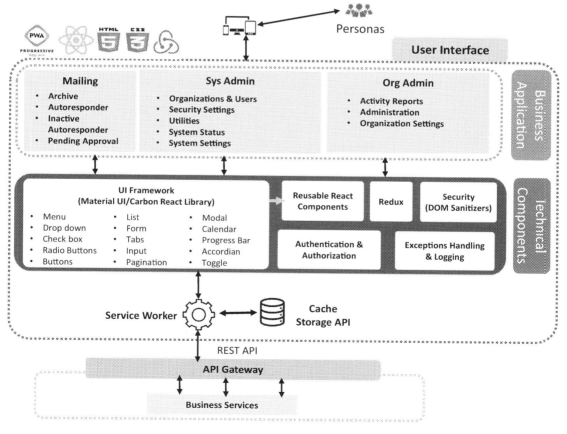

Figure 5-6. *React application request processing*

117

CHAPTER 5   MODERN WEB PLATFORM PERFORMANCE PRINCIPLES

The React framework is based on component design. In React, you can create components that can be reused. The reusable components are added into a separate JavaScript file, and can be used in another component by importing it. React uses virtual DOM for changing and updating the DOM in memory leading to faster performance.

React follows the atomic design pattern, where the system is designed through a combination of five fundamental building blocks: atoms (basic building blocks), molecules (a combination of atoms), organisms (a combination of molecules such as a form), template, and page. The atomic design provides modularity, scalability, flexibility, and reusability.

Reference Architecture: Angular-based Modern Web Application

A sample Angular-based modern web application is depicted in Figure 5-7.

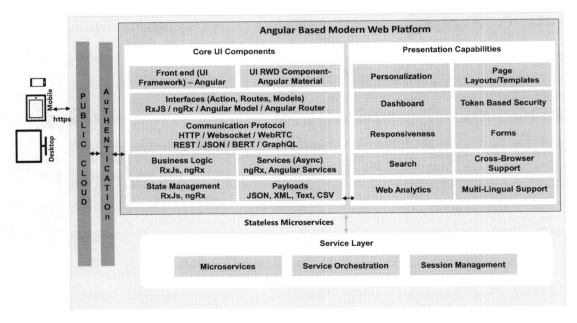

Figure 5-7. Angular-based modern web architecture

Angular core UI components use a responsive web design (RWD) concept to render various browsers and devices. A few examples of Angular UI modules are the home module, admin module, and dashboard module. Angular UI components include

CHAPTER 5 MODERN WEB PLATFORM PERFORMANCE PRINCIPLES

header, footer, navigation components, charts, lists, and sort filters. The UI component tree encapsulates the UI logic, styles, and views. The interface module consists of the Angular Model and Angular Router for routing the requests.

The business logic modules maintain the business rules and interact with services. The state management is responsible for the immutable application state. The async services interact with external systems and transform the data as required.

Various communication protocols such as HTTP, WebSocket, REST, and GraphQL are supported with diverse payloads such as JSON, XML, text, and CSV.

The Flow of Angular Solution Components

Figure 5-8 shows the flow and role of each of the Angular framework solution components.

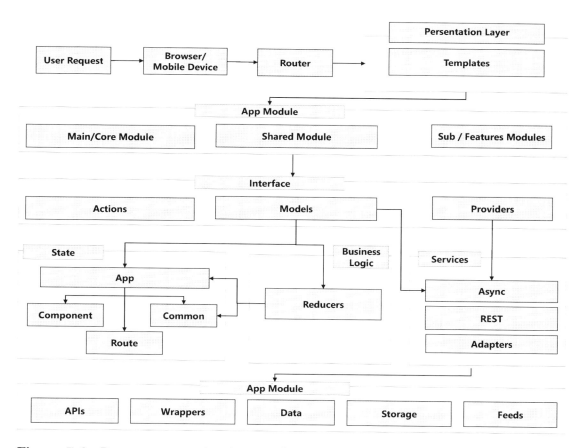

Figure 5-8. *Request processing in Angular*

119

CHAPTER 5   MODERN WEB PLATFORM PERFORMANCE PRINCIPLES

Let's briefly look at the design best practices for various solution components in the Angular framework.

Modules

Angular app modules are the core solution component of the framework. To enable modularity and reusability, Angular app modules are logically categorized based on the concerns handled by the modules. You can have user experience modules, business logic modules, common modules (alerts, configurations, directives, pipes, etc.), and core modules (loggers, audit services, etc.). Common components are shared across the application.

Components

Components are responsible for rendering views. The components are modular and scalable, and they optimize the app using the lifecycle hooks. As a best practice, you need to use a singleton pattern for the components. To optimize the change detection strategy, you can use state management and Redux architecture.

Interfaces

The interface defines the contract of a function for the function arguments and its types.
For interfaces, you can use the Reactive design pattern to handle views, state, models, and actions.

State Management

Managing state among various Angular solution elements such as modules, components, services is one of the challenging tasks for a single-page application. The following are key states and the design guidelines for the states.

- A persistent state acts as a global state for the dynamic data and can be used across components while interacting with the back-end services.

CHAPTER 5 MODERN WEB PLATFORM PERFORMANCE PRINCIPLES

- A local UI state is used for customizations (notifications display, enablement, and disablement of button) and component-level controls.

- The router/URL state is used for prefetching data, sending data to child components, and so forth.

You can use the Redux pattern to manage predictable and immutable state management.

Services

Async services invoke external services to get the required response. The services also play a role in data transformation to fit the defined business schema. Async services ensure stateless payload. Asynchronous services, coupled with a stateless payload, provides high performance and scalability.

You can use REST APIs, HTTP clients, adaptors, and wrappers for implementing services. RxJS handle all the asynchronous events.

Payload

When Angular services invoke the upstream services and third-party services, you get the response data in the payload. An Angular application needs to process the data as per the application's needs.

The application can receive payloads in various formats, such as JSON, CSV, XML, text, blobs, and Excel. You need to transform and process the application payload to suit the application's needs.

Realization of Modern Web Solution Tenets

Table 5-2 highlights modern web design principles and how they are fulfilled in modern UI frameworks.

Table 5-2. *Modern Web Design Principles*

Modern Web Design Principles	Description	Solutions
Access from any device and Intuitive UI	• Responsive design • Mobile app for Android and iOS • Hybrid mobile app for non-Android and non-iOS • Design-centric UX (design thinking)	• Material design/Native design/CMS/RWD/Design thinking • Push notifications
User Engagement	• Engaged learning • Virtual assistant for FAQs • Integration with a social channel like slack • Design-centric UX • Design-centric content delivery • Fast response	• LMS/Virtual assistance/Chatroom plugin • BI dashboard • Data analytics
Offline accessibility	• Offline storage for browser and mobile app • Seamless data synchronization with the server	• PWAs provide the option to cache the data in the browser and use it when there is poor or no connectivity. PWAs use service workers and cache for providing offline storage. • The best of the caching strategy is applied based on the outcome of the discovery to provide an effective offline experience.
Access to information	• Access to social channels • Updated content delivery • Content in preferred languages • Highly flexible search	• Search engine integration • Chat/Virtual assistants • Guided navigation • Multilingual support
UI Framework	• Component library to develop a modern, responsive web app • Modular and reusable components	• Angular, React, Vue

(continued)

Table 5-2. (*continued*)

Modern Web Design Principles	Description	Solutions
UI Component Model	• Atomic design approach to break down components at their most granular level to provide the business and application with reusable, flexible, and scalable components • Storybook, a component explorer tool, demonstrates the workings of individual component in isolation	• React components
1-click operation	• Business orchestration to orchestrate services like a business process (BPM) • Service orchestration to achieve composite service	• Business process management • Service mesh • Event mesh
Data visualization	• Data aggregation • Analytics-driven visualization for better decision making	• BI dashboard • Data analytics
Self-service	• Self-managed content • Self-service dashboard • Minimum IT support for operational activities	• Chat • Search • AI-driven automation
Personalization	• Customer insight • Data-driven analytics • Customer single view	• Web analytics • Role-based access
Responsive	• Responsive design for omnichannel delivery • Mobile-first approach with multi-device support • Intuitive design is achieved • Customer single view	• HTML5, CSS3 • Media queries • Progressive web apps (PWA) • Web analytics

(*continued*)

Table 5-2. (*continued*)

Modern Web Design Principles	Description	Solutions
Design centric	• Prioritizes customer experience over features • Engages agent more closely	• Web analytics
Customer preference	• Data analytics to understand behavioral trends • Personalized delivery	• Web analytics
Network Interaction	Leverage service workers for the following • To control network requests • Cache requests to improve performance • Push notifications, offline support discussed during the discovery and design phase • Router/Navigation to handle screen navigation within the web application • Authentication and authorization token-based authentication requests	• PWA service worker
Quick time to market	• MVP/Phase approach to releasing quickly to market • PWA is developed using a headless approach on top of the existing ecosystem • Minimal development or modification at back-end services	• DevOps processes • Responsive design • Progressive Web Apps (PWA)
Personalized recommendation	• Recommendation based on customer profile • Personalized delivery	• Web analytics • Rules engine

(*continued*)

Table 5-2. (*continued*)

Modern Web Design Principles	Description	Solutions
Continuous integration/Delivery	• DevOps for continuous integration • Continuous code integration • Continuous testing • Automated deployment • Automated code analysis	• DevOps • CICD pipeline
Process optimization	• Process evaluation • Continuous incremental improvement	• Highly flexible BPM

Modern Web Platform Governance

Governance is a crucial aspect of a project's success. You can implement many performance optimizations, such as automated code reviews, metrics-based monitoring, and automated notification using a well-defined governance processes. Governance also impacts the time to market, release time, and other project metrics.

This section looks at the development tools modern web platforms need to implement an automation strategy, a robust DevOps setup, and governance metrics.

Modern Web Platform Development Tools

Integrated development environment (IDE) and tools play crucial role in reducing the overall delivery timelines. The right set of tools in the right project phase helps us in implementing the performance based design. Using automated tools for code quality control, performance testing helps us to improve the overall performance of the deliverable. The key development tools for modern web platforms are shown in Figure 5-9.

CHAPTER 5   MODERN WEB PLATFORM PERFORMANCE PRINCIPLES

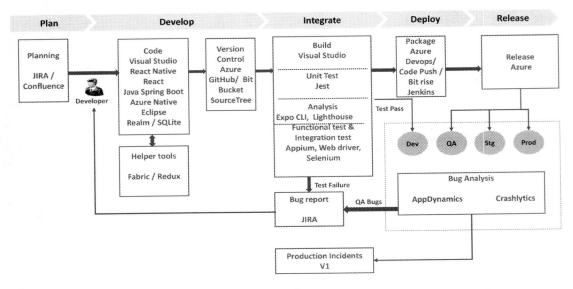

Figure 5-9. *Modern web development tools*

During the planning phase, you can use Jira or Confluence to log Jira stories. During the development stage, you can use IDEs such as Visual Studio and frameworks such as Spring Boot (for server component development), React framework, Redux, and Fabric. Source code is managed in version control tools such as GitHub and BitBucket. During the integration and testing phase, you use auditing tools (e.g., Lighthouse), testing tools (e.g., Selenium). Deployment uses Azure DevOps and tools such as Jenkins.

The following are other tools you can leverage in modern web platforms.

- The Jest Enzyme library for front-end automated unit testing
- ESLint and Sonarqube static code analysis tools for code quality checking
- Google Lighthouse for performance audits of PWA solutions
- Redux to handle asynchronous service calls and state management
- DOM Sanitizers to handle secure connection and communication
- Exception handling and logging to capture exception or error within UI components NgxLogger for error logging
- Automation of Restful API using Rest Assured, and SOAP protocols using SOAP UI /Postman to support both XML and JSON formats
- Leverage tools such as Selenium, Appium, BrowserStack, and Applitools for automated testing

CHAPTER 5 MODERN WEB PLATFORM PERFORMANCE PRINCIPLES

DevOps for Modern Web Platforms

DevOps is the key enabler of agile deliveries and performance based design. DevOps defines the processes, tools, and automation opportunities for project governance. A robust DevOps platform provides various features, such as metrics-based monitoring, automated code reviews, enforce security guidelines, automate testing, automated release management, and automated deployment. Many cloud platforms provide native support for DevOps capabilities.

This section looks at migrating traditional CI (continuous integration) to cloud-native DevOps. It also looks at a comprehensive cloud-based DevOps setup.

Note Azure DevOps are used as an example to illustrate the concepts. Similar DevOps capabilities can be enabled on other cloud platforms.

Migration of CI Platforms to Cloud-based DevOps

Figure 5-10 depicts the various steps to migrate a traditional on-premise Jenkins-based CI setup to a cloud-native DevOps platform.

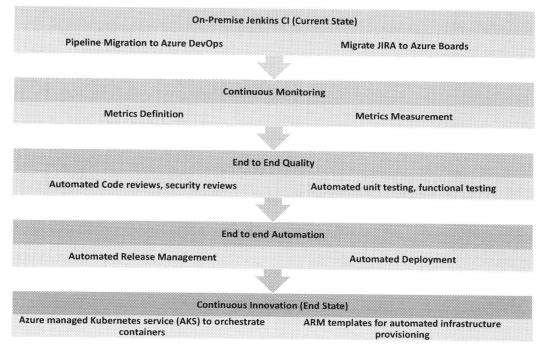

Figure 5-10. *On-premise CI migration to cloud-native DevOps*

On-premise Jenkins CI is the starting point for this migration. Normally, you deploy Jenkins in an on-premise environment and develop the Jenkins pipeline for build and deployment. The first step in the migration journey is to migrate the Jenkins pipeline to Azure DevOps (or any cloud-native DevOps service). The JIRA tasks and stories are migrated to Azure Boards.

The next step in the migration is to set up monitoring for the application. You define the metrics and set up the monitoring jobs (performance monitoring, availability monitoring, response time monitoring, etc.) to track and monitor the metrics.

Set up quality-related jobs for code reviews, security reviews, and performance reviews. Set up testing jobs such as unit testing, functional testing, and web testing.

Identify various automation opportunities and set up the corresponding jobs for the same. You can set up the jobs for automated builds, automated publishing, automated deployment, and so forth.

The end state in a robust DevOps setup enables continuous innovation by leveraging the cloud's platform services. For instance, you can use the Azure-managed Kubernetes service (AKS) to set up container orchestration and use ARM templates to automatically provision the infrastructure.

Cloud-based CICD Setup

Figure 5-11 depicts a robust cloud-based CICD setup based on the Azure platform.

CHAPTER 5 MODERN WEB PLATFORM PERFORMANCE PRINCIPLES

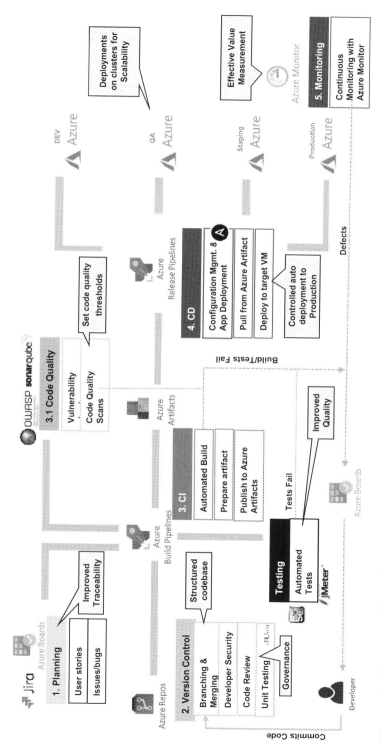

Figure 5-11. *Azure-based CICD setup*

In the project planning phase, you track the user stories, tasks, and bugs in Jira or Azure Boards. For source code management, you leverage Azure Repos to implement features such as branching, merging, and other version control features. You can set up the Azure build pipelines to implement the code governance (automated code review and automated testing using JUnit and JMeter) for improved quality.

As part of the continuous integration (CI) process, the Azure build pipeline automates the build, and prepares and publishes artifacts to Azure Artifact. You can also set up automated code scans and code vulnerability scans to set the code thresholds. You can leverage tools such as SonarQube for automated code reviews.

The continuous deployment (CD) process involves Azure release pipelines to pull artifacts from the Azure artifact repository and deploy it to the target Azure VM. You can deploy artifacts to dev, QA, staging, and production environments.

Finally, you can monitor the production environment (performance, error, availability, etc.) using Azure monitors, which notify system administrators about errors.

Agile Delivery of Modern Web Platforms

Figure 5-12 depicts the sprint-based agile delivery of modern web applications.

CHAPTER 5 MODERN WEB PLATFORM PERFORMANCE PRINCIPLES

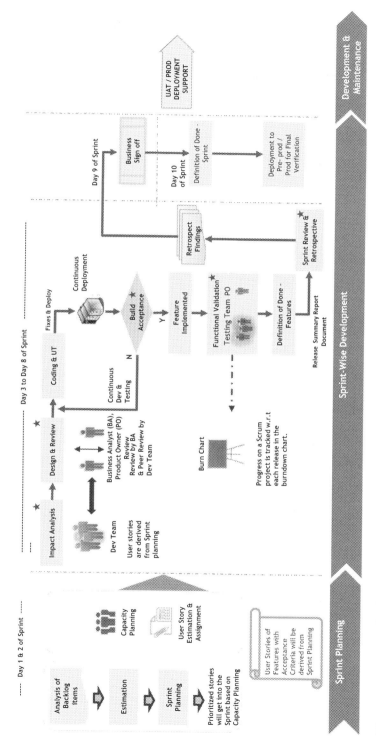

Figure 5-12. *Agile delivery steps*

CHAPTER 5 MODERN WEB PLATFORM PERFORMANCE PRINCIPLES

Figure 5-12 represents a typical 9-day sprint delivery model. During the sprint planning phase, the sprint master analyzes the backlog, prioritizes the stories, and estimates the stories. Based on the estimates, the sprint master comes up with capacity planning and assigns the prioritized stories to the development team.

In the sprint development phase, the business analysts (BA) and product owner (PO) hands over the stories to the development team. The development team analyzes the stories and creates low-level design and develops the code along with unit testing. The developed stories are continuously deployed to implement sprint features. The PO and testing team validates sprint functionality. The scrum master plans for a sprint retrospective and documents the learnings, improvements, and key success factors for the sprint. At the end of this phase, the sprint is handed over for business validation.

Once the business signs-off the sprint in the UAT environment, it deploys the build to the pre-production and production environments. Post-production maintenance is done during the deployment and maintenance phase.

Governance Metrics

Table 5-3 highlights the key metrics for tracking project governance at various stages. It includes examples of monitoring metrics.

Table 5-3. *Key Project Governance Metrics*

Project Phase	Reason for Monitoring	Metrics
Development	To measure the performance and quality of delivery	• Predictability (planned vs. actual stories/sprint): 95% • Code coverage: 90% • Code quality score: 90% • Code complexity
Testing	To identify the effectiveness of testing and quality	• Defect leakage: 0.2 (Per person per sprint) • Test coverage: 95% of the features • Defect validity: 95%

(continued)

CHAPTER 5 MODERN WEB PLATFORM PERFORMANCE PRINCIPLES

Table 5-3. (*continued*)

Project Phase	Reason for Monitoring	Metrics
Maintenance	To gauge fulfillment of end-user commitments	• Impact analysis: 100% • Root Cause Analysis (RCA): 100% (For all Severity-1 and Severity-2 defects) • First Time Right Fix: 95% (For break fixes)
Process	Check the impact the new process on the results	• DevOps pipeline: 100% (Dev and test environments) • Offshore leverage: 100% • Metrics, SLA, KPI reporting compliance: 100% • Risk reporting and mitigation: 95%
Delivery and Sprint Management	To track the effectiveness of sprint delivery	• Release automation: 70% • Velocity • Burndown charts • Commit to complete

The following describes each of the key governance metrics.

- **Velocity**: The number of story points that are completed in a Sprint

- **Defect leakage**: Defects that are found outside of a sprint through acceptance, integration, performance, and usability (AIPUS) testing

- **Code complexity**: Typically, an automated test done with tools like SonarQube that looks at coding standards and cyclomatic complexity

- **Burndown charts**: Looks at project progress; the average delivery timeline compared to the actual delivery progress

- **Commit to complete**: The ratio of committed stories to completed stories

- **Code coverage**: The percentage of unit test cases written

133

CHAPTER 5   MODERN WEB PLATFORM PERFORMANCE PRINCIPLES

Progressive Web Apps (PWA)

Progressive web apps (PWAs) are the most popular frameworks for building modern web platforms. Progressive web apps leverage the features of modern web browsers to provide offline-capable, native app-like user experience using device-hardware accessibility support. They are built with responsive web design (RWD) and are flexible enough to cater to various browsers and devices. PWAs progressively cache the data based on user interaction, making the application lightweight, and minimizing network interactions. PWAs can provide the look and feel similar to a native mobile app. PWAs also support other features like push notifications.

PWAs are discoverable by search engines. They are accessible on browsers and installed on mobile device home screens to provide an app-like experience.

PWA patterns are discussed in Chapter 10.

Performance Optimization of Modern Web Apps

This section discusses the design best practices and principles for modern web platforms.

Design Best Practices for Modern Web Applications

Now let's go over the best practices for building a seamless omnichannel experience.

- **Single responsibility principle (SRP)**

    The SRP principle states that modules *do one thing*. By applying the SRP to components and services, it is easier to maintain the code, modularize the code, test the code, and extend the code. The following are some best practices of SRP.

    - The services handle a single concern, and the context encapsulates it.

    - The UI component only handles the logic related to the view. The services handle all other logic.

    - Develop reusable services so that components are simple and reusable.

CHAPTER 5   MODERN WEB PLATFORM PERFORMANCE PRINCIPLES

- Develop smaller, modular, and reusable functions.
- Presentation logic is separated from business logic.
- Follow the DRY (Don't Repeat Yourself) approach. The DRY approach ensures reusability, maintainability, testability and reduces complexity.
- Each solution module is focused on a single concern, and each module has a well-defined boundary.

- **Responsive design**

  Leverage responsive design to cater to multiple devices and multiple browsers. The responsive design leverages the HTML5, CSS3, and media queries to render the web page across various browsers and devices.

- **Single code base**

  Develop the web platform using a tool to use a single code base for the web and various mobile devices. Isomorphic applications use a single code for the client side and the server side. For instance, you can use IONIC4-based hybrid cross-platform development using Angular7 with a single source code for mobile web and iOS and Android mobile apps.

- **Optimal maintenance cost and shorter time to market**

  A single code base improves maintainability and results in effective cost reduction for implementation and support and maintenance. The single code base also improves time to market.

- **Separation of concerns**

  Create different modules and components to handle data, UI rendering logic, business logic, and communication logic. This pattern improves code testability, code reusability, and code extensibility.

- **Testability**

  The modules use a single responsibility principle that are modular, decoupled, and easily testable.

135

CHAPTER 5   MODERN WEB PLATFORM PERFORMANCE PRINCIPLES

- **Extensibility**

    The modules and components are reusable and extensible to follow the open-closed principle. The solution is extensible to easily onboard new features and integrate new systems. The APIs are decomposed based on business functionality. API-driven design enables the incremental addition of business capabilities.

- **Maintainability**

    If there are new UI requirements in the future, the UI components are reused so that there is no need to rewrite the entire UI.

Modern Web Key Design Principles

Based on our analysis of modern web requirements and industry trends, this section defines the core solution principles. The platform principles define the overall design, architecture, and execution approach for the modern web platform. These solution principles are well-aligned to fulfill the long-term digital vision and feature roadmap for a digital enterprise.

The platform provides forward-looking, proven, and best-in-class architecture principles. The solution is well-aligned with the emerging architecture industry trends. The following are the salient features of the recommended solution architecture.

- **Omnichannel, intuitive, and personalized user experience**

    The user experience is designed to cater to various devices and personas seamlessly. Omnichannel enabled user interface based on responsive design provides a seamless omnichannel experience. The platform supports implicit and explicit personalization. Implicit personalization involves leveraging the user's attributes (e.g., location) to personalize content, and explicit personalization leverages the user's explicit preferences to personalize the experience. The platform supports localization and targeted communications. For instance, personalized product recommendations based on the user's transaction history. The solution provides intuitive experience with a responsive, personalized, and omnichannel experience to provide self-service functionality.

- **Collaborative**

    The platforms provide collaborative features, such as blogs, wikis/articles, chat, and people searches. Users can share information seamlessly.

- **Robust architecture**

    The platform provides scalability and high performing solution components. The architecture is future-ready with a cloud-ready and flexible architecture. Reusability, configurability, and extensibility are key features of a robust architecture.

- **Separation of concerns**

    The modules within each layer have high cohesiveness, and the modules across different layers have low coupling.

- **User engagement**

    Engage users through various features such as chatbot, user collaboration, polls and surveys, blogs, communities, and articles.

- **Platform principle**

    The solution is based on platform principles providing the framework and reusable building blocks for continuous development and integration.

- **Modular**

    Decompose the solution modules based on business capability. The modular design enables reusability.

- **Ease of use**

    The platform is intuitive and is easy to use with a simple and minimalistic design. The platform is easy to learn, easy to navigate, and easy to find the relevant information. The platform provides single-click features for key business transactions such as checkout, registration, and so forth.

- **Open standards**

  Modern web platform uses open standards and specifications (REST, SOAP, OAuth) at all layers for better interoperability, so it is easy to integrate and extend.

- **User-centric approach**

  You identify personas and the unique requirements for each persona. Information delivery and tools are personalized for each persona. The site structure, navigation model, and information architecture are designed to cater to all personas. The self-service tools and services are developed to empower associates and improve their productivity.

- **Agility**

  Agile methodology is adopted for solution delivery. The execution methodology consists of sprints for MVP (minimum viable product) delivery for quicker time to market. You need to implement agile and unified DevOps practices with continuous integration and continuous deployment along with two-week sprints.

- **Reliability**

  Build a scalable and fault-tolerant integration between on-premise and cloud platforms. To implement the reliability, you need to build the disaster recovery systems, multi-node cluster, distributed database, redundant services to handle the failure.

- **Future readiness**

  The platform support forward-looking features such as advanced analytics, chatbots, artificial intelligence, robo-advisory, and so forth.

Modern Web Integration Design Principles

Integrations are an essential part of modern web platforms as modern web platforms need to onboard new features or extend the existing features.

Modern web platforms use API-driven and contract-based approach for integration. Modern web platforms use modular, lightweight, and granular microservices for integrations. The services are decomposed based on the business capabilities required

CHAPTER 5 MODERN WEB PLATFORM PERFORMANCE PRINCIPLES

for the web platform. This section defines the main design principles for the integration modules within modern web platforms.

- **Stateless integration**

    Server APIs are stateless with well-defined contracts and use the security tokens for security scenarios. Stateless APIs complement the lightweight nature of the APIs and can be used with various consumers (web platforms, mobile apps, etc.).

- **High performance**

    The server APIs respond within the defined performance SLA. To render the entire page within two-second response time, each of the underlying APIs responds within 0.5 seconds. Additionally, the performance of the server APIs should not degrade in the normal load. The solution is built for high performance through lightweight UI and lightweight integration. For instance, in the Angular or React frameworks, you can adopt these design guidelines.

    Service workers run separately from the main UI thread to provide good performance. Use lightweight design for decoupled architecture with headless content, with a lightweight, front-end façade, which also helps improve performance.

- **Scalability**

    The solution modules and integration modules are scalable and provide an autoscalability pattern. API-driven and stateless integration provide higher scalability.

    Normally a single web page needs data from multiple server APIs, and the web page or the screen invokes the APIs asynchronously. To support multiple invocations, you need to test the scalability and performance of the server APIs at normal load and peak load. The APIs also be scalable to dynamic requirements.

- **Microservices**

    The integration across layers use granular decomposed microservices to provide a lightweight and stateless integration model.

CHAPTER 5   MODERN WEB PLATFORM PERFORMANCE PRINCIPLES

- **Decoupled**

    Decouple systems of engagement (SOE) from systems of record (SOR) to provide architecture flexibility. The data exchange contract is clearly defined.

- **Cloud-ready**

    All the layers and solution components are made cloud-ready. It is recommended to develop the new applications as cloud-native systems leveraging the cloud services and migrating existing legacy and on-premise systems to cloud platforms.

- **Headless integration**

    Use a headless mode of integration between systems of record and systems of engagement. Headless architecture to provide flexible and scalable integration based on the lightweight microservices model.

- **Fault tolerance**

    The server APIs gracefully handle error and exception scenarios. For instance, if the API cannot get the source data, they fall back to cached data, or it sends a friendly error message. In a transaction failure, the server API, or the orchestration layer must ensure the data integrity and data consistency through rollback mechanisms.

- **End-to-end security**

    The server APIs are secured to ensure data sensitivity, resource authorization, and API security. The security governance process enforces security checks before invoking the APIs. The API itself validates the invoker's permission and accordingly provides the data. All sensitive data is encrypted. Enterprise security standards are defined to provide data isolation, privacy and security, and information integrity. Build a solution that is compliant with the organization's security guidelines and requirements. The solution provides data isolation, privacy, and security, information integrity.

CHAPTER 5   MODERN WEB PLATFORM PERFORMANCE PRINCIPLES

- **Lightweight design**

    The server APIs for modern web platforms use lightweight data exchange format such as JSON. APIs serve the response based on the request channel; for instance, the API provides minimal data to the mobile app request compared to a web request.

- **Testable**

    The APIs specify the well-defined contracts, and you can test the APIs to validate the request and response contract. You can conduct various tests (regression testing, automated testing, etc.) on APIs with the proper tools.

- **Plug-and-play architecture**

    The server APIs is flexible enough to support various clients (browser, mobile apps, tablets, wearable, watch, kiosk, etc.), various deployment models (on-premise or cloud or serverless architecture), various protocols (HTTP, HTTPS, REST, SMTP, etc.), and platform-agnostic (cloud, database, UI framework, etc.).

- **Service governance through middleware**

    Normally, the integration of middleware systems provides service governance. A centralized middleware manages the service orchestration and provides other features such as service monitoring, metering, auditing, and auto scalability. You define the policies, processes, standards, and templates for APIs.

    The middleware system handles the following concerns.

    - Parsing incoming requests or inject headers in the response; for example, you can use *body-parser* middleware for parsing the HTTP request

    - Authenticating requests before processing; for example, you can use a *passport* to handle various authentication strategies (OAuth, email, AD, third-party authentication, etc.)

    - Middleware such as *helmet* secures the APIs through headers.

CHAPTER 5   MODERN WEB PLATFORM PERFORMANCE PRINCIPLES

- Logging request and response; for example, you can use *morgan* middleware for logging

- Handling CORS (cross-origin resource sharing)

- Proxying requests through middleware such as `http-proxy`

- Error handling by gracefully handling application errors, connection errors, and data errors

- Compressing the HTTP response; for example, *compression* middleware is used for HTTP response compression

- Cache static data and service response and database response.

- Perform any required data transformation.

The API façade pattern can be used in middleware to orchestrate system-specific calls and abstract information from the caller.

- **Asynchronous API invocations**

    Most of the modern web platforms invoke server APIs asynchronously. The asynchronous calls prevent blocking request processing, and you can execute the tasks in parallel.

Summary

- The drivers for the modern web design are hyperconnectivity, enabled and empowered users, collaboration, business model transformation, AI and automation, discoverability, user engagement, quick time to market, performance, and cost optimization.

- The key capabilities of a modern web platform are responsiveness, personalization, search, security, enterprise integration, web analytics and page analytics, content management and document/asset management, collaboration, and AI advancement modules.

- Business imperatives of modern web platform are seamless omnichannel user experience, enterprise integrations and DevOps.

- Progressive web app (PWA) leverage the features of modern web browsers to provide offline-capable, native app-like user experience using device-hardware accessibility support.

- The key design best practices of modern web platforms are the single responsibility principle (SRP), responsive design, a single code base, optimal maintenance costs, shorter time to market, separation of concerns, testability, extensibility, and maintainability.

- The modern web key design principles are omnichannel and personalized user experiences, collaboration, separation of concerns, the single responsibility principle and segregation, user engagement, the platform principle, scalability, extensible, modular, decoupled, cloud readiness, headless integration, ease of use, open standards, user centric approach, high performance, centralized service governance, microservices, data security, and reliability.

- The key modern web integration design principles are stateless integration, high performance, scalability, fault tolerance, end-to-end security, lightweight design, testable, plug and play architecture, service governance, extensibility, and asynchronous API invocations.

PART III

Performance Validation and Infrastructure

CHAPTER 6

Web Performance Validation

Performance validation ensures that various layers of the application conform to predefined performance service-level agreements (SLAs). You need a robust performance-testing plan to validate all aspects of the application. It is a critical success factor to ensure the optimal performance the overall solution. A performance testing exercise analyzes the performance needs of the application, characterizes the workload, scripts performance scenarios, executes performance scripts, and reports the findings. The performance findings and recommendations are used by various teams to address performance issues. Performance validation and sign-off are crucial aspects of the system acceptance criteria and are part of the production readiness decision.

This chapter describes various topics of performance testing. It discusses the trends, types, and attributes of web performance testing. The next section defines the approach to web performance validation, including performance validation prerequisites and phases, performance prediction models, testing tools, and application testing. The chapter also covers the prerequisites and processes for workload modeling. Later sections define the web performance test methodology and performance testing maturity model. We have provided a detailed example of Performance Test Strategy in Appendix D and we have given the template for Performance Test Report in Appendix C.

Performance engineers, web developers, digital architects, project managers, and program managers will find this chapter useful.

What Is Web Performance Validation?

Web performance validation is a crucial activity for the success of a digital platform. Robust web performance testing requires a deep understanding of the application's domain, technology stack, solution ecosystem, and functional domain knowledge.

CHAPTER 6   WEB PERFORMANCE VALIDATION

Business organizations plan to exceed end-user expectations. Companies aim to develop a reliable application that doesn't experience performance bottlenecks and has minimal failures. Organizations always try to optimize maintenance costs, downtime, and production outage costs. Performance testing enables these goals.

As per the IEEE,[1] performance testing is "conducted to evaluate the compliance of a system or component with specified performance requirements." During performance testing, you aim to identify and isolate system performance issues, bottleneck scenarios, and system scalability issues. Organizations conduct performance testing to meet performance SLAs and develop a reliable and predictable response time with high availability.

Performance testing helps with the following.

- Uncovering the **performance issues** early in the project lifecycle, thereby reducing cost and effort.

- Understanding the **resource utilization** and **throughput** of various system components. The outcome of performance testing can fine-tune the capacity and size of the infrastructure.

- Assessing the **perceived performance** from an end-user standpoint across various geographies and browsers.

- Creating a **performance baseline** for future performance validations.

- Identifying **performance bottlenecks** in the solution ecosystem across various layers.

- Understanding **server configuration** (e.g., OS configuration, application server configuration, web server configuration, database configuration, and hardware configurations) that impacts overall performance.

- Supporting the performance **fine-tuning exercise**.

A good performance test covers various aspects of solution performance.

- **System availability** to understand the uptime of the system and the service

- **Transaction throughput** to understand the workload (number of transactions or requests handled per second) by the system

- **Response times** to understand various response times at all layers
- **Resource consumption** to understand resource utilization on all servers
- **Bottleneck analysis** to identify any existing performance bottlenecks in the system
- Various kinds of **load testing** to understand the ability of the system to handle various workloads

Trends in Web Performance Testing

The following are emerging trends in web performance testing.

- **Holiday readiness assessment**: Most of the B2C e-commerce digital organizations carry out holiday readiness performance validation and identify performance vulnerabilities. The performance test is carried out with the peak user load expected on holidays to assess the performance, scalability, and availability of the system. During the validation, application performance monitoring (APM) monitors resource utilization. Based on the performance assessment, performance bottleneck analysis is done across all layers.

- **End-user experience management**: Organizations want to measure the actual performance experienced by the end users. As part of this capability, you need to get insights into the end-user transactions, browsers and devices, geographies, and the application performance across various channels.

- **Load testing for cloud-based applications**: As many modern digital applications are cloud-native, you need to understand methods and processes for testing cloud-based applications.

- **Mobile web application performance testing**: Mobile apps and mobile web applications are popular user experience platforms. Hence testing the performance of mobile apps is an essential part of application validation.

CHAPTER 6 WEB PERFORMANCE VALIDATION

Types of Web Performance Testing

You need to understand the application usage patterns and simulate the user load during performance testing.

Based on the application needs and performance SLAs, various kinds of performance testing are conducted. The common types of performance testing are as follows.

- **Load testing**: Measure the system performance at predefined load conditions and for specified concurrent user load. You record the change in system behavior and performance with the increase in the load. You monitor the system resources such as CPU, memory, network utilization during the load testing.

- **Stress testing**: The system is subjected to peak loads, sudden spikes, extended high load scenarios, and subject the system to stress conditions and measure system performance and system behavior as part of this testing. You find out the breakpoint of the application and learn the maximum load levels that the system can handle without degradation in the performance. The system suffers from resource depletion during this testing. You use the following inputs for stress testing.

    - Identify peak limits: number of transactions, concurrent users, 24/7 availability, and so forth

    - The number of concurrent users at peak and average loads.

    - The number of concurrent transactions at peak and average loads.

    - Average and peak data and content volume

- **Endurance testing**: The system is subjected to load testing for a long duration (usually 48–72 hours) to measure system performance and system behavior. You identify any potential memory leaks, buffer overflow issues, timeout issues, exception handling scenarios, hardware-related issues during this testing.

- **Scalability testing**: You test the system with various workloads based on the workload model. You iteratively increase the concurrent user load and check the system performance. You identify the key workload and mitigate the bottlenecks that impede the application scalability. You start with 10% of data, scale up to the maximum with increasing data volume periodically.

- **Reliability and availability testing**: As part of the reliability testing, you check the MTTF (mean time between failures) to test the reliability and availability of the application.

- **Performance benchmarking testing**: You compare the application performance vis-à-vis the performance of earlier versions of the application. You also compare the application performance with the same category of application and with same domain applications.

- **Volume testing**: This tests the system with data volume and content volume similar to that of the production environment.

Key Performance Testing Metrics

During performance testing, you record and report key performance metrics, as follows.

- **Response time**: You test the overall response time for pages, transactions, and business processes. You test the response time at various user loads. For a web page, you measure various timing metrics such as total page response time, time to first byte, first meaningful time, and time to interactive.

- **System scalability**: You test the system with various workloads based on the workload model. You iteratively increase the concurrent user load and check if the system scalability at various loads.

- **Resource utilization**: You monitor the system resources such as CPU, memory, network bandwidth, input/output (IO), disk utilization activities during various loads.

- **Efficiency**: You check if the resource utilization is healthy and within the agreed thresholds during various loads. For instance, you monitor if the CPU utilization is within 80% during the entire duration of load testing.

- **Recoverability**: You test the system resiliency and how well the system recovers from failure and how well the system handles the errors gracefully.

CHAPTER 6 WEB PERFORMANCE VALIDATION

Common Performance Issues Across Tiers

In this section we identify the most commonly occurring performance issues across various tiers. Long wait times, frequent system errors, frequent production outages, and frequent service timeouts are symptoms of the underlying performance issue. The following are some of the common performance-related issues across various tiers.

End-user layer

- Slow response times for the web pages due to absence or inefficient browser-level caching
- Heavy page size, heavy static assets, high asset count
- Chatty server calls
- Inefficient JavaScript execution

Network layer

- Low firewall throughput leading to dropped requests
- Inefficient load balancing policies
- Suboptimal network bandwidth
- Absence of CDN level caching

Web server layer

- Inefficient asset caching
- Inefficient load balancing policy
- Inefficient clustering
- Inefficient size (CPU, memory)
- Inefficient number of threads to handle incoming requests

Application server layer

- Inefficient connection pool settings, thread pool settings
- Improper timeout configurations
- Suboptimal heap size, garbage collector (GC) settings
- Frequent and chatty database and service calls

- Heavy sessions and inefficient session management
- Inefficient size (CPU, memory)
- Absence of server-side caching
- Inefficient object lifecycle management
- Memory leaks

Database layer

- Absence of indexes for columns used in query conditions
- Lower buffer caching
- Absence of query caching
- Frequent full table scans
- Presence of database deadlocks

Services layer

- Absence of service caching
- High granularity of the services leading to chatty calls

Approach to Web Performance Validation

A comprehensive performance validation involves phase-wise performance testing. This section discusses various testing phases, testing tools, and performance prediction models.

Prerequisites for Web Performance Testing

A complete understanding of requirements and solution ecosystem is needed for a successful performance testing strategy. This section discusses various inputs needed for performance testing. These inputs are needed to craft efficient test cases and do efficient workload modeling. The performance testing team can use the following list as a checklist for the deliverables.

CHAPTER 6   WEB PERFORMANCE VALIDATION

Generic requirements

- Understand the current performance-related challenges with the solution. The challenges include slow response time, frequent production outage, or existing performance bottlenecks.
- Understand the growth rate of the application in terms of user traffic rate, content volume rate, and data volume rate.

Solution ecosystem

- Understand the various solution components, technologies, information flow of the entire application. A deeper understanding of the solution ecosystem helps a performance testing team create layer-specific performance test cases and to identify the performance bottlenecks easily.
- Understand the core functionality, use cases, business scenarios of the application.
- Understand various tiers of the applications such as web server, application server, database server, and so forth.
- Understand the various protocols, such as HTTP and LDAP, used by the application.
- Understand various enterprise interfaces and their integration methods.
- Understand all the software and the versions used in the application.

Infrastructure details

- Understand the capacity, throughput, and sizing details of various servers used in the application.
- Understand various servers and network details of the application.
- Understand the complete deployment architecture of the application.

User profile details

- Understand various types of users and their roles.
- Understand the traffic patterns of the user based on geography and timings.

154

CHAPTER 6   WEB PERFORMANCE VALIDATION

- Understand the user mix (ratio of repeated users to new users).
- Understand the average and peak concurrent user load.
- Understand the average session time for the user.
- Understand the expected total number of users.
- Understand the browsers and mobile devices used by the users.

Performance goals

- Understand the main performance goals and performance metrics such as expected response times, performance SLAs, scalability SLAs, expected user load, availability SLAs.
- Understand the performance expectation from the end user of the application and the performance expectation from the business stakeholders.
- Understand the current performance challenges and pain points.
- Understand the current scalability and performance of the system.
- Understand the existing performance bottlenecks at various layers and systems.
- Understand the performance requirements for reporting functionality.
- Understand the scope of performance testing (performance reports, performance fine-tuning recommendations, performance bottleneck analysis, etc.).

Data details

- Understand the data flow across various layers.
- Understand the data volume needs of the solution.
- Understand the special needs of the data such as encryption policies (at rest and in motion), data archival policies, reference data policies, GDPR policies.
- Understand the main data stores in the application (relational database, cloud database, enterprise database, NoSQL database, etc.).

155

CHAPTER 6 WEB PERFORMANCE VALIDATION

- Understand the data-related regulation needs of the application (data sharing policies, personally identifiable data needs, GDPR compliance, etc.).

- Understand the details of all reference data stores used by the application.

- Understand any functional domain-specific data requirements (e.g., HIPAA standards).

- Understand the details of data-related scripts and batch jobs for data synchronization and data backup activities.

Security details

- Understand the security features of the application, such as authentication, authorization, and single sign-on.

- Understand the security protocols used across various solution layers.

- Understand the specific security needs of the application, such as security policies for information sharing, access policies, security needs for third-party plugins and services.

Web Performance Testing Phases

Web performance testing closely follows software development lifecycle (SDLC) phases. The following are the key phases.

- **Performance evaluation and requirements elaboration**: The requirements for performance testing are gathered using the finalized requirements document.

- **Performance test planning**: The testing team develops the test design, plan, and test strategy for performance testing in this phase.

- **Performance test scripting**: During this phase, the performance testing team scripts the test scenarios.

CHAPTER 6 WEB PERFORMANCE VALIDATION

- **Performance test execution**: The performance testing team executes the scripts and records the timing metrics.
- **Result reporting and tracking**: The performance testing team reports the findings for easier tracking.

Table 6-1 highlights the activities and deliverables for each of the performance testing phases.

Table 6-1. *Performance Testing Activities and Deliverables*

Phase	Performance Validation Activities	Deliverables
Performance Requirements and Analysis	- Understand the application architecture and functional domain - Determine performance testing needs - Requirements validation - Usage analysis and understanding user characteristics - Performance metrics finalization - Understand non-functional requirements (NFR) and SLAs - Understand current performance challenges - Understand business-critical transactions - Collect data required for workload modeling - Gather load numbers, content volume, and data volume - High-level estimation - Identify the key performance metrics such as average page load time and TTFB	- Clarification of requirements - Signed-off content volume, data volume, user traffic details. - Signed-off NFR requirements
Performance Test Planning	- Performance test environment setup - Test data preparation - Performance test strategy and workload model development - Finalize performance test scenarios - Identify the performance testing tools - Devise performance testing roadmap	- Performance test plan and strategy - Workload model - A finalized list of performance testing tools

(*continued*)

157

CHAPTER 6   WEB PERFORMANCE VALIDATION

Table 6-1. (*continued*)

Phase	Performance Validation Activities	Deliverables
Performance Test Scripting	• Performance test scripting • Create test data requests (transactional and master) • Develop automation scripts • Develop baseline and benchmark tests	• Performance test scripts • Automation scripts
Performance Test Execution	• Baseline and load testing • Benchmark testing • Performance measurement • Performance and resource monitoring • Identification of performance bottleneck • Sanity testing • Conduct load tests and other tests (stress/endurance/volume) • Record test results against the executed test cases • Defect logging and tracking • Results analysis and reporting	• Test result and defects • Performance baseline numbers
Reporting and Recommendation	• Provide QA sign-off • Report and publish test metrics • Document best practices and lessons learned • Recommend the go/no-go decision	• Test summary and recommendation report • Trend report • Performance tuning recommendations • Performance bottleneck analysis report

CHAPTER 6 WEB PERFORMANCE VALIDATION

Web Performance Prediction Model

You can also use the workload model to predict the performance of different workloads. As a rule of thumb, you consider a 15% increment in the user traffic, content volume, and data volume on a yearly basis. Because the changes in user traffic, content volume, and data volume impact the workload, you can use the web performance prediction model to predict the performance numbers.

Generally, you conduct the performance test in the preproduction environment, which closely mirrors the production configuration. Based on the performance findings of the preproduction environment, you predict the performance of the production environment.

A workload-based web performance prediction model is depicted in Figure 6-1.

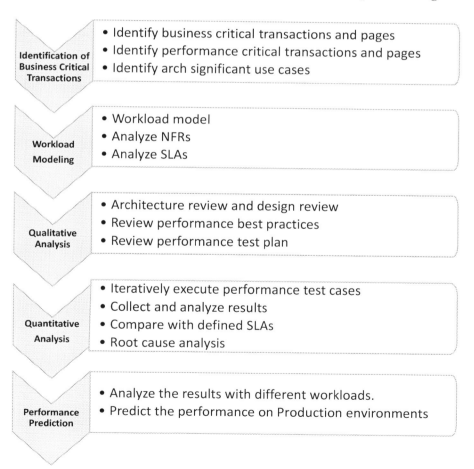

Figure 6-1. *Workload based web performance prediction model*

159

CHAPTER 6　WEB PERFORMANCE VALIDATION

The steps in the workload-based web performance prediction model closely follow the performance testing phases. As part of the regular performance testing planning, you identify the business-critical transactions and performance-critical transactions and pages. Architecturally significant use cases are validated.

Based on the data gathered in the previous step, the performance testing team creates the workload model. The workload model identifies the peak user load, maximum content load, and maximum data load that needs to be handled by the application. Workload models develop performance test strategies needed for the application. The performance testing team analyzes non-functional requirements (NFR) and performance service-level agreement (SLA).

As part of qualitative analysis, the performance testing team reviews the current architecture, design, performance recommendations, and best practices. The team also reviews the performance test plan.

The performance testing team iteratively executes the performance scripts during quantitative analysis. The team then compares the obtained results with the predefined performance SLAs. The performance testing team identifies performance bottlenecks and performance issues.

For performance prediction, the performance testing team analyzes the results with various workloads and uses the data for predicting the performance data for different workloads.

Web Performance Testing Tools

Table 6-2 shows the key testing tools for web performance testing.

Table 6-2. Key Performance Testing Tools

Category	Performance testing tools
Web Page Testing	Google Chrome Lighthouse
	Google PageSpeed Insights
Application Profiling	Open Source: JProbe, Eclipse Profiler
	Commercial: JProfiler, OptimizeIt,
Load testing	Open Source: Apache JMeter, Grinder, Apache Bench, HTTPPerf
	Commercial: HP LoadRunner, NeoLoad, BlazeMeter
Service testing/API Testing	LoadUI, SOAPUI, Rest-Assured
Client-side performance testing	https://www.webpagetest.org
Real-time web performance monitoring	Open Source: Nagios, Hyperic – HQ, PERFMON, NMon
	Commercial - HP SiteScope, Wily Introscope
Application Performance Monitoring (APM)	Dynatrace, AppDynamics, New Relic
Mobile App testing	Appium, UI Automator
Analysis tools	GC Analyzer, JVM Analyzer

Mobile App Performance Validation

As mobile apps are gaining prominence and are shaping the end-user experience for many digital platforms, it is imperative to evaluate the mobile app from a performance standpoint. Mobile app testing is different from the regular application testing, as there is variation in device form factors, network connections, mobile OS platforms, and limited resources for mobile.

This section discusses the performance validation for mobile apps.

Mobile applications come in three flavors: mobile web, native mobile apps, and hybrid mobile apps. You look at the performance validation approach for each of these scenarios.

CHAPTER 6   WEB PERFORMANCE VALIDATION

Performance Validation for Mobile Web Applications

The high-level steps for mobile web application performance validation are shown in Figure 6-2.

Figure 6-2. *Mobile web application performance validation*

The mobile web application performance testing is like the normal web application testing that follows web performance test methodology. One major difference is the simulation of network conditions as the mobile web is accessed from mobile devices.

The main performance metrics you measure the following metrics.

- **Page response times or latency** represents the overall time taken for the user to see the response. The overall latency is the total of network latency (time taken for the data to be transferred over the wire between client and server), application latency (time taken by the server to respond), and client latency (time taken by browser to render the page).

- **Server response time** indicates the total time taken by the server to respond to the request.

- **Throughput** defines the number of transactions that a mobile app can handle per second; it is normally measured in TPS (transactions per second).

- **Component-wise load times and sizes** provide details of size and load time for each of the web components like images, JavaScript, stylesheets, and so forth.

- **Resource utilization** of the device provides the utilization of resources such as CPU, disk I/O, and memory.

- **Cache utilization** indicates the amount of cache for serving requests.

Performance Validation for Native Mobile Apps

The high-level steps for native mobile apps are shown in Figure 6-3.

Figure 6-3. *Mobile web application performance validation*

In the performance test strategy, you learn the mobile app landscape, device, and network matrix. You use this information to design performance metrics and workload.

Once you define the workload model, you simulate the user actions through scripts on the device/emulator. You then collect the performance metrics (e.g., response time and resource utilization) for the device. The performance and stability of the mobile app are tested under a normal load and an anticipated peak load.

The main performance metrics you measure the following metrics.

- Mobile app response times
- Server response time
- Resource utilization of the device (CPU, memory, network, battery, etc.)

Performance Validation for Hybrid Mobile Apps

The high-level steps for hybrid mobile apps are similar to the steps defined in Figure 6-2 except for "conduct load testing for the web." step. Instead of load testing for the web, you simulate user actions on both the web and a native device to collect performance metrics.

Non-Functional Testing

As part of non-functional testing for mobile apps, you test battery usage, memory usage, network calls, responsiveness to various screen sizes, form factors, multilingual, multi-time zone support, and other user actions (e.g., pinch, zoom, and swipe). For mobile web testing, you also test the application responsiveness and performance on various browsers.

CHAPTER 6   WEB PERFORMANCE VALIDATION

Workload Modeling

As workload modeling is an important activity for overall performance validation, this section explains the details of workload modeling. The workload is modeled based on the percentage of users executing specific functions over a while.

The workload modeling uses the application usage pattern, transaction distribution, log analysis to characterize the application load.

Prerequisites for Workload Modeling

Before developing the workload model, you need to have the full details of the following.

- You need the complete details of all performance SLAs, such as response times across all geographies.
- You need the complete details of all load numbers, such as user traffic, content volume, and data volume.
- All applicable types of performance tests need to be identified.
- Understand the user behavior pattern and usage of the application. You need to understand the heavily used pages, popular flows, busy hours of the day, and so forth.
- Identify all performance testing scenarios and transactions.
- Collect the application logs to understand user behavior patterns.
- Identify the scenario mix that needs to be simulated.
- Identify the browsers and devices that need to be supported.

Process of Workload Modeling

To model the workload, you need the key details such as application usage pattern, session duration, and request count. Figure 6-4 depicts the high-level steps in workload modeling.

Figure 6-4. *Workload modeling process*

Application and Load Analysis

This phase explains the application and the users' navigation flow. By analyzing the user navigation flow, you understand the popular paths. You also need to understand the key performance indicators (KPI) and performance goals of the application, such as expected response times, expected resource utilization, and application scalability.

User and Data Load Analysis

You profile application users to understand the type of users, average and maximum concurrent user load, the growth rate of users per year, average user volume per day/week/month/year, and the average session time per user. You also need to check the average think time for the user (time taken by the user on a page for completing an activity).

You learn the data and content volume of the application. This includes average data transferred between various tiers and data volume growth.

Scenario Identification

You identify the key business scenarios of the application. The most common categories for scenarios are as follows.

- The most popular business scenarios that get higher user traffic
- Business scenarios that need integrations with other systems
- Scenarios that consume a relatively high amount of resources (CPU, memory, network, file storage)
- Scenarios that expect optimized performance
- Scenarios that are of high business value and the ones that generate high revenue
- Scenarios that need stricter transaction management and has strict data integrity constraints
- Scenarios that are time-dependent and that are mission-critical
- Scenarios that handle bulk data volumes and huge files such as file upload and file download

Load Distribution

Identifying loads for each of the scenarios is one of the crucial steps of the workload modeling exercise. Based on an analysis of the application log files, user behavior analysis, A/B testing, beta testing, and stakeholder interview, you need to know the load distribution across key application pages. A sample load distribution for financial application is shown in Table 6-3.

Table 6-3. Sample Load Distribution

Scenario	Percentage Load Distribution
Product details scenario	10%
Search product scenario	30%
Dashboard view scenario	50%
Others	10%

You also need to know the average and peak load per day, week, month, and year. Use the load growth rate to predict the expected load for the future.

Scenario-based load distribution, coupled with time-specific load prediction, can script the load test scripts and stress test scripts.

Sample Workload Model Template

Table 6-4 is a sample workload model template capturing all the details discussed previously.

Table 6-4. Sample Workload Template

Scenario	Average Concurrent User Load per hour/day/week /month/year	Peak User Load per hour/day/ week/ month /year	Average User Think time	Average time per page	Average session time	Average number of sessions	Growth rate(Yearly)	User Mix	Scenario Mix

Web Performance Test Methodology

A web performance test methodology defines the sequence and activities for various performance testing phases. Figure 6-5 highlights the performance test methodology.

CHAPTER 6 ■ WEB PERFORMANCE VALIDATION

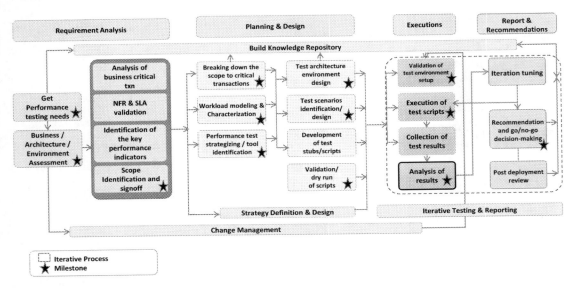

***Figure 6-5.** Web performance test methodology*

During the **requirement analysis phase**, the performance testing team gets the complete performance test requirements and documents the requirements. During this phase, the testing team assesses the architecture and design documents. The team also analyzes the business-critical and performance-critical transactions. The performance validation team gets sign-off on performance-related metrics (such as peak user load, peak content volume, etc.) and performance-related SLAs (timing metrics for the defined NFRs) during this phase. The team identifies the key performance indicators (KPI), such as average page response time across all geographies, availability metrics, performance metrics, and performance SLA adherence rates. Some of the common performance-related questions are as follows.

- Which pages receive the highest traffic?
- How many pages have an acceptable performance above the configured performance thresholds?
- Which pages have poor performance?
- What is the caching strategy used?

In the **planning and design phase**, the performance testing team breaks down the scope into business transactions that need separate performance scripts. You also characterize the workload model based on the load numbers you have gathered. The testing team develops the test plan and sets up the testing environment.

During the **execution phase**, the performance test team executes all the scripts and records various timing metrics that are defined in the requirements analysis phase. The performance testing team executes load tests, stress tests, endurance tests, volume tests, and other performance test scenarios. Automation scripts automatically execute the performance tests after each major release. The results are analyzed and documented.

Reports are published in the **reporting and recommendation** phase. Performance testing teams recommends a "go" or a "no-go" decision based on the overall performance reports and adherence of the performance results to the defined SLAs. Performance testing and reporting are done iteratively for various sprints of the release.

Continuous Performance Testing

Agile projects have shorter release cycles requiring continuous integration and continuous performance testing. Continuous performance testing uncovers the performance issues early in the game, thereby greatly reducing the application performance risks and defect fix effort.

Figure 6-6 depicts the performance continuous testing process.

CHAPTER 6   WEB PERFORMANCE VALIDATION

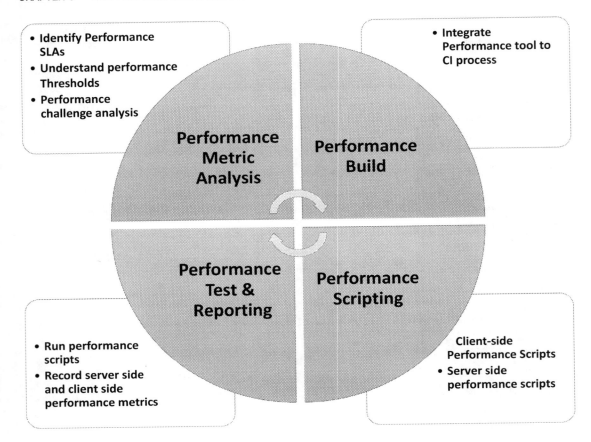

Figure 6-6. Continuous performance testing

The first step in the process is **performance metrics analysis**, where you identify the performance SLAs and metrics. You gather the performance thresholds and identify the key components that contribute to the overall size, response time.

In the **performance build** step, you integrate the performance tool with continuous integration (CI) tools such as Jenkins. The performance tool is used during the validation step of the release management process.

As part of the **performance scripting** step, you develop the performance scripts to validate the client-side and server-side performance scenarios.

During the **performance test and reporting** step, you execute the performance scripts as part of the release management process, and you capture the server-side metrics (e.g., server response time, number of calls, resource utilization) and client-side metrics (size, response time, etc.)

Performance Testing Maturity Model

The performance testing maturity model defines various stages and associated capabilities. Organizations can use the maturity model as a reference guide to enhancing their performance testing practice.

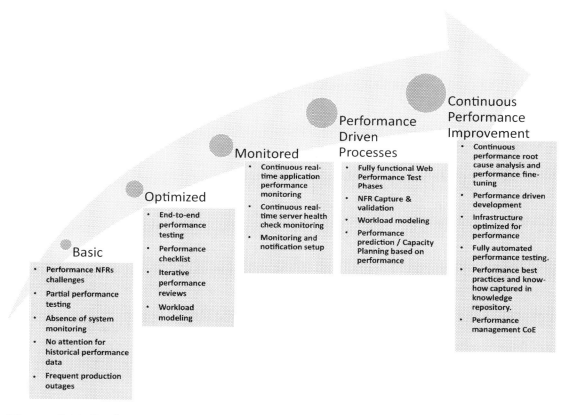

Figure 6-7. Performance testing maturity model

Various stages of the performance testing maturity model are depicted in Figure 6-7.

In the **basic** stage, performance practice is reactive. The performance-related NFRs and SLAs are not fully defined. Performance testing is done during the end-stage of the project. Historical performance data is not analyzed, and historical metrics do not predict and improve performance. Real-time monitoring and notification infrastructure are not present. As a result, you notice frequent production system outages related to performance.

CHAPTER 6 WEB PERFORMANCE VALIDATION

The next stage in the maturity model is **optimized.** In this stage, performance testing is done in all layers, such as UI, server-side, integration, and infrastructure. The workload is modeled based on the identified load numbers. Iterative performance testing is carried out for each release. During the design phase, you create a performance checklist used for performance reviews during the development stage.

In the **monitored** stage, a continuous real-time monitoring infrastructure is set up. The monitoring infrastructure is configured to monitor the system health check (CPU, memory, logs, errors, performance), system heartbeats (system availability, service availability), and performance monitoring (page response time). The notification setup is configured to notify the system administrators about performance SLA violation or availability issues.

In the **performance-driven processes** phase, performance-related NFRs and SLAs are fully identified and maintained. The workload is modeled based on the expected load numbers. All the activities of web performance test phases (Requirement Analysis, Planning & Design, Executions, Report & Recommendations) are carried out. Performance prediction activity is carried out to predict the expected performance at various loads and in a production environment. The capacity and sizing of the infrastructure are based on the predicted performance. Performance profiling is actively carried out in the build phase to troubleshoot performance issues. The application performance times are continuously captured iteratively during the build phase. You define the standard templates for NFR, performance test design, and strategy.

The final stage in the performance testing maturity model is **continuous performance improvement**. In this stage, the organization has an active performance management center-of-excellence (CoE) that owns the performance testing practice of the organization. In the performance-based development, performance best practices, principles are followed in all stages of the SDLC**.** The performance management CoE champions continuous performance improvement initiative; this involves performance root cause analysis and development of performance knowledge base. The lessons learned and the performance best practices are captured in a centralized knowledge base. The infrastructure is fine-tuned based on the expected performance. A fully automated performance test is established to improve testing productivity and to uncover any regression issues.

Summary

- A performance testing exercise analyzes the performance needs of the application, characterizes the workload, scripts performance scenarios, executes the performance scripts, and reports the findings.

- Performance testing is required to meet the performance expectations of the end users, to analyze performance bottlenecks, and to reduce the maintenance costs and efforts.

- Performance testing identifies performance issues, resource utilization, perceived performance, performance baseline, performance bottlenecks, and server configuration and supports fine-tuning performance exercises.

- The main trends in web performance validation are Holiday readiness assessment, end user experience management, load testing for cloud-based applications, mobile app performance testing.

- The key types of performance testing are scalability testing, stress testing, load testing, endurance testing, reliability and availability testing, and performance benchmarking testing.

- Key performance testing metrics are response time, system scalability, reliability and availability, resource utilization, efficiency, and recoverability.

- Before initiating the performance validation exercise, you need to know the solution ecosystem, infrastructure details, user profile details, performance goals, data details, and security details.

- The main web performance testing phases are performance evaluation and requirements elaboration, performance test planning, performance test scripting, performance test execution, and reporting and tracking.

- The performance prediction model includes identifying business-critical transactions, workload modeling, qualitative analysis, quantitative analysis, and performance prediction.

CHAPTER 6   WEB PERFORMANCE VALIDATION

- Workload represents the function used by the user community. The workload is modeled based on the percentage of users executing specific functions over a period.

- Workload modeling includes application and KPI analysis, user and data load analysis, scenario identification, and load distribution.

- The performance testing maturity model consists of basic, optimized, monitored, performance-driven processes, and continuous performance management stages.

CHAPTER 7

Web Performance Monitoring and Infrastructure Planning

A performance monitoring exercise defines a comprehensive set of monitoring processes, methods, and tools for enterprise applications. Continuous and real-time performance monitoring helps organizations proactively monitor server health, performance issues, and availability issues enabling organizations to adhere to performance and availability SLAs. A robust performance monitoring setup involves defining the monitoring infrastructure, monitoring metrics, and monitoring processes.

Robust performance monitoring enables organizations to deliver a predictable, high-performing user experience and conform to performance, scalability, and availability SLAs. Organizations can monitor production errors and production outages and take proactive, responsive steps to address issues.

This chapter discusses various aspects of performance monitoring. You define the performance KPIs and metrics that are required from a performance standpoint. The next section describes performance monitoring tools, migration best practices, and real user monitoring. The following section discusses the infrastructure planning and sizing process and a disaster recovery strategy. The last section discusses the performance monitoring ecosystem.

Performance engineers, web developers, digital architects, project managers, and program managers will find this chapter useful.

Performance Monitoring Metrics

The performance monitoring process is set up to record and report performance monitoring metrics. The performance monitoring metrics provide measurable and quantifiable values for measuring the success of monitoring. By continuously monitoring performance metrics, you can adhere to the defined performance and availability SLAs and take real-time corrective actions.

In a typical n-tiered enterprise application, the monitoring tool needs to record the response time at various layers involved in the request handling. For example, for a single web request, you need to record the database query response time, web service response time, application server response time, web server response time, and the browser render time. This isolates performance bottlenecks to a specific layer.

Let's now define the core metrics for monitoring the service, system, business goals, and web systems.

Service Metrics

The monitoring metrics for web page URL/endpoints, web services, and microservices are included in the service metrics. The services process incoming requests and provide a response. The following are the key service metrics.

Response Time or Latency

Response time, or *latency*, refers to the overall time elapsed between client request initiation and the last byte of the server response. The latency includes the client latency (the time it takes the browser to render a page), network latency (the time it takes for data to be transferred over the wire), and server latency (the time it takes the server to respond). The overall latency (round-trip time) is represented by time to last byte (TTLB).

You need to collect the response time for every tier (i.e., web server, application server, middleware, messaging servers, and database servers). You usually take the average, maximum, minimum, and 95th percentile values for response times. The following are the response time-related metrics.

CHAPTER 7   WEB PERFORMANCE MONITORING AND INFRASTRUCTURE PLANNING

- **Average page load time** is the average time it takes the web page to fully render on the browser.

- **First meaningful paint (FMP)** indicates the time it takes to load the primary content on the page. Generally, FMP should be less than a second.

- **Time to interactive (TTI)** indicates the time it takes to render the interactive user components (input box, buttons, link, etc.) on the page. It is recommended to have the TTI to be less than 2 seconds.

- **Perceived page load time** is the page load time perceived by the end user.

- **Total page size** is the total size of the page, including the static assets and the HTML content.

- **Total static asset size** is the total of all the assets (JS/CSS/image/JSON) on a given page.

- **Total asset count** is the total number of all the static assets on the page.

- **Time to first byte (TTFB)** is the time elapsed between the browser initiating the server request and sending the first response. TTFB is the measure of server responsiveness.

- **Average transaction completion time** is the average time it takes for the end user to complete a business process.

- The **speed index** is the average time it takes to render the visible parts of a page. It is recommended to have a speed index value of less than 1250.

The generic rule of thumb for response time is that if the end user receives a response within 100 milliseconds, the user perceives it instantly. Any response time more than 1 second is considered a delay. If the response time takes more than 10 seconds, the user is more likely to abandon the page.

Throughput

The throughput represents the total number of requests handled within a specified time. Throughput is usually measured by transactions per second (TPS). It is also measured with requests per second, hits per second, or pages per second. Usually, the throughput increases with the increase in load; once the resources are exhausted, the throughput decreases. With the increase in the number of requests, the response time also increases based on the available resources.

The following are the throughput-related metrics.

- **Total page views per day/week/month** provides a total number of page views for a given time.
- **Total hits per week** provides the total number of requests per week.
- **Total user sessions per week** indicates the total number of distinct user sessions per week.
- **Average session duration** provides the average session time of the user.
- **Average hit size** provides the average size of the request.
- **Average pages per session** provides the average number of pages that the user uses for a given session.
- **Average hits per page** provides the average number of requests for a given page.
- **Average page viewing time** provides the average time spent by the user for a given page.
- **Error rate** is the ratio of the average number of error requests to the total number of requests.

Error Handling

The error-handling metric measures the error-handling capability of the system. If the application is resilient, the errors are gracefully handled. When there are errors, the application should provide robust error-handling capabilities. As part of the error-handling capability, you need to check the following aspects.

CHAPTER 7　WEB PERFORMANCE MONITORING AND INFRASTRUCTURE PLANNING

- Handling errors related to timeouts from upstream systems
- Handling errors related to the availability of the upstream systems
- Tracing errors across various layers using unique error identifier
- Handling errors in transaction management scenarios
- Handling retries in recoverable errors

System Metrics

The system metrics define the metrics for system resources, infrastructure components, and servers. This section explains the system metrics.

Resource Metrics

- **CPU utilization** indicates the average CPU utilization over time. Normally the desired CPU average utilization should be less than 80% per day. If the CPU utilization consistently stays above 90% for an hour, it calls for a root cause analysis.

- **Memory usage** indicates the amount of available memory and the amount of memory used. Consistent usage of more than 80% memory indicates inefficient caching and degrades the system performance. For Java based applications it is recommended to monitor the heap size.

- **Cache utilization** indicates the cache usage and is measured by metrics such as cache hits, cache miss, and cache hit ratio.

- **Disk I/O** provides the amount of data read and written to disk.

- **Disk utilization** provides the available disk space.

- **Network I/O** provides the available network bandwidth utilized.

- **Thread pool utilization** provides information on active threads and maximum threads.

For Java-specific servers, you monitor garbage collector (GC) metrics and Java virtual machine (JVM) metrics.

The monitoring tool should constantly monitor the system metrics for various workload capacities.

Network Metrics

The following are key network-related metrics.

- **DNS lookup time** is the time needed to convert the DNS name to the IP address.
- **TCP connection time** is the time it takes the browser to connect to the origin server.

Server Metrics

In an n-tier enterprise application, the web/application server provides server components such as page code, portlets, widgets, UI modules, servlets, libraries, utilities, and helpers. The server metrics define the core metrics at the web server and application server layer. The following subsections describe the main metrics of the application server.

Number of Sessions

The total number of sessions represent the concurrent usage of the application. To support high concurrency, you need to increase the system memory, CPU, heap size, and adjust the connection timeout accordingly.

The monitoring tool needs to monitor the session count, memory utilization, and cache utilization.

Thread Pool Size

The servers use the thread pool to spin off the processes for serving the incoming requests. If the thread pool size is small, the incoming requests are queued up; if the thread pool size is large, it utilizes a large amount of memory. Hence, the thread pool size is fine-tuned based on the concurrent user load.

The monitoring tool should constantly monitor the server thread pool size and alert administrators if the used thread count crosses a predefined threshold value.

Connection Pool Size

The connection pool maintains a pool of reusable database connections. Based on the concurrent user needs, you need to fine-tune the connection pool size appropriately.

The monitoring tool should continuously monitor the pool size and the number of active connections and notify administrators according to predefined thresholds.

Java Virtual Memory (JVM) Parameters

For Java-based servers, the monitoring tool should monitor the Java heap size and garbage collection frequency at various workloads. Based on the analysis, you need to fine-tune the Java heap size to handle various workloads and various memory requirements.

Cache Parameters

You maintain the frequently used static data, lookup values, results from costly queries, and service responses in a server-side cache. The monitoring tool should constantly record the cache hit ratio, cache size, and cache miss to know the cache effectiveness. You need to fine-tune the cache timeouts, cache replacement algorithms based on the cache effectiveness.

Business Metrics

Business departments such as sales and marketing teams want to monitor the critical business-impacting metrics in real time. The following are the key business metrics.

- **Conversion rate** indicates the rate of conversion from visitors to buyers.

- **Top pages** indicates the most popular pages of the web site receiving the maximum percentage of user traffic.

- **Task completion rate** indicates the percentage of users who ended up completing the task.

- **New/unique visitor traffic** provides the unique visitor volume for a specified duration for the site.

- **Engagement metrics** depict what users are doing with the web pages. Engagement metrics are measured by pages per visit, bounce rate, average session time, average time on page, and more.

- **Average order value** is the average value of the orders by a user for a specified time duration.

- **Page views** depict the total number of page views per user session. A popular page is the one with the greatest number of page views.

- **Sessions** is the total number of user interactions with the web site over time.

- **Users metric** covers site visitors related numbers. You could use metrics such as average monthly visitors and average daily visitors.

- **User satisfaction score** is an indicator of the users' satisfaction with the web site.

- **Ad revenue** indicates the total ad revenues obtained from the web site.

- **Traffic source** indicates the major sources of the incoming traffic for the web site. The incoming traffic sources could be search engines, social media platforms, affiliated sites, referrals, or advertisements.

- **Pages per session** indicates the average number of pages a user browses in a single session.

- **Bounce rate** indicates the number of users who exit the site after viewing single page.

- **Time on site** indicates the average time spent by a user on the site.

- **Abandonment rate** indicates the users who abandon their ongoing business transaction (such as checkout process) in the middle of the process.

Also, the business wants to know the users' access channels (devices, browsers), demographic information (geographies, languages), user segmentation information (new user, repeat user, user group), and page performance (response time, load time, page weight).

Web Application Performance Metrics

Many of the digital platforms are delivered through web channels such as web site or mobile web. Hence, it is imperative to monitor the web application performance metrics for complete performance monitoring. The following are the main monitoring types.

- Uptime monitoring to monitor the availability of the web system
- Performance monitoring through metrics such as response time and asset load time
- Multi-geo monitoring of web platforms from various geographies
- Synthetic monitoring with real browsers to understand the performance in a real-world scenario
- Get insights about various web page optimizations that can potentially improve the page performance
- Error metrics related to page errors

Building Performance Monitoring Ecosystem

The performance monitoring ecosystem needs the tools, methods, frameworks, and the best practices to implement a robust performance monitoring system. This section defines the key performance monitoring tools and describes the performance monitoring best practices.

Performance Monitoring Tools and Frameworks

You could leverage many open source and commercial tools for performance monitoring. Table 7-1 features some of the popular performance monitoring tools.

Table 7-1. Performance Monitoring Types and Tools

Monitoring Type	Monitoring Tool
System monitoring (CPU, memory, and disk)	• Windows performance monitor (PERFMON) • NMon for AIX servers • System activity report (SAR) for Unix systems • Node exporter for container pods
File monitoring	Filebeat (www.elastic.co/guide/en/beats/filebeat/6.8/monitoring.html)
Network monitoring, System monitoring and infrastructure monitoring	• Nagios (www.nagios.org) • ELK (Elastic search, Logstash and Kibana) (www.elastic.co) • Grinder (http://grinder.sourceforge.net) • AppDynamics (commercial) http://grinder.sourceforge.net/g3/features.html • New Relic (commercial) (https://newrelic.com) • Zabbix (www.zabbix.com)
Statistics dashboard and visualizations	• Kibana (www.elastic.co/guide/en/kibana/current/kibana-page.html)
Alert and monitoring dashboard	• Grafana (https://grafana.com)
Real time event monitoring Visualizations and data queries	Prometheus (https://prometheus.io) and Grafana
Search engine	Elasticsearch (www.elastic.co/home)
Synthetic monitoring tool	• DynaTrace (commercial) (www.dynatrace.com/solutions/application-monitoring/) • Selenium (www.selenium.dev) • Lighthouse (https://chrome.google.com/webstore/detail/lighthouse/blipmdconlkpinefehnmjammfjpmpbjk?hl=en) • WebPageTest (https://webpagetest.org)
Database monitoring	• Automatic Workload Repository (AWR) • Fluentd (www.fluentd.org)

(continued)

Table 7-1. (*continued*)

Monitoring Type	Monitoring Tool
Log monitoring	• Splunk (www.splunk.com) • Fluentd
Message streaming	Apache Kafka (https://kafka.apache.org)
Notification	Alert Manager
Container Monitoring	• Node Exporter • Docker Stats • cAdvisor • Prometheus
Web page monitoring (page size, page response time, number of requests, asset load time etc.)	• WebPageTest.org • Site Speed (www.sitespeed.io) • Google Page Speed Insights (https://developers.google.com/speed/pagespeed/insights/) • Pingdom (commercial) www.pingdom.com • Silk performance Manager (commercial) (www.microfocus.com) • Uptrends (commercial) (www.uptrends.com) • https://web.dev/measure/
Development tools/Page Auditing	• Google Chrome Developer Tools • Test My site (www.thinkwithgoogle.com/feature/testmysite/) • Google Chrome lighthouse • HTTP Watch (www.httpwatch.com) • https://speedrank.app/en • Fiddler (www.telerik.com/fiddler) • Firefox Dev Tools • Web Tracing Framework http://google.github.io/tracing-framework/ • Timeline tool https://developers.google.com/web/tools/chrome-devtools/evaluate-performance/timeline-tool#profile-painting

(*continued*)

CHAPTER 7   WEB PERFORMANCE MONITORING AND INFRASTRUCTURE PLANNING

Table 7-1. (*continued*)

Monitoring Type	Monitoring Tool
Multi-geo web performance testing	• https://performance.sucuri.net
Cloud monitoring	• AWS CloudWatch, Azure Monitor
Website speed test	• https://tools.keycdn.com/speed
Load testing	• BlazeMeter (www.blazemeter.com) • Apache JMeter (https://jmeter.apache.org)
Web site latency test	• Ping Test (https://tools.keycdn.com/ping)
Real user monitoring (RUM)	• New Relic • SpeedCurve (https://speedcurve.com) • DynaTrace • Akamai mPulse (commercial) (www.akamai.com/us/en/products/performance/mpulse-real-user-monitoring.jsp) • AppDynamics (commercial)
Analyze network timings	• Resource Timing API (https://developer.mozilla.org/en-US/docs/Web/API/Resource_Timing_API/Using_the_Resource_Timing_API) • Network Information https://developer.mozilla.org/en-US/docs/Web/API/NetworkInformation

Performance Monitoring Best Practices

This section discusses the performance monitoring best practices to build a robust performance monitoring system.

Figure 7-1 depicts the performance monitoring related best practices.

CHAPTER 7　WEB PERFORMANCE MONITORING AND INFRASTRUCTURE PLANNING

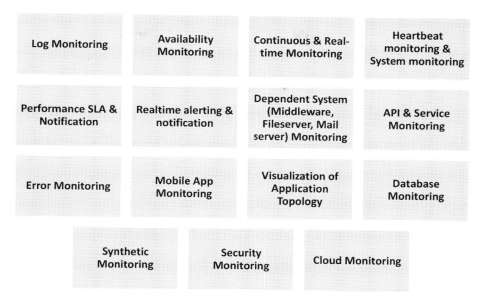

Figure 7-1. *Performance monitoring best practices*

The monitoring setup should be designed to fulfill the non-functional requirements (NFR) of the application. Sample NFR requirements are covered later in the chapter.

Continuous and Real-Time Monitoring

The monitoring system should monitor the defined monitoring metrics continuously in real time. This enables the organizations to take corrective action quickly and minimize the performance and availability issues. The monitoring frequency and monitoring method should not cause any overhead to the overall system performance. Minimal intrusive tools such as passive monitoring, low-frequency monitoring bots are used for continuous monitoring.

Performance SLA and Notification Thresholds

You should be able to configure the performance and availability SLAs in the monitoring system. For instance, a page performance SLA is defined as follows: "If the average page load time is more than 30 seconds continuously for more than 2 hours, then notify the system administrator through pager alert."

Usually, the thresholds are defined to identify the recurring problem patterns and avoid any one-off or abnormal anomalies.

187

CHAPTER 7 WEB PERFORMANCE MONITORING AND INFRASTRUCTURE PLANNING

Real-Time Alerting and Notification

If the monitoring system detects any SLA violation, the monitoring system should trigger the notification in real time. Normally, the monitoring system triggers an email, SMS, slack message, or a pager message in an SLA threshold violation to the configured contact.

The monitoring system should also record the historical data and provide intuitive visualizations (e.g., time-based charts) for system administrators to monitor the performance trend and take timely corrective actions.

Heartbeat Monitoring and System Monitoring

A comprehensive monitoring infrastructure should also check the server resources (the system availability and utilization of CPU cores, memory, disk, endpoints, APIs, etc.). You should also define the SLAs and notification thresholds.

The metrics and KPIs for the heartbeat monitoring are explained in the "System Metrics" section in this chapter.

Log Monitoring

The monitoring system should continuously monitor the application log files and system log files. Log monitoring systems should identify critical system errors (out of memory exception, HTTP 500, and HTTP 404) and critical application errors (file not found exception, connection time out exception, malformed URL exception, etc.) and security exceptions (failed login attempts and invalid certificates). System administrators are notified about any critical errors.

Table 7-2 shows key log files for Apache server. You can use the appropriate server log file for troubleshooting application and system errors.

Table 7-2. Apache Server Log Files

Log File Name	Brief Description
startserver.log stopserver.log	Server status logs, written to during server start and stop
systemErr.log	Contains exception and stack trace information
systemOut.log	Monitors the health of a running server. The application logger statements are logged in this log file.

Error Monitoring

The monitoring system should monitor the page errors, application errors, and system errors regularly. The performance KPIs, such as page error rate, requires continuous error monitoring. The monitoring system should report recurring errors and critical errors.

System administrators need to address critical errors (connection timeouts, page errors, system errors) as soon as they are reported (see Table 7-3).

Table 7-3. Sample Error Codes

Error Codes	Brief Summary and Recommendation
HTTP 404 error in the log files	The error happens when the resource is not available. Check the resource URL. Deployment status and other details. Review the systemout.log file for information.
Error: 503 Failed to load target	This error occurs if the application cannot connect to back-end systems. Check if all the back-end systems are available. Setup continuous real-time health check monitoring of all dependent and upstream systems.
HTTP 500 – Internal server error	This is related to an application exception. Check the exception trace and application log files to the root cause of the error.
Login failed. Please enter a valid user ID and password.	Look for error messages in the systemout.log and systemerr.log.
Out of Memory error, cannot allocate initial heap	Adjust and fine-tune the heap size in the JVM parameter. Identify and isolate the component causing the memory leak. Perform the scalability testing of the application. Perform the endurance testing to identify the memory leaks.

Availability Monitoring

One of the core requirements for a monitoring system is to monitor the availability of the servers, APIs, and services and notify the operations team in any availability incidents. The "service down" and "system down" scenarios are severity 1 incidents for organizations. Hence, it is critical to monitor the availability of systems and services continuously on a real-time basis.

A sample availability-monitoring rule is as follows: "If the service response is HTTP 404 or HTTP 500 continuously for 5 minutes, notify the system administrators via configured email."

API and Service Monitoring

The monitoring system should also monitor all the key APIs and services used by the application. Generally, APIs and services are available over HTTP, HTTPS, and TCP protocols. You need to identify all the APIs and services needed by the application. The monitoring system should monitor the performance and availability of the APIs.

Many API frameworks, such as the Spring Boot framework, support the health check endpoint out of the box. You could enable and leverage the health check endpoints to monitor the API health.

Dependent System Monitoring

The monitoring system should monitor the availability and performance of the dependent systems, such as database systems, enterprise services, caching services, third-party services, web services, microservices, middleware systems, messaging systems, mail servers, and feeds.

Mobile Monitoring

As mobile apps are an integral part of the digital strategy, you should monitor the end-user experience and the performance of mobile apps as well.

Database Monitoring

Use the monitoring jobs to monitor the database performance parameters such as query performance, database CPU utilization, database memory utilization, average response time, and throughput.

Visualization of Application Topology

Generally, enterprise applications are integrated with various internal and external systems and services. The monitoring system identifies the performance at all points in the application topology, which helps you understand the bottlenecks in the connected ecosystem.

CHAPTER 7 WEB PERFORMANCE MONITORING AND INFRASTRUCTURE PLANNING

Synthetic Monitoring

As part of synthetic monitoring, you record and simulate the mission-critical transactions, business-critical processes, and multi-step workflows without using real-user data. Synthetic monitoring happens in a controlled environment with artificial page loads. You could use tools such as Selenium to playback the recorded scripts for user navigation paths on real browsers from various geographical locations. The tool monitors the performance of various web components on multiple browsers from geographically distributed locations. Synthetic monitoring assesses and benchmarks complex multi-page workflows such as logins, checkout processes, and so forth.

Cloud Monitoring

For cloud-native solutions, you need to monitor the following.

- The infrastructure as a service (IaaS) resources, such as virtual health checks, CPU, and memory utilization.

- Monitor the performance, availability of the services deployed as a software-as-service (SaaS) model.

- Monitor the performance and availability of the systems (i.e., database deployed as a platform-as-service (PaaS)).

- Monitor other cloud services such as storage, virtual network, and the application endpoints.

Amazon CloudWatch and Azure monitors are a popular cloud monitoring service that provides configurable metrics, SLA-based alarms, metrics dashboard, events management, logs management, anomaly detection, container insights, and end-user monitoring.

Virtual Machine Monitoring

You need to monitor the resources of the cloud virtual machine. Usually, you monitor the CPU, memory, availability, start/restart timings of the virtual machines

Containers Monitoring

You monitor the availability, memory and CPU utilization of the controller, nodes, and the containers.

Security Monitoring

All security incidents and events should be monitored, and anomalies should be captured proactively. The key security events include authentication, delegated access, secured resource access, and password reset. You also should perform real-time monitoring to capture and analyze data, review logs to ensure compliance with operational and security requirements. All suspicious activities should be identified, mapped, and marked for further analysis.

Application Performance Monitoring (APM)

APM covers various aspects of the live digital application monitoring, such as performance, health, availability, and other performance metrics. The key APM metrics are CPU utilization, average page response time, error rate, and availability. A comprehensive APM setup also monitors the dependent infrastructure elements such as database server, Redis cache server, and web services.

Once the application is deployed to the production environment, it is important to constantly monitor the application in real-time and maintain the performance SLAs. A robust monitoring and performance maintenance framework are shown in Figure 7-2.

CHAPTER 7 WEB PERFORMANCE MONITORING AND INFRASTRUCTURE PLANNING

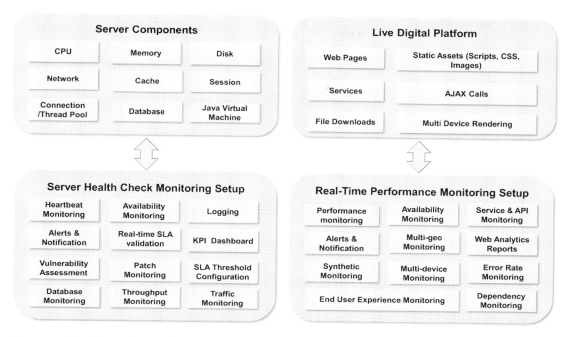

Figure 7-2. Sample application monitoring setup

Server Health Check Monitoring Setup

The infrastructure constantly monitors the internal servers, network, and interfacing systems. An internal server health-check monitoring infrastructure includes components to regularly monitor the health of internal systems and services. The primary component of the health-check monitor is the heartbeat monitor, which frequently pings all the involved systems and services to check their availability. In case of a system outage incidence, there are components to alert and notify appropriate system administrators. The CPU, memory, disk utilization, cache, session, connection and thread pool, database, and JVM parameters of all servers are monitored during testing and post-production deployment. Its main responsibilities are as follows.

- Constantly check the servers' health check by heartbeat messages.
- Constantly monitor the CPU and memory status of all participating servers and interface systems.
- Log the server status in the centralized log system.
- Constantly monitor the throughput of all the servers.

CHAPTER 7   WEB PERFORMANCE MONITORING AND INFRASTRUCTURE PLANNING

- Automatically alert and notify when the server is down, the service is unavailable, or the metrics exceed the configured SLAs.

- Perform regular server maintenance activities like patching and updates through automatic scripts.

- Constantly run the security scripts for threat and risk assessment.

Real-Time Performance Monitoring Setup

The real-time performance monitoring setup includes distributed automated monitoring agents to access the live web pages to check the response time. The infrastructure also provides flexibility to configure the SLA threshold alerting mechanism. Automatic alerting and notification components send email/pagers to specific site administrators support these components.

In this setup, you monitor the web page, static assets, services, AJAX calls, and the end-user performance experience.

The following monitoring methods are for real-time performance monitoring setup.

- Performance monitoring of all web components to record and report response time metrics.

- Availability monitoring of all web components and services.

- API and service monitoring to check their availability and performance.

- Monitor the application and services from various geographies.

- Leverage synthetic monitoring to enable end-user experience monitoring.

- Leverage web analytics reports monitoring real-time performance.

- Monitor the dependent systems such as ESB, middleware systems, services, and feeds.

CHAPTER 7   WEB PERFORMANCE MONITORING AND INFRASTRUCTURE PLANNING

Real User Monitoring (RUM)

Real user monitoring (RUM), also known as end-user experience monitoring, is a passive monitoring setup that records the perceived user performance, user navigations, application availability, overall performance, and application responsiveness. RUM provides insights into how real users perceive the performance of the web site in real time. Normally, RUM needs a JavaScript code fragment inserted into the web page. JavaScript continuously collects the user activity data and transfers it to the cloud-based server. RUM tools provide nice visualizations that can provides performance reports. Business users can visualize the perceived end-user performance based on the browser, geography, and so forth. Business users can also view end-user navigation paths, popular pages, and availability. RUM involves the real user base.

For a globally distributed website, real-time monitoring is done from various geographies to test the performance of various languages and geo-specific sites. You can also implement multi-geo monitoring for multilingual sites using RUM.

A RUM tool monitors a live application in real-time and has the following responsibilities.

- Uses end-user experience monitoring tools like multi-geo bots to ping the live web pages in real-time to check for availability and response time

- Automatically triggers alert if the page response time or component load time falls below the performance SLA/preconfigured threshold time

- Provides the performance metrics for each web page and various web components (JavaScript, images, CSS, etc.)

- Provides performance metrics for various browsers

- Provides performance information for single-page applications (SPA) and AJAX calls

- Creates web performance analytics reports by tagging business-critical page/processes with web analytics (reports provide insights into performance of pages and components)

- Performs real-world last mile and backbone load testing and monitoring

CHAPTER 7   WEB PERFORMANCE MONITORING AND INFRASTRUCTURE PLANNING

The automatic alert and notification mechanism helps system administrators take the corrective actions as soon as they are notified about an issue. This drastically improves availability and average performance SLAs.

Complementing RUM and synthetic monitoring helps you get crucial insights about end-user experiences in real time.

Infrastructure Planning for Performance

The performance, scalability, and availability of the system are dependent on the underlying infrastructure. The infrastructure includes the right-sized servers, hardware, network, caching systems, and monitoring systems. To establish and sustain the desired performance, you need to properly do capacity planning. NFRs define the metrics and SLAs for system performance, availability, and scalability. The infrastructure capacity should be designed to fulfill the defined NFRs.

This section explains the key aspects of infrastructure aspects. It discusses the NFR requirements to learn the common non-functional requirements for the application. You need to define the monitoring setup and the infrastructure setup based on the defined NFRs.

Non-Functional Requirements (NFR)

NFRs define an organization's requirements for system performance, availability, security, and scalability. During the requirement analysis we learn what's needed to design the applications infrastructure and other solution components. This section looks at the common NFRs.

Availability

The following are the common availability requirements.

- The availability of enterprise-critical applications should be 99.99999% apart from scheduled downtime.

- The availability of non-critical applications should be 95%.

- The availability of all critical services (web services, databases, etc.) should be 99%.

Application Growth Rate

The following applies to the application growth rate.

- User traffic increases yearly by 15%.
- Content volume and data volume increase yearly by 10%.

Security

This section covers various aspects, such as data security, authentication, authorization, and access control.

- **Authentication**
  - The application supports various authentications, such as form-based authentication and OAuth-based authentication.
  - The application supports single sign-on (SSO) with secured enterprise applications.
- **Access control and authorization**

  Access control in the application is driven by a module/role-wise CRUD matrix and associated rules.
- **Data security**
  - The various types of data involved in the solution should be identified and assigned an appropriate classification label according to the data protection policy.
  - The system must enforce data retention requirements in line with business requirements and compliance with data management policy.
  - A secure method must be used when transferring confidential data between organization networks/systems and between organization systems and external networks/third-party systems.
  - No data should be transferred outside of the organization network to a third-party without the approval of the data owner.

- The systems must protect all data/information from unauthorized access and unauthorized alteration and destruction (i.e., always maintain and validate the integrity of data).
- The solution must have a means of scanning / checking the Rich Media data, or any data uploaded/imported.
- The solution must be capable of protecting the privacy, personally identifiable data (PII), and confidentiality of data (e.g., protect against disclosure of client sensitive information or inappropriate company information to unauthorized persons).
- **Session control**
  - The system must provide a log-out facility, which should effectively terminate a user's session.
  - The application must ensure that cookies and other user identification information stored on the client/browser interface are protected from disclosure and tampering, including ensuring its removal at session termination.
  - The system should automatically terminate the session if there is no activity for 20 minutes.

Auditing and Logging

The following are auditing and logging requirements.

- The application should be compliant with statutory and compliance requirements for PII data.
- The application should provide audit capability to allow data from key activities to be tracked so that who/what/why/when data are captured for analysis, per the organization security policy.
- Additionally, the audit report should be in an easily readable, user-friendly format.

- The solution must be capable of recording a log of system/user-related security-relevant events, including.

    - Login attempts (successful and unsuccessful)

    - Changes to system/user permissions and access rights, including password changes

    - Actions performed by users, including administrators;

    - Read, write, modify, delete actions to data and metadata (data attributes)

    - Changes to system configurations

- The solution should provide central audit logs protected from amendment or deletion and retained per the organization retention policy and schedule. Audit logs must be tamper-proof and provide integrity through hashing algorithms, offline storage, or written to write-only-once media.

Archival

The following are archival requirements.

- The system should archive all data older than specified time duration in an easily restorable format.

- The system should provide appropriate housekeeping, archiving, and retrieval processes to ensure that the solution capacity and performance is maintained.

- An archival system design should do the following.

    - Maintain good operational system performance

    - Support data retention for legal compliance, business controls, and due diligence.

    - The reference and compliance methods of storing data should take less storage.

CHAPTER 7 WEB PERFORMANCE MONITORING AND INFRASTRUCTURE PLANNING

Internationalization

The following are internalization requirements.

- The application should support multiple languages, including the RTL (Right to Left) languages.
- The application should support multiple currencies and date/time formats.
- The application should localize holiday calendars.

Performance

The following are performance requirements .

- In mission-critical and enterprise-critical applications, the performance of lightweight web pages should be less than 1 second.
- The performance of all other web pages should be less than 3 seconds.
- The response time of all APIs exposed by the upstream systems should be less than 0.5 seconds.
- All database operations should be completed within 2 seconds.

Scalability

The following are scalability requirements .

- The application should support more than specified number of registered users.
- The application should support specified number of concurrent users

Multitenancy

The following are multitenancy requirements.

- The application should provide data separately for each country.
- The application should provide configurable parameters that are independently configured at the country level.

Infrastructure Planning Process

The infrastructure planning exercise defines the initial size and capacity of the infrastructure, validates the infrastructure configuration, and continuously fine-tunes the infrastructure. Infrastructure planning is necessary to comply with the scalability and performance SLAs of the application.

Figure 7-3 depicts the high-level infrastructure planning process.

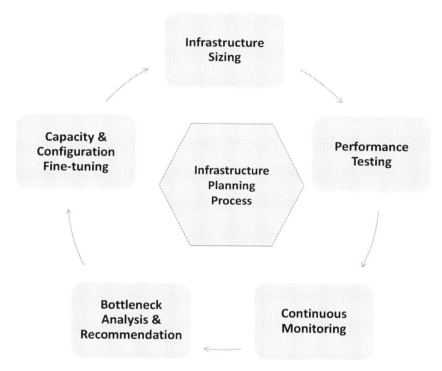

Figure 7-3. Infrastructure planning process

As the first step of the process, you do the initial **infrastructure sizing**. The initial infrastructure sizing uses various parameters such as user traffic volume, growth rate, content volume, concurrent user count, and maximum user count. The next section explains the initial infrastructure sizing process.

In the next step, you conduct **performance testing** of the infrastructure based on the workload model. You carry out various types of performance testing, such as load testing, stress testing, volume testing, endurance testing, and API testing.

CHAPTER 7   WEB PERFORMANCE MONITORING AND INFRASTRUCTURE PLANNING

During performance testing, you **monitor** infrastructure components such as the CPU, memory, disk, and network to understand the infrastructure's scalability at various loads. You log all the recorded metrics in the performance testing report. System monitoring metrics and the monitoring process were discussed in previous sections.

Based on the SLA violations in the performance testing report, you carry out the **bottleneck analysis** and performance analysis. The analysis explains the performance bottleneck at various infrastructure layers (low memory, lesser number of CPU cores, lower network bandwidth, etc.) are reported. The performance improvement recommendations are one of the main outcomes of this exercise.

You carry out the **capacity and configuration fine-tuning** of infrastructure components based on recommendations. You resize the CPU cores, increase memory, network bandwidth, disk size, and cache size based on the recommendations.

You monitor the production application continuously in real time to track the performance of the SLAs. You also monitor the infrastructure resources in real time to record and notify utilization SLAs.

Initial Infrastructure Sizing Process

During the initial infrastructure sizing process, you define the size of the infrastructure components to handle the peak application load. You use the recommended infrastructure configuration given by the product vendor or performance benchmark studies or sizing calculator to arrive at the initial sizing numbers.

A typical n-tier enterprise infrastructure is depicted in Figure 7-4.

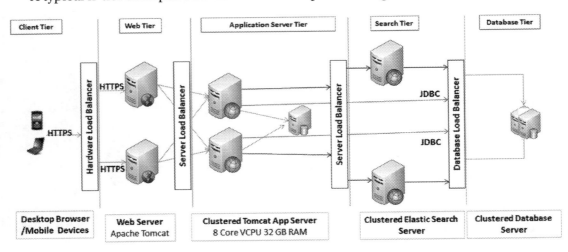

Figure 7-4. *Regular n-tier enterprise infrastructure*

CHAPTER 7   WEB PERFORMANCE MONITORING AND INFRASTRUCTURE PLANNING

The corporate load balancer handles incoming web request and routes it to the web server nodes. The web server forwards the request to a cluster of application servers. Identity and Access Management system (IAM) provides the necessary security services such as authentication, authorization, and single sign-on. Based on the application requirements, you use the services from the search engine and database server. As a rule of thumb, each of the servers in the production environment should use a multi-node cluster topology to provide high availability and scalability.

To do the initial infrastructure, you consider the following parameters.

- **User volume**: You need user-related data such as peak user count, concurrent users, maximum user count, average session time, average session object size, think time, anonymous user count, and logged-in user count. The user volume data affects memory sizing and CPU core sizing.

- **Data volume**: You need the average and maximum data volume and content volume for the application. The data volume requirements affect the storage and capacity planning for disks and file share components.

- **Disaster recovery requirements**: Many organizations have strict disaster recovery (DR) requirements. You collect the metrics such as recovery time objective (defines the maximum downtime for a production system) and recovery point objective (defines the maximum allowed data loss). Based on these metrics, you set up the DR infrastructure consisting of mirror sites, data sync-up jobs, failover methods, and load balancer.

- **Availability requirements**: The availability SLAs dictate the number of server nodes needed to handle the server failures.

- **Scalability requirements**: The scalability requirements provide the maximum content volume and peak user traffic for the system. Based on the scalability needs, you need to size the CPU cores, memory, and the server nodes to handle the peak user traffic and peak content volume.

CHAPTER 7   WEB PERFORMANCE MONITORING AND INFRASTRUCTURE PLANNING

- **Performance SLAs**: Based on the performance SLAs (i.e., response times), you carry out the performance test to validate the performance of the system. Based on the performance testing results, you could explore the CDN and other caching infrastructure to improve the performance.

Disaster Recovery (DR) Strategy

Enterprises use DR strategy to implement high availability and manage the performance SLAs. This section discusses the DR strategy for the AWS cloud.

Modern solutions are cloud-native using PaaS services. You could automate environment creation using Infrastructure as code as part of DR process. Let's define the preparation phase and the recovery phase for DR management.

Preparation Phase

In preparation for a disaster, the one-click environment provisioning AWS-based DevOps pipeline is readied by following these steps.

1. The AWS cloud environment is scripted using ARM templates, and the code is checked-in to the code repository.

2. A DevOps pipeline is created, which pulls the infrastructure-as-cloud (IaC) templates from the code repository. This creates the environment in a secondary region.

3. Separate the DevOps pipeline to deploy the application's front-end code to web app services and the back-end code to app services.

Recovery Phase

During a disaster scenario, the following steps are executed.

1. Re-create the environment using the DevOps pipeline in the secondary region.

2. Deploy the latest code to the secondary environment using the DevOps pipeline.

3. Reconfigure the traffic manager endpoints to point to the secondary region.

CHAPTER 7 WEB PERFORMANCE MONITORING AND INFRASTRUCTURE PLANNING

A sample DR strategy for the AWS cloud is depicted in Figure 7-5.

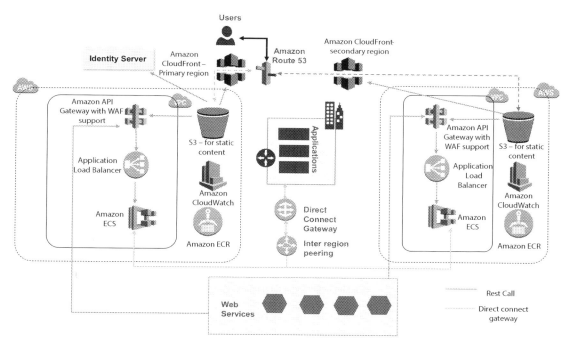

Figure 7-5. *AWS DR setup*

Proactive Robust Monitoring and Alerting Setup

A robust monitoring and alerting setup captures the system metrics (e.g., CPU, memory), log metrics (e.g., system logs, application logs), errors, and performance. The monitoring setup should be flexible to monitor various systems, including Linux OS, database servers, and stand-alone servers. The alert and notification setup should be flexible enough to send notifications to various channels such as email, pager, incident management system, and so forth. You should be able to configure the performance thresholds and resource utilization thresholds that can trigger the notification.

CHAPTER 7 WEB PERFORMANCE MONITORING AND INFRASTRUCTURE PLANNING

A comprehensive monitoring tool should support the following features.

- Core monitoring capabilities including the monitoring of the following:
  - Resource (CPU, memory) monitoring at normal and peak loads and during synthetic monitoring
  - Network (router, switch, and firewall, etc.) monitoring during normal and peak content loads
  - Windows event log monitoring to report any critical error
  - Applications monitoring for performance and availability
  - Virtual instances monitoring
- Server monitoring capabilities including the monitoring of the following:
  - Database monitoring to report the CPU, memory, and query response time
  - Web page, web server/web services monitoring for performance and availability
  - Middleware monitoring for availability and performance
  - Custom application monitoring for performance
- Reporting dashboard
  - Business service management views
  - Comprehensive dashboard
  - Real-time trends and availability of devices
  - Events and correlated alarms
- Reporting
  - Standard daily, weekly, monthly, quarterly, and yearly reports

This section discusses a comprehensive monitoring and alerting setup using open source tools. Figure 7-6 depicts a sample monitoring and alerting setup.

CHAPTER 7　WEB PERFORMANCE MONITORING AND INFRASTRUCTURE PLANNING

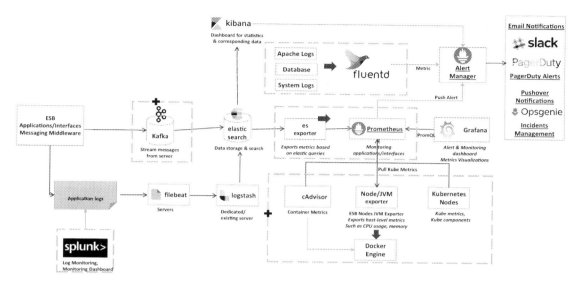

Figure 7-6. *Proactive monitoring and alerting setup*

Let's now look at various monitoring components used in Figure 7-6.

- Prometheus server collects the metrics and stores it in the time-series database. You can query the Prometheus through PromQL language. Prometheus exporter can scrap the performance metrics from various systems (e.g., Linux, MySQL database) and feeds them into the Prometheus database. Prometheus can monitor endpoints such as HTTP, HTTPS, DNS, TCP, and DNS.

- Grafana is the visualization tool for the Prometheus database. The Grafana dashboard provides an intuitive visualization of various metrics.

- Kibana provides data visualization based on Elastic search indexed content. Kibana supports graphs, including line graphs, bar graphs, scatter plots, and so forth.

- Node Exporter provides the metrics related to CPU, memory for the configured nodes. Prometheus can scrape the metrics from Node Exporter.

- Logstash provides a data processing pipeline for Elasticsearch by collecting and transforming various sources of data.

207

- Filebeat monitors file events on log files and forwards the log events to Logstash.

- Kafka is a distributed stream processing software that provides high-performance, low-latency real-time data feed. Kafka provides publishing and subscribing capabilities for data streams.

- Elasticsearch is a popular open source search engine that supports various types of document indexing.

- Fluentd collects data from various sources to supports unified logging.

- Alertmanager provides a notification feature in Prometheus. You can configure the alert rules and metrics thresholds that trigger the alert if the metrics values exceed the configured threshold. The alert manager can send notifications to various channels such as Slack, email, push notifications, PagerDuty alerts, and OpsDuty incident management, WeChat alerts, and so forth.

- Splunk provides rich, real-time, and centralized log monitoring capability along with a flexible query feature.

The various monitoring methods are detailed in next section.

Container Pod Monitoring

You can get the cluster metrics for Kubernetes clusters, such as pod availability status, CPU/memory/network usage for each of the pods. cAdvisor (container advisor) monitors and exposes the running container resource metrics and performance metrics compatible with the Prometheus database. Node Exporter provides various OS metrics and server metrics. Prometheus pulls the pod metrics and container metrics from the node exporter.

The metrics pulled from cAdvisor and Node Exporter are stored in the Prometheus database, and you can view the visualization in the Grafana dashboard.

Log Monitoring

Splunk and Fluentd are popular tools for log monitoring. Splunk collects the log data from various log files, analyzes indexes, and visualizes and queries it. Log monitoring helps you analyze and troubleshoot issues quickly using a powerful query language to trace the log events. Fluentd monitors various systems, like databases and log files, and feeds the metrics to Prometheus for storage and visualization.

Database Monitoring

Tools like Fluentd monitor databases. These tools can get insights into CPU, memory, and utilization of the database server. You learn the slow database calls, long-running queries, and overall database performance.

Application Monitoring

The monitoring tools should provide fine-grained analysis of the methods and the code segments that result in errors. The log messages and event streams can be streamed through Kafka and fed into Elasticsearch. Kafka collects data from various sources, such as services, web applications, and data lakes. Once the metrics are stored and indexed in Elasticsearch, Kibana can provide intuitive visualizations for analyzing the metrics.

Alerts and Notification

You can configure the Prometheus alert manager to define the triggering SLAs. Once the metrics exceed the configured SLAs, the alert manager triggers alerts to various channels, such as mail, Splunk, PagerDuty, pushover notifications, and the Opsgenie incident management system.

CICD Setup

The continuous integration and continuous development (CICD) setup streamlines and automates the release management process, reducing the deployment timelines. Figure 7-7 depicts a sample CICD setup on the AWS cloud.

CHAPTER 7   WEB PERFORMANCE MONITORING AND INFRASTRUCTURE PLANNING

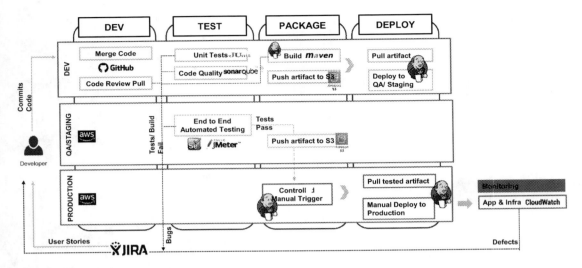

Figure 7-7. Sample CICD setup

During the development stage, the code is managed in the GitHub code repository. You define the code governance processes related to code merge and code review and approval. During the test stage, you conduct automated unit testing using JUnit and conduct an automated code review using SonarQube. The testing team conducts end to end automation testing. In the packaging stage, the code artifacts are built using build tools, and the code artifacts that clear the testing are pushed to the S3 bucket. Finally, the code from the code artifact repository is pulled and deployed to various environments. Once the code is live, you can monitor the application through AWS CloudWatch.

Summary

- Performance monitoring provides a comprehensive set of monitoring processes, monitoring tools for enterprise applications.

- A robust performance monitoring enables organizations to deliver predictable, high performing user experience and conform to performance, scalability, and availability SLAs.

- The performance monitoring metrics provide measurable and quantifiable values for measuring the success of monitoring.

- The monitoring metrics for web page URL/endpoints, web services, and microservices are included in the service metrics.

CHAPTER 7   WEB PERFORMANCE MONITORING AND INFRASTRUCTURE PLANNING

- Response time is the overall time elapsed between client request initiation and the last byte of the server response.

- The throughput represents the total number of requests handled within a specified time.

- The error handling metric measures the error handling capability of the system.

- The system metrics define the metrics for system resources, infrastructure components, and servers.

- The server metrics define the core metrics at the web server and application server layer.

- The key server metrics are the number of sessions, thread pool size, connection pool size, Java virtual memory (JVM) parameters, and cache parameters.

- The main web monitoring types are response times, uptime monitoring, multi-geo monitoring, synthetic monitoring, and error metrics.

- The main performance best practices are managing logs, availability, mobile app, error, database, API and service, security, synthetics, cloud and enabling continuous and real-time monitoring, heartbeat monitoring, performance SLA, real-time alerting, and dependent system monitoring.

- Application performance monitoring (APM) includes monitoring of server components (e.g., CPU, memory, disk, network, cache, session) and live digital platform (web pages, static assets, services, AJAX calls, etc.)

- Real user monitoring (a.k.a. end-user experience monitoring) is a passive monitoring setup that records the perceived user performance, user navigations, application availability, overall performance, and application responsiveness.

- The infrastructure planning exercise defines the initial size and capacity of the infrastructure, validates the infrastructure configuration, and continuously fine-tunes the infrastructure.

CHAPTER 7   WEB PERFORMANCE MONITORING AND INFRASTRUCTURE PLANNING

- The infrastructure planning process involves infrastructure sizing, performance testing, monitoring, bottleneck analysis, capacity, and configuration fine-tuning.

- To perform the initial infrastructure, you consider user volume, data volume, disaster recovery requirements, availability requirements, and performance SLAs.

- A robust monitoring and alerting setup can capture system metrics (CPU, memory), log metrics (system logs, application logs), errors, and performance.

PART IV

Performance Case Studies

CHAPTER 8

Web Performance Optimization Case Study

This chapter discusses a real-world case study related to the performance optimization of a legacy application. The case study covers various performance challenges that you normally face with legacy applications. You look at various methods to optimize the performance of a legacy application. In this case study, you leverage the performance assessment framework from Chapter 3. You start with a performance assessment approach, including a scope and assessment checklist. The next section discusses a complete performance assessment exercise across all layers. Based on the outcome of the assessment exercise, performance optimization recommendations, and best practices are provided.

This chapter also covers the design revamp to align with forward-looking and modern architecture principles for optimal performance.

Case Study Background

For this case study, we have considered a finance application that is built on a legacy portal technology. The web-based financial application is used by financial brokers, retail users, and admin users to manage insurance data.

The finance application has various features, such as a dashboard view, financial reports, investment recommendations, personalization, role-based access, collaboration between brokers and users, user registration, product search, product information, and user account information. Users can collaborate with brokers and compare products before purchasing financial products. The users can also search for products and view the performance of their products on a dashboard.

CHAPTER 8 WEB PERFORMANCE OPTIMIZATION CASE STUDY

Due to heavy user volume, the current application suffers from performance, scalability, and availability issues. The home page, landing page, and key features (search and registration) take an amount of time that violates the performance SLAs. The expectation is to optimize the existing applications.

The performance assessment in this chapter covers the end-to-end assessment and analysis of layer-wise components. Key performance issues and improvement themes for web components and server-side components are identified.

The discussion focuses on the scope of design, architecture, and governance improvements based on the analysis of the current solution ecosystem.

High-Level Architecture

The finance application was developed using legacy portal technology built of portlets and web components. The legacy portal technology is a server-side application that includes JSR-complaint portlets, ESBs, services, and WSRP-based integration.

The high-level architecture of the legacy application is shown in Figure 8-1.

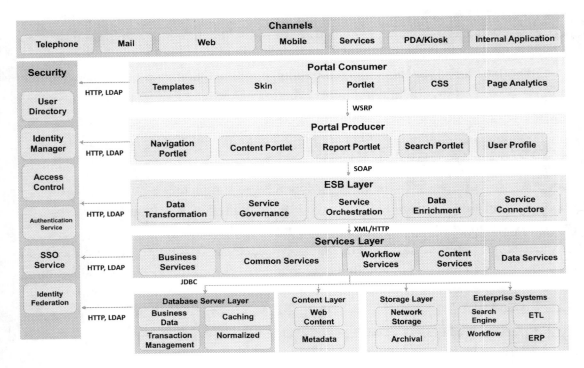

Figure 8-1. *High-level architecture of a legacy application*

As shown in Figure 8-1, the finance application is an n-tier application consisting of the following layers.

- **Channels**: The application users access the finance application through these channels. The application is accessible through various digital channels such as web, mobile, email, services, tablets, PDAs, and telephone. The finance application exposes various applications and services to cater to the digital channels.

- **Portal consumer layer**: The web components in this layer consume the services from the portal producer layer through a WSRP (Web Services for Remote Portlets) protocol. The layer provided themes, skins, stylesheets, and JavaScript to provide the functionalities. This layer provides key services, such as role-based access, personalization, and the dashboard for the end users. The components in this layer are based on JavaScript.

- **Portal producer layer**: The layer primarily provided the portlets, pluggable, and reusable web components for the users. The portlets provided various functions such as navigation, content authoring, reporting, search, and user profile information. The components in this layer are based on JSR-168 based portlets. The portlets use SOAP-based services to get the required information from the ESB.

- **ESB Layer**: ESB (Enterprise Service Bus) provides centralized access to back-end services. The ESB layer is responsible for data transformation, service governance, service orchestration, data enrichment, and provides inbuilt service connectors to the upstream systems. The ESB connects to the services layer to fetch the required application data.

- **Services layer**: The services layer provides many services from the back-end systems. Content services provide web content from the CMS layer, data services provide data from enterprise data systems, and workflow services provide workflow management services. Common services cater to cross-cutting concerns such as logging, auditing, exception handling, and so forth.

CHAPTER 8　WEB PERFORMANCE OPTIMIZATION CASE STUDY

- **Back-end systems**: The systems (enterprise databases, enterprise CMS, and enterprise systems) store the enterprise data. The data in the enterprise database layer is highly normalized and structured.

- **Security layer**: The security layer handles the security concerns such as authentication, user directory services, identity management services, single sign-on (SSO) service, and user federation service. All layers leverage the security services to provide secured access to data and functionality.

Key Solution Components

The financial application was built on legacy portal technologies. The following are the core solution components.

- **JSR portlets**: Portlets are independent, pluggable web components that form the basic building blocks of an application. They are configurable, JSR-compliant, web applications that provide personalization, data configuration, and security.

- **WSRP-based portlet communication**: The portal consumer layer communicates with the portal producer through the WSRP protocol that is heavy.

- **SOAP-based web services**: Portlets consume the ESB services through XML-based SOAP protocol.

- **RDBMS database**: The business and application data is stored in the highly normalized form in the RDBMS database that formed the source of truth for the enterprise systems

Core Performance Challenges

Due to the legacy nature of the solution components, the finance application suffered from multiple performance challenges. The key challenges are as follows.

- **Heavy web pages**: Many of the web pages' size exceeded 2 MB due to large images, duplicate scripts, 404 errors, and heavy HTML content. All the scripts and stylesheets are delivered without minification.

- **Slow page-response times**: Due to the heavy-sized pages and slow integrations, the page response time was close to 60 seconds for most pages. The slow response time led to low user satisfaction scores.

- **Slow web services**: The application used a legacy WSRP protocol that largely contributed to the slow service response time. Additionally, to serve each page, you needed multiple service calls between the portal consumer, ESB layer, and services layer.

- **Integration issues**: Many pages make more than five heavy-duty server calls to get the needed information. The numerous chatty calls blocked the page load, which further impacted the page response time.

- **Availability issues**: Sometimes, the services in the services layer went down, and due to the absence of service monitoring, the application faced many user complaints.

- **Database performance issues**: The data in the RDBMS was structured and normalized. The application used multiple queries that required complex table joins, leading to performance issues on the database end.

- **Scalability issues**: The application was not tested for maximum user load, and hence, the infrastructure was not properly sized to handle peak user traffic.

Web Performance Assessment Approach

This section explains the scope and approach of the financial application's performance optimization.

Performance Assessment Scope

The following are included in the scope of the exercise.

- Analyze various layers and layer-wise solution components from a performance standpoint.
- Assess the performance issues and bottlenecks at all layers.

- Identify the performance antipatterns across all layers.
- Provide recommendations and long-term changes from a performance standpoint.

Performance Assessment Exercise Approach

The performance assessment framework is discussed in Chapter 3. The web reference architecture provides layer-wise performance optimizations. As this is an existing application, you follow a top-down approach for the performance optimization exercise.

Top-down performance optimization

- Identify the key pages and transactions for each of the applications using the 80/20 approach.
    - The pages and transactions are used most often (e.g., home page and search page).
    - The pages and transactions that are business-critical and that have a high impact on business revenue.
- For each of the identified pages and transactions, analyze the following.
    - End-to-end performance across all layers.
    - Analyze the performance manually and by leveraging the tool
    - Identify web components, server-side components, services components, and infrastructure components affecting the performance.
    - Based on the performance analysis, recommend short-term tactical interventions and long-term strategic interventions.
    - Identify the list of design and architecture changes that can impact the long-term performance of the end-to-end application.
    - Proactively define other frameworks such as an early warning system, monitoring system that is needed to sustain overall performance.
    - Proactively call out any process gaps, governance gaps, or process interventions that impact the overall performance.

CHAPTER 8 WEB PERFORMANCE OPTIMIZATION CASE STUDY

For the performance analysis, you analyzed the end-to-end analysis of web pages most frequently used by the end users. The pages in the following list are the key landing pages for various user groups. A better user experience in these pages directly impacts overall user satisfaction, user traffic, and online revenue.

The following briefly describes each of the key pages.

- **Registration page**: Users and brokers register through the registration page. A smoother and faster onboarding is vital for the success of the platform.

- **Home page**: The home page provides the dashboard view of user products, transaction history, service request history, personalized offers, and more.

- **Search page**: Retail users search for products on the search page. Faster and relevant search results impact the likelihood of the product selection

- **Product information page**: Users can view and compare information about the products.

- **Account page**: Users can change their preferences and profile information.

The next section discusses the performance assessment checklist for this exercise.

Performance Assessment Checklist

Table 8-1 is the performance assessment checklist we used for the performance optimization exercise.

CHAPTER 8 WEB PERFORMANCE OPTIMIZATION CASE STUDY

Table 8-1. *Performance Assessment Checklist*

Category	Question/Information Needed
Web Performance	Response and page load times for different critical pages/flows such as home page, search, product, account details, and so forth. This data is needed at different levels (min, max, 90/95/99 percentile) based on what they record and measure.
	Was there any analysis done for tracing a web request end-to-end to analyze the layer-wise, component-wise, and API-wise performance? If so, you need that data.
	If this application is accessed from multiple geographies, you want to know if the performance problems exist in all geographies and the data around the same.
	If any application profiling is done, you need the data about it.
Infrastructure	Throughput and utilization information on different components of Infrastructure components such as application server, web server, database server. You collect information such as the number of concurrent requests, number of concurrent sessions/VM, memory utilization, and CPU utilization.
	Workload model for performance testing
	Production and performance environment specifications (number of servers, number of app servers, number of JVMs, OS and JVM configurations, number of DB nodes, etc.).
	Does the existing architecture leverage custom or in-built caching framework? If so, you need to collect the information.
AS-IS Scenario	Existing performance issues and known performance challenges.
	Were there any recent changes (software upgrades, patches) that caused this performance issue?
	Is there any particular pattern (e.g., geo-specific issues, time-specific issues, load-specific issues, page-specific, device-specific) to the performance problem? If so, you need to collect the information.
Technology	You need the existing technology stack and logical architecture and technology ecosystem

(*continued*)

CHAPTER 8 WEB PERFORMANCE OPTIMIZATION CASE STUDY

Table 8-1. (*continued*)

Category	Question/Information Needed
Testing	Was any analysis done by product vendors for this issue? If so, you need to collect the information.
	What are the open-source frameworks used in the solution?
	Which performance tests (load testing, stress testing, endurance testing, etc.) have been done? You need to collect the information.
	If there is any benchmark data done periodically, you need it for trend/pattern analysis.
Security	You want to get high-level security requirements of the application.
Database	If there is any database performance analysis or fine-tuning done recently, you need to collect the information.
	You also need data volume and content volume used by the application.
Enterprise Integrations	What are the enterprise integrations for the application? What is the mode of integration?
	Are there any external applications or third-party applications integrated with the application?

Web Performance Assessment Exercise

This section discusses the layer-wise performance assessment exercise adopted for the financial application. Performance assessment tools are covered in the next section.

Performance Tools for Performance Assessment

Table 8-2 shows various tools for performance assessment at various layers.

CHAPTER 8 WEB PERFORMANCE OPTIMIZATION CASE STUDY

Table 8-2. *Layer-wise Performance Assessment Tools*

Layer	Tool	Brief Description
Presentation layer	Google Chrome Lighthouse	The browser plugin evaluates the web page on various parameters such as overall performance score, best practices and provides an aggregated score and performance improvement suggestions
	Fiddler, Firefox Firebug, Fiddler	The tools provide the network timings details for various resources such as load times (DNS lookup time, connection time, download time), size for various assets such as scripts, stylesheets, images, and XHR.
	Web performance checklist	The checklist describes web performance best practices. A sample checklist is in Appendix A.
Server layer	Apache JMeter	The tool is for load testing and stress testing the server-side components.
	Performance checklist	A server-side performance checklist is in Appendix A and a database performance checklist in Appendix B
Services Layer	SOAPUI, Postman, Rest-assured	The tools are for API testing
Database Layer	Query Performance Testing	After the identification of heavy queries, you tested and analyzed the queries

Starting with the presentation layer, you trace the request end-to-end across all layers. For the presentation layer, you used the performance metrics from the Google Chrome Lighthouse tool and Mozilla Firebug tools. For the server-side components, you can enable instrumentation to understand the component level and service level timing metrics. The timing numbers for the database layer and web service layer were individually verified through the service invocation and database query execution, respectively.

CHAPTER 8 WEB PERFORMANCE OPTIMIZATION CASE STUDY

Performance Assessment of Presentation Layer

Let's analyze the key parameters for each of the in-scope web pages.

- **Page size**: The overall size of the page that impacts the page performance
- **Average Page Load Time (PLT)**: The average response time recorded by the tools. The time to first byte indicates the server response time. Perceived load time measures the page performance perceived by the end user.
- **Asset count**: The total number of static assets (Scripts, stylesheets, Images) for a given page.

Table 8-3 shows the performance metrics for all the in-scope pages.

Table 8-3. Page Metrics

Page	Page Size	Average Page Load Time	Number of Assets
Registration Page	1.7 MB	1.5 secs	CSS: 13 Scripts (JS): 19 Images: 10
Search Page	1.9 MB	7 secs	CSS/Stylesheets: 3 Scripts (JS): 14 Images: 16
Product information page	1.2 MB	3.3 secs	CSS/Stylesheets: 1 Scripts (JS): 14 Images: 16
Home page	1.3 MB	27.68 secs	CSS/Stylesheets: 19 Scripts (JS): 34 Images: 53
Accounts page	1.1 MB	14.45 secs	CSS/Stylesheets: 18 Scripts (JS): 17 Images: 50

225

CHAPTER 8   WEB PERFORMANCE OPTIMIZATION CASE STUDY

As you can see, the key landing pages are very heavy due to numerous images, scripts, and stylesheets. The heavy web pages impact the average page load times for the page.

Performance Assessment of Server Layer

For most of the pages, the time to first byte (TTFB) is about 4.5 seconds, indicating that server response time is very high. The application faced the following key challenges.

- Multiple service hops for a single service (the first call from portal producer to ESB, the second call from ESB to services, and the third call from services to the database)
- XML-based heavy web service calls
- Not modular code where a lot of code is rewritten and duplicated across various modules with minimal reusability
- WSRP-based portlet communication leading to heavy-duty calls
- The model layer used the Hibernate framework that faced performance issues during complex queries
- Service availability issues due to poor service governance and absence of monitoring infrastructure

Web Performance Optimization Recommendations

Based on the challenges identified, this section goes over performance improvement recommendations.

Performance Improvement Recommendations for the Presentation Layer

Based on the performance analysis, the following are recommendations to improve the overall page performance.

Minimize HTTP Calls

You need to minimize the number of server resource calls that impact performance.

Recommendations

The following are the changes done to improve the page load time and reduce the HTTP requests.

- **Creation of combined files through merging the files**: To load each static file, you need to make a separate request to the server. So, as the number of page files increases, the number of requests to the server increases. This adds the additional performance overhead. Combining the JS files into a single file reduces the number of calls.

- **Having the CSS sprite images**: In this method, you combine all the page images (e.g., background images, product images) into a single image and serve it to the browser. This eliminates multiple image request calls.

- **Inline images**: By avoiding the inline images and using a combined image reduces image-related calls.

gzip Static Components

As the financial application has large-sized pages, you need to explore opportunities to reduce the page size.

You can compress the application images, HTML content using gzip. Image compression would decrease the size by approximately 25%.

Put CSS at the Top

You need to place the CSS files inside the head element to enable progressive rendering. The CSS files need to be included at the top of the page before any scripts are loaded.

Move Scripts to the Bottom of the page

You need to place the JavaScript at the bottom of the page to not block the page load. JavaScript placement improves the perceived load time. It is recommended to have the third-party scripts (i.e., web analytics scripts) be placed at the bottom of the page. Minify scripts and stylesheets.

Minification removes unnecessary characters such as white space, to reduce the overall asset size. Minification reduces the overall page size.

CHAPTER 8 WEB PERFORMANCE OPTIMIZATION CASE STUDY

Avoid Redirects

The client side redirects or the server side redirects slows down the overall page load time; hence, you should avoid any unnecessary redirects.

For optimal performance, you need to load the content in the proper order.

Recommendations

The following is the recommended order for loading static resources.

1. Place the titles at the top.
2. Place the meta-content.
3. Place all the SHC config entries.
4. Place the combined CSS files.
5. Place the combined JS files.
6. Place the individual JS files.
7. Move all the inline JS code under one <script> tag.

HTML Compression

You can enable the HTML compression at the web server level. You can also reduce all gaps and white space in the server pages. HTML compression reduces the overall page size of the application. Enable gzip compression for HTTP traffic.

JavaScript Refactoring

The main purpose is to alter the inclusion of JS files so that the static content is loaded quickly. The loading of static content takes most of the page loading time; hence, if you can reduce JS inclusion loading time, performance increases.

Recommendations

The following are the changes that need to be done as a part of JavaScript refactoring.

- All the JS files need to be packed in the corresponding combined files, until and unless it needs to be loaded separately.

- All the JS files that are not required on the page load need to be removed or used in a deferred function. By placing the files in the deferred functions, the content of these JS files is loaded after the document.ready(), so the page loading time is improved.

Fixing the Height and Width of Images

The purpose is to modify the dimensions of the images to the suggested size. This helps in using the image directly without any resizing while rendering the page.

Recommendations

Specify the exact image dimensions; you get the various images that do not have the proper dimensions. When you hover on the image, it specifies the suggested size. You need to make the recommended size. Whenever an image is added, please check whether the image dimensions are as per the suggested size.

Fixing 404 Errors

The main objective is to remove the 404 errors for all the static content to avoid delays in retrieving a file that is not present in the specified location.

Recommendations

When the page is loaded, open Firebug and click the Network tab. It shows all the 404 Errors that are present while loading a page. Once you identify these errors, you need to check the actual file from where you are loading this content and check whether the actual content is present in that location. If, not present then the proper location of the file needs to be mentioned.

Multiple Domains

The main objective is to make multiple domains available to retrieve the static content. Multiple domains are useful in fetching the JS files from one domain and CSS and images from other domains. When multiple domains are used, the browser can download the static resources in parallel.

CHAPTER 8 WEB PERFORMANCE OPTIMIZATION CASE STUDY

Removal of Duplicate Calls

The main objective is to remove the duplicate calls that perform the same task to reduce the page load time.

Recommendations

The duplicate Ajax calls and resource calls happen because the same call is present in different JS files (or) in different functions. If both the JS files are included for any page, then the duplicate call retrieves the same data. So, you need to identify all the calls and avoid duplicate calls.

Removal of the Duplicate Functions in Various JS Files

The main objective is to eliminate the functions which have the same function definitions and are present in various JS files. This removes the redundant function definitions.

Recommendations

Identify various methods that perform the same functionality but are present in various files. This reduces the code size, ambiguity in function definitions, and improve the performance.

Removal of Duplicate Loading of Files

The recommendation is to remove all the duplicate files loaded for a page. The duplicate calls for loading a particular file increases the page load time and hence reduces the performance.

Recommendations

There are a few files that are loaded twice: once by the combined file and once by the individual file. Eliminate this redundant loading of individual files.

CHAPTER 8 WEB PERFORMANCE OPTIMIZATION CASE STUDY

Caching AJAX/XHR Call

Modern web applications heavily use AJAX calls to load data asynchronously. In many Web applications, the user is made to wait for the response because the response time varies with the type of data it retrieves and the network speed.

Recommendations

Cache the AJAX response to improve the performance of the AJAX response. You need to add the details of the AJAX call in the caching file (cachespec.xml) to be cached.

Caching Static Assets

Cache static assets such as JS, CSS, and images so that the browser can cache these assets. Configure entity tags (ETags) by specifying a Last-Modified or ETag header to enable cache validation for the resources. Leverage browser caching by setting a long expiration for static assets. Leverage web server caching by adding the expires header in the web server config file.

Recommendations

You can set the cache headers for static assets such as images, scripts, and stylesheets to enable browser caching.

Server-Layer Performance Improvement Recommendations

Most of the pages have high TTFB, indicating that server-side calls (web services and database calls) need to be optimized.

The server-side performance optimizations reduce TTFB. This section covers the key server-related performance optimizations. The optimizations are categorized into database query optimizations and service optimizations.

Database Optimizations

Based on the analysis of the query performance in the performance assessment phase, the following describes database performance optimizations.

231

- Reduce the number of database calls. You can batch the database calls and reduce the frequency of database calls. Use the batch/bulk query call supported by Hibernate.

- Move the heavy-duty database operations to a database stored procedure to avoid multiple database calls. For database-intensive operations, leverage database stored procedure instead of JDBC calls.

- You should completely avoid database calls in a loop. To avoid this, you can either create a stored procedure to do all the database heavy lifting operations and invoke the stored procedure only once from application passing all needed parameters.

- You can cache the query result values to increase the performance of the application using Hibernate caching, such as supported multi-level caching.

- On the database end, create indexes for columns used in the "where" clause of the frequently used queries. Database performance optimizations are in Appendix B.

Service Optimizations

The following are service-related performance optimizations.

- Replace the heavy WSRP calls with lightweight REST calls.
- Leverage the asynchronous service to load the data only on demand.
- Minimize the number of service call hops needed for servicing a single request. Currently, a single request triggers three network hops: the first call from client to ESB, the second call from ESB to the corresponding service, and the third call from the corresponding service to the source system.
- Cache the service responses for a fixed duration to avoid the fresh server calls.

Server Code Optimizations

The following are server code optimizations.

- Cache the frequently used data and data that needs heavy computation. Look up data, costly service responses, and costly query responses can be cached for a fixed duration with appropriate caching policies.

- Refactor the server-side code to create reusable and modular components.

Infrastructure Optimizations

The following are infrastructure optimizations.

- Review the web server and application service configurations to ensure that key configurations related to connection pool size, memory settings, and so forth are configured properly. A server configuration checklist is in Appendix 1.

- Set up a robust real-time application monitoring and server health check monitoring infrastructure to monitor the service availability and system availability in real time and notify of any errors.

- Conduct load testing to check the scalability and capacity of the existing infrastructure. Based on the sizing recommendations from the product vendor, and based on the performance findings from the load testing, you need to fine-tune the infrastructure capacity.

CHAPTER 8 WEB PERFORMANCE OPTIMIZATION CASE STUDY

Recommended Tools for Performance Optimization

Table 8-4 shows the tools recommended to improve the overall performance.

Table 8-4. Tools to Improve Performance

Category	Tool	Brief Description
Minification	JSMin, YUI Compressor	Minification of JavaScripts
Image Compression	Smush It	Provide loss-less image compression
Application Monitoring	Nagios, AppDynamics	Provide service monitoring, service and application availability
Error monitoring	Splunk	Monitor the errors in the application log files
Edge side caching/Content Delivery Network (CDN)	KeyCDN, jsDeliver, BootstrapCDN	Caching of static assets (images, CSS, JS, Videos)
Load testing	Apache JMeter, SOAP UI	Application load testing

Performance-related Design Recommendations

During our performance assessment, you noticed the scope for design improvements for the existing application. Fundamental design recommendations from a performance standpoint are provided.

Proposal for Early Warning System (EWS)

An early warning system is a set of systems that proactively monitor the key systems with defined parameters. Once the specified SLA is violated, it should trigger an email notification to the configured admins

You recommend using the EWS for proactively following parameters.

- **System availability**: Notify if the system or server is down or is not available
- **Service availability**: Notify if the service is down or is not available
- **CPU usage (>90%)**: Notify if the CPU usage exceeds 90% over a period of time

- **Memory usage (>90%)**: Notify if the memory usage exceeds 90% over a period of time

- **Disk usage (>90%)**: Notify if the disk usage exceeds 90% over a period of time

Implementation

A comprehensive monitoring solution involves application and services health check monitoring through tools such as AppDynamics and real user monitoring/synthetic monitoring through Nagios.

Sample AppDynamics-based Application/Services Health Check Monitoring

You can leverage AppDynamics to build the health check/heartbeat monitoring of the services and systems.

For this scenario, you can develop a comprehensive monitoring solution using three out-of-the-box components.

- **Health rules**: You can create health rules for key performance metrics that you would like to monitor.

- **Policies**: You can define policies to link the health rule violations to the appropriate actions.

- **Actions**: You can create notification alerts for serious health rule violations.

System and Service Availability Monitoring

As availability is of critical importance, you need to prioritize the availability monitoring. The following defines the availability monitoring steps.

1. Create a health rule to detect errors for HTTP response code 404 (Not Found), 500 (Internal Server Error), and 502 (Not Available).

2. The health rule can be configured for all critical services. You can start with the registration page and include all key services that impact the application.

3. An email notification action can be configured to trigger the email when there is a violation.

4. You need to create server metric monitoring for all servers. You can monitor the CPU utilization (with threshold of >60% utilization), memory utilization (with threshold of >80% utilization). An email notification can be tied to the health rule violation through policy.

5. A distribution list (DL) can be created for the emails to receive the notification.

Nagios-based Synthetic Monitoring

Nagios can be used for real-time application monitoring/synthetic monitoring. For real-time monitoring of the finance application, you can follow these steps.

- Configure the production URL for the core pages of the application.
- Nagios can be configured to monitor the performance of the servers.
- You can configure email addresses in Nagios to send the alert notifications.

Note Nagios can monitor server resources. You can use check_nrpe plugin to monitor the disk usage and average load of the servers. Configure email to alert the admin once the disk usage/CPU utilization reaches the configured threshold.

Splunk-based Error Reporting

Splunk can be configured to monitor critical errors. You can configure Splunk to alert for HTTP 500 errors. You can create a search query for key errors and configure real-time alerts for notification.

Application Monitoring

As part of best practice, you need to monitor the servers/applications that you are looking for performance. You need to monitor the infrastructure and applications from a 360-degree perspective. The advantages of monitoring the systems and applications are as follows.

- Continuous monitoring for vulnerabilities and threshold configurations

- Instant alerts and notifications when a downtime incident is reported

- Faster root cause analysis of the production issues.

- Reduced cost of ownership

- Improved productivity and accelerated turnaround

- Health dashboards with in-depth reporting features on busy hours, trends, downtime

- Improved customer satisfaction

Recommendations

I recommend a holistic performance governance plan that covers all the project lifecycle stages. The following are the key aspects of performance governance.

- During the application design stage, you need to define the performance guidelines, best practices relevant to the application. You should also clearly define the performance SLAs (page load times, page response times, etc.) used in the development and testing phase.

- During the application development stage, the developers should follow the specified guidelines. The QA team should iteratively validate the performance of the application based on the defined SLAs.

- During the user experience testing phase, the QA team must validate the performance across devices, geographies, and supported user agents/browsers.

A robust monitoring infrastructure should be set up to do the following.

- Real-time monitoring of heartbeat of internal systems and services. This should cover the availability of systems and CPU/memory/disk usage metrics.

- Real-time production application monitoring to get live performance numbers.

CHAPTER 8   WEB PERFORMANCE OPTIMIZATION CASE STUDY

Design recommendations for Server-side Components

The following are the main design recommendations for server-side components for the financial application.

- **Transition to microservices**: Legacy web server services need to be remodeled into granular, modular, and independently scalable microservices. Microservices can be closely modeled based on the presentation needs. Microservices provide independently scalable, granular, and extensible service architecture. The main advantages of using a microservices-based integration model are as follows.

    - Modular microservices bring in decoupled architecture.
    - Enhances reusability of microservices
    - Lightweight microservices invoked in asynchronous mode improve the performance.

- **Lightweight integrations**: Design and deploy REST-based services instead of SOAP-based web services. REST-based services support JSON data formats that are lightweight. The JSON-based service performs better than the XML-based SOAP service.

- **Service choreography**: Replace the ESB-based orchestration with event-based choreography.

- **Event-driven architecture**: Migrate from the services-based integration to an event-based model.

Architecture and Design Recommendations

This section offers recommendations for the existing architecture elements.

Lean Architecture

Modern web platforms use lean architecture consisting of lean UI and lightweight integrations.

Current Context and Observations

Currently, the Portal consumer (based on JavaScript framework) and portal producer (based on JSR-compliant portlets) components are used as presentation components. This leads to the following challenges.

- Presence of multiple presentation components: Both portal consumer and portal producers have presentation capabilities.

- Usage of heavyweight portal components (such as portlets) increases the page size impacting performance. The home page has a size exceeding 1 MB and takes more than 20 seconds to load due to the heavyweight components and numerous JS/CSS/Images.

Recommendations

Across the digital ecosystem traditional horizontal portals are being replaced by lean portals and digital experience platforms based on lightweight JavaScript frameworks using microservices.

Hence portal consumer and portal producer be replaced by a JavaScript framework-based (such as Angular or React) lightweight UI using microservices for data interactions. Microservices can use the ESB to interact with upstream systems.

Services Façade

Multiple calls are invoked from the presentation layer. For instance, the home page makes multiple synchronous calls for login functionality.

You need to create a service façade that handles the sequencing and orchestration of calls so that the presentation layer can make a single call to the service façade.

Leverage Open Source CDN for Serving Static Assets

As many of the pages have more than 15 static assets (images), you can leverage open source CDNs such as KeyCDN, jsDeliver, and BootstrapCDN to improve the asset loading time.

All the static images, JS files, and CSS files can be served from the CDN locations wherever possible.

Open source CDNs provide high availability and high performance. Ideally, you should use the minified version of the JS files to be served from CDN locations.

User Experience Redesign

The user experience design greatly influences the overall page performance. Here are a few points in this regard.

- The home page is heavy with numerous page sections/portlets, images, JS/CSS files, and XHR calls.
- The best practice is to have a minimalistic design for home pages/landing pages so that the page performance is optimal.
- Ideally, you should have three to five UI modules on the home page, and all other rarely used functionalities should be moved to other pages.

Layer-wise Caching

The principle of layer-wise caching states that you need to cache the frequently used data values at every layer.

- The user-agent/browser layer can cache the assets such as JS/CSS and images. You can set the appropriate cache headers for this.
- The service layer can cache the application objects, lookup values, and service responses for frequently used service invocations.
- The database layer can cache the query results for frequently used queries.
- You noticed that many applications are making repeated database calls for user profile information. For instance, the home page makes a database call for getting user profile and status information. The user values are ideal candidates for server-side caching with appropriate cache TTL values.

Stricter Compliance to Architecture Layers

Few components and flows bypass the ESB services and directly interact with the database. Though this provides short-term performance gain, this approach poses scalability challenges and extensibility challenges in the future. You recommend to expose data services from ESB and use it for all data interactions.

ESB provides service governance, caching, and security controls in this context.

Performance Best Practices

This section goes over the performance best practices recommended for the financial application.

Performance by Design

Adopt the performance-driven development strategy as a crucial development guideline. The following are some of the performance-by-design principles.

- Simple and lightweight: Keep the frequently used pages like the home page and landing page simple yet effective. This would involve the following.

    - Include only key functionalities on the home page, landing page to keep it lightweight.

    - Have optimized marquee images.

    - Provide search feature to reach any page using the keyword search functionality.

    - Provide an elaborate menu to allow the user to navigate to any sublevel page.

- Fine-tune the key functionalities for performance.

- Maximize client-side components: Wherever possible, employ partial page rendering to avoid a full page refresh.

- Avoid third-party plugins unless required. Even when they are included, only load the scripts on-demand, and keep the third-party scripts at the bottom of the page.

- Think caching: Apply caching at all possible layers (such as web server, application server, database server) to get optimum performance.

- Performance guidelines: Create organization-level performance guidelines involving images, JS/CSS coding, and other aspects. Some of them could include

    - Use the PNG format of images

    - Use CSS sprites

CHAPTER 8 WEB PERFORMANCE OPTIMIZATION CASE STUDY

- Use JS code validation with JSLint
- Use lazy loading of content wherever possible
- Avoid iframes and redirects to the best extent possible

Summary

- The case study discusses finance application that is built on legacy portal technology that has n-tier architecture.
- The main layers of the financial application are channels, portal consumer, portal producer, ESB layer, services layer, security layer, database server layer, content layer, storage layer, and enterprise systems.
- The key solution components are portlets, WSRP based interportlet communication, and SOAP-based web services and relational databases.
- The key challenges are heavy pages, slow page response time, slow web service, availability issues, integration issues, and database performance issues.
- The key performance improvement recommendations for the presentation layer are to do the following: minimize HTTP calls, use gzip static components, put CSS at the top, move scripts to the bottom, minify scripts and stylesheets, avoid redirects, use sequence loading of scripts and stylesheets, use HTML compression, use JavaScript refactoring, fix the height and width of images, fix 404 errors, use multiple domains, remove duplicate calls, remove duplicate functions in various JS files, remove duplicate file loading, cache AJAX/XHR calls, and cache static assets.
- The key performance improvement recommendations for the server layer are database query optimizations and service optimizations.
- The key performance-related design recommendations are a proposal for an early warning system (EWS), lean architecture, services façade, leverage open source CDN for serving static assets, user experience redesign, layer-wise caching, and stricter compliance to architecture layers.

CHAPTER 9

Performance Engineering Case Study

In this chapter, you do a performance engineering exercise that provides a holistic and end-to-end performance analysis of an application. As part of the performance engineering activity, you analyze the web performance, server-side performance, and infrastructure to identify the performance bottlenecks and performance challenges. You also carry out performance testing to validate the performance issues identified. Once the application is deployed to production, you set up the monitoring infrastructure.

This case study covers various aspects of performance engineering. You look at the legacy n-tier application and apply the performance engineering process steps discussed in Chapter 3. The approach and methods for analyzing the performance of web pages, server-side components, and infrastructure components are covered.

Based on the findings, you identify the key performance challenges and scenarios and recommend methods to fine-tune the performance.

Performance engineers, web developers, digital architects, project managers, and program managers will find this chapter useful.

Performance Engineering Overview

Performance engineering is a holistic exercise to identify, test, analyze, and report performance issues and suggest recommendations. As part of performance engineering, you establish a performance strategy to improve the overall system performance and identify key performance indicators (KPIs) and metrics that measure improvement.

CHAPTER 9   PERFORMANCE ENGINEERING CASE STUDY

Performance Engineering Process

The end-to-end steps of the performance engineering process are shown in Figure 9-1.

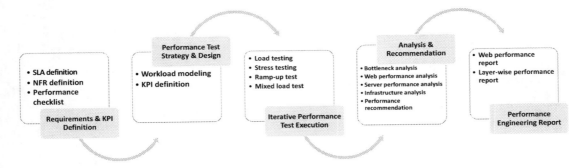

Figure 9-1. *Performance engineering process*

Requirements and KPI Definition

Performance-related requirements and SLAs are defined in this step. You identify the key business transactions and non-functional requirements (NFR) in this phase. NFR gathering is done using the following sources.

- **Existing application logs** of applications to better understand the transactions and transaction mix
- **Live application logs** of applications to better understand the SLA of downstream response time SLAs
- **Volumetric requirements** for the application

You define performance best practices and checklists so that the development team can adhere to performance-based design.

Performance Test Strategy and Design

You define the workload model for load testing. You identify the KPIs that align with business goals and have a positive impact on the user experience. You get the information for these performance metrics from business stakeholders and industry standards and best practices. The following are the main performance KPIs.

CHAPTER 9   PERFORMANCE ENGINEERING CASE STUDY

- Response time, such as page response time, load time, and DOM-ready time
- Response times for key business transactions and processes
- The page size of key pages
- Throughput for all systems and interfaces
- Peak throughput requirements per application
- Average throughput requirements
- Response time SLAs
- Downstream response time SLAs

Iterative Performance Test Execution

You execute the performance testing in iterations. You also carry out a mixed-load test per workload modeling. Performance test execution was covered in Chapter 6.

Performance Analysis and Recommendation

Based on the performance testing, you do the bottleneck analysis and layer-wise analysis. The focus is on web performance analysis, server performance analysis, infrastructure analysis, and performance optimization recommendations. Because this step is a crucial part of performance engineering, layer-wise performance recommendations are discussed.

Performance Engineering Report

As the final step in the performance engineering process, the performance engineering team provides the recommendations and performance reports to management. The project management team should act on the recommendations.

Chapter 9 Performance Engineering Case Study

A Brief Overview of the Application

You provide a performance engineering approach for an n-tier application in this case study. Performance engineering can be applied to any generic multi-tiered application. The solution involves legacy Java Server Pages (JSP) that heavily uses database queries.

High-Level Flow

The solution needs five web service calls, on average, to serve a single web request. For instance, to retrieve the data from a relational database, the JSP page invokes the gateway service, which uses the corresponding controller. The controller then uses the database handler to invoke the corresponding database service that executes the needed JDBC query on the relational database.

The application uses an XML-based SOAP protocol for integration across all layers. The high-level flow of the application is depicted in Figure 9-2.

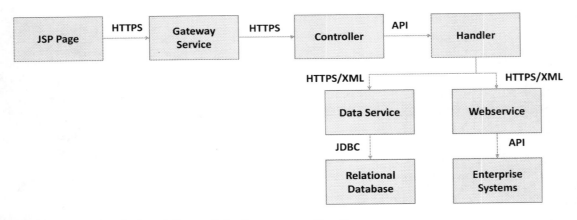

Figure 9-2. High-level flow of the legacy application

Technology Ecosystem

The existing platform is built on legacy technologies. The following are technologies used in the presentation layer, services layer, and database layer.

- **Presentation components**: The legacy application is built on the Struts framework. The application package is deployed on the Oracle WebLogic server. A few of the UI components use the jQuery JavaScript framework. AIX OS is used on production servers.

- **Service components**: The legacy platform uses XML-based SOAP web services. All services are HTTPS-based.

- **Database components**: Oracle 11g is deployed as the core database engine. JDBC APIs are used for database interaction.

- **Security components**: Microsoft Active Directory (AD) stores user information and digital certificates for security.

- **Infrastructure components**: All production servers are clustered. Sizing and capacity planned are not based on the load and performance requirements. A monitoring setup is missing in the infrastructure.

Web Performance Analysis

The first step in a performance engineering exercise is to analyze the web pages. This analysis focuses on web and presentation components. It provides insights into the performance of web components. You use tools such as HTTPWatch, Google PageSpeed, Google Lighthouse, and Firebug to collect the network-related information about web components.

This section discusses an approach for analyzing the web components as part of web performance analysis.

Web Frameworks and JavaScript Framework

You analyze the usage of web frameworks and the JavaScript framework used in existing solutions web applications. The solution uses the Java-based struts framework as a web framework. The web framework renders the web components through Java Server Pages (JSP). JQuery is the main JavaScript framework used in the application.

Page Load Times and Page Size Analysis for Key Pages

You analyze the load times and page size for key pages such as the home page, gateway page, and landing pages. You benchmark them against the industry standards, best practices, and performance SLAs.

CHAPTER 9 PERFORMANCE ENGINEERING CASE STUDY

As per the industry standards, you need to have a two-second page load time for main HTTP pages and five-second page load time for HTTPS pages.

You also test the performance on multiple devices and supported browsers. Tools like Google Lighthouse are used for testing web performance.

Presentation Component Analysis

This includes understanding the number of static global assets (images, JavaScript, CSS, video, JSON, HTML content, XML, text, etc.) and the size of each of the components. For each of these assets, you record the following performance metrics using the network analysis tools (e.g., Firebug and HTTPWatch).

- Response time of the web component from various browsers
- Response time for AJAX/XHR calls
- Size of the component
- Caching status of the asset
- Asset count

Web Analytics Report Analysis

Web analytics tools such as Omniture and Google Web Analytics (GWA) passively track the user activities such as navigation, clicks along with other parameters such as performance, availability. The web analytics tool's cloud-based dashboard provides good insights into the performance. The web analytics reports are analyzed to understand performance, bounce rate, exit ratio, conversion ratios, and pages flows, which have challenges in user experiences.

The server-side components include the servlets, portlets, services, and persistence layer components. The server-side components are deployed on the application server.

All server-side components are analyzed to understand their contribution to the overall performance. The following are the main activities in this analysis.

Business Components Performance Analysis

The main business components for a Java-based enterprise application are servlets, custom business components, and portlets. Handler classes and helper classes form part of the business components in Figure 9-1. The response time of business components directly affects the time to first byte (TTFB) metric, thereby impacting overall page performance. To analyze the performance of the business components, you can follow the following methods.

- Instrument the code to get the time taken for each of the business components.
- Analyze the layer-wise timing metric using application monitoring tools (e.g., AppDynamics)
- Log the timing information for each of the business components
- Analyze the server-side cache and the cache utilization metrics

You need to record the timings at various loads to understand the scalability and performance behavior. Workload modeling is used for load testing. If the performance degrades at high loads, it indicates possible insufficient server configuration, which means fine-tuning the server configurations (thread pool, connection pool, heap size, etc.) and infrastructure (adding cluster nodes, increasing memory, etc.).

Usually, business components invoke services such as database services and web services. Let's look at those services in the next section.

Service Performance Analysis

The main services of the application are data service and web services, as depicted in Figure 9-1. To analyze the performance of the services, you can use the application-monitoring tool to get the average response time of each of the services.

Once you get the cumulative response time of the services, you can trace the time taken by individual methods, APIs, database queries, utility/helper classes to understand the most time-consuming component.

You should also record the cache utilization of the services. As part of this analysis, identify the most used services, most resource-intensive and costly services, time-consuming database queries, and identify the potential cache candidates.

The various integration patterns are discussed in Chapter 12 that can be used for services design.

CHAPTER 9 PERFORMANCE ENGINEERING CASE STUDY

Database Performance Analysis

As part of the database analysis, you can identify the most time-consuming queries. You can test the performance of the queries at the database level. You can use tools like Oracle Database Explain Plan to explore the query's fine-tuning measures, such as the following.

- Creating indexes for columns for filtering
- Logical partition of the tables data
- Leveraging the views and denormalized tables to cater to reporting needs
- Exploring the database stored procedures to execute a database-intensive operation

The various data patterns are explained in Chapter 11.

Infrastructure Analysis

As part of infrastructure analysis, you analyze the as-is capacity, server configuration, cache configuration, and you provide infrastructure-related recommendations.

AS-IS Capacity and Network Analysis

In this phase, you use load-testing tools to understand the following key performance parameters.

- System availability at normal loads and high loads
- Transaction throughput of various servers at normal loads and high loads
- Response times for various business transactions at normal loads and high loads
- Resource consumption of various servers at normal loads and high loads

Server Configuration Analysis

You look at the main server configurations to determine if they are in line with the vendor-recommended configurations. Some of the key server configuration parameters are.

- Heap size of the servers
- CPU cores and memory size of the severs
- Disk capacity of the servers
- Connection pool settings, such as max pool size, min pool size, and so forth
- Thread pool parameters such as pool size
- Session parameters such as timeout parameters

Cache Configuration Analysis

As part of the exercise, you explore the usage of a cache at various layers of the application. The following are some of the cache opportunities.

- Edge caching with a content delivery network (CDN) to cache static assets, such as images, videos, scripts, and CSS
- Client-side caching by leveraging the browser caching feature
- Server-side caching or object caching for caching the static and frequently used values (Redis cache, Memcached, and EhCache are some of the caching frameworks.)

Infrastructure Recommendations

Based on the current and anticipated load, the testing team comes up with a recommendation for the sizing and capacity for all servers. Some of the common infrastructure-related recommendations are listed next.

- Conduct performance testing to validate infrastructure sizing.
- Resize the server capacity to scale and perform at peak loads.

- Based on the analysis of the application response time, report the specific business transactions and processes that need performance fine-tuning.

- Report the application errors at high loads for the business transactions and business processes.

- Set up real-time application monitoring and the server health-check service.

Performance Testing

The section discusses the performance testing process. Follow the performance testing process, as described in Chapter 6.

Performance Testing Tools

The team conducts performance testing from various dimensions. The following are some of the tools to collect the performance data from various servers.

- Use a load runner to run load testing across various servers to get the performance metrics.

- Use the NMON tool to get the performance data from AIX servers.

- Use the Windows PERFMON tool to get performance data from Windows Server.

- Use Apache JMeter for load testing and API testing.

- Use JProfiler to profile and analyze a Java application.

- Use Google Chrome Lighthouse tool to identify the performance and areas of improvement for the web pages.

Performance Test Setup and Execution

The following are the main activities in the performance test setup.

Performance Test Design

The following are the main activities in the performance test design.

- Involves identifying interfaces, per transaction request/response for each simulator, building simulator, and load testing to prevent bottlenecks
- Application setup
  - Set up the application server and configure parameters, data sources, connection pool, and so forth
- Testbed preparation
  - Data priming and simulator data setup
  - Sanity test the application
- Workload analysis
  - Identify the key transaction mix and load values
- Test script preparation and parameterization
  - Analyze the different transactions based on NFR and business inputs
  - Analyze the different types of upstream interfaces that need to be tested
  - Build scripts for each interface
  - Build the script data

Performance Test Execution

The following are the main activities in the performance test execution.

- Ramp-up tests
  - For each transaction
  - For mixed load

CHAPTER 9 PERFORMANCE ENGINEERING CASE STUDY

- Isolated tests at different workloads for testing scalability
  - For each transaction
- Mixed-load test at different workloads
  - All transaction with a particular transaction mix

Load Testing and Stress Testing

During load testing, you apply the normal expected load for the system and check the system behavior. Load testing measures the performance of the application under a statistically representative load, and you simulate the real-life usage patterns. During stress testing, you subject the application to peak loads to ascertain the performance of the platform under abnormal load. Stress testing also determines the application's failure points, degradation points, exception handling, and transaction handling capabilities.

The key steps in this testing are as follows.

- Ramp-up and mixed load test at different workloads (all transactions with a particular transaction mix). Maintain user load for some duration and then ramp up the user load in steps. A sample ramp-up test template is shown in Table 9-1.

Table 9-1. Sample Ramp-up Test

Number of Users	Time (Mins)	Server CPU Utilization	Average Throughput (requests/second)	% Failures	Response Time (Seconds)
5	10	30%	3.1	0	3
10	20	35%	4.8	0	3.2
15	30	35%	6.2	0	4.6
20	40	40%	8.9	0	4.8
25	50	45%	10.4	0	5.2
30	60	50%	15.3	0	5.5
35	70	50%	18.3	0	6.2
40	80	55%	22.4	0	6.8
45	90	60%	25.9	0	7.2
50	100	70%	30.2	2%	8.1

CHAPTER 9　PERFORMANCE ENGINEERING CASE STUDY

- Load system with concurrent users over time and check system behavior
- Isolate single transaction tests with varying loads. A sample template is shown in Table 9-2.

Table 9-2. *Isolated Load Test*

Number of Users	Server CPU Utilization	Throughput (requests/second)	% Failures	Response Time (Seconds)
5	30	3.2	0	4.6
10	53	5.9	0	9.8
15	74	7.8	0	13.9
20	81	8.4	0	18.6
25	85	9.1	0	24.4

- Multiple rounds of the testing is needed to identify and resolve performance issues each time
- Mixed load testing through multiple transactions and a particular transaction mix and multiple tests with increasing load and same transaction mix. Sample reports are shown in Tables 9-3 and 9-4.

Table 9-3. *Mixed Load Distribution*

Transaction Mix	
Transaction	Weightage
Transaction A	55
Transaction B	25
Transaction C	10
Transaction D	10
Total	100

CHAPTER 9 PERFORMANCE ENGINEERING CASE STUDY

Table 9-4. *Sample Mixed Load Testing Results*

Transaction	50 Users Number of users	No of requests processed	% of Failures	Throughput (requests/second)	Response Time (seconds)
Transaction A	55	2004	0.4	0.54	42.4
Transaction B	25	6854	0	1.8	8.8
Transaction C	10	289	1.9	0.04	15.4
Transaction D	10	65	1.2	0.02	40.4

- Monitor the response time for each test iteration. A sample response-time test report is shown in Table 9-5.

Table 9-5. *Response Time Report*

Workload	Transactions	Response Time Minimum	Average	Maximum	90 Percent	Think Time	Completed Transactions	Workload Mix %
W1	W1_TXN1	6	8	20	8	42	120	
	W1_TXN2	0.5	0.6	2.2	0.7	15	2300	
	W1_TXN3	71	75	80	79	40	18	45
W2	W2_TXN1	4	4.5	8	4.3	20	20	
	W2_TXN2	6	7	7.5	7.2	92	180	55

Concurrent User Testing

You test the maximum supported concurrent user load, transaction load, and data load. The performance testing team uses a combination of open-source and commercial tools for this exercise.

Performance Bottleneck Analysis and Problem Patterns

You compile the list of all existing performance challenges in this phase. Based on the bottleneck analysis, you also compile the key problem patterns for the application.

Bottleneck Analysis

You analyze any potential bottlenecks existing in the request-processing pipeline. This is identified in the following test scenarios.

- End-to-end performance testing and layer-wise performance testing
- Profiling for server-side code components to test for memory leaks
- Analyzing service calls and enterprise integration components
- Recording and analyzing the system behavior at various loads

Availability Analysis

You check the current availability of all systems and interfaces and benchmark it against business requirements and industry standards.

Common Performance Problem Pattern

Based on the insights from the bottleneck analysis and the performance challenges you identified, the main problem patterns are discussed next.

Application Not Scalable

The application is facing challenges with scalability upon an increase in the load.

- **Problem symptoms**
  - Response time increases drastically at all layers, with an increase in load
  - Some queuing observed with an increase in load
  - CPU utilization at some layers increases with an increase in load
  - Memory utilization increases with an increase in load
  - Timeouts at the service layer at high loads with an increase in load

CHAPTER 9   PERFORMANCE ENGINEERING CASE STUDY

- **Root cause analysis**
    - Suboptimal database connection pool settings
    - Suboptimal Oracle database's session and process parameters
    - Suboptimal connection pool settings
    - Suboptimal session settings
    - Absence of timeout configuration
    - Suboptimal sizing at the infrastructure layer
    - Code not built with modular and extensible design
    - Absence of layer-wise caching
    - Absence of iterative performance testing

Suboptimal Deployment Architecture

The deployment topology of the application is not optimal, leading to decreased performance.

- **Problem symptoms**
    - The CPU and memory utilization of the servers was more than 80% at a normal load and exceeded to 95% at peak load.
    - The response time and performance of the application gradually decrease with an increase in load.
- **Root cause analysis**
    - Multiple applications deployed on the same physical server in production
    - Three applications were deployed on the same server in the production and the disaster recovery (DR) environment. The topology shared the CPU and the memory of the server leading to scalability issues.
    - Performance testing revealed that this setup was not scalable.
    - CPU utilization graphs show peaks and troughs. This is attributed to problems with one of the applications that was not scalable.

- Due to the non-scalable behavior of the application, dependent applications were not able to support the projected volumes with this setup

- After the team simulates a non-scalable application on a separate server, see if projected volumes were met and if the system is scalable.

- With this new setup, the system was scalable and supported the projected volumes.

- **Applications deployed on admin server**

  - Admin servers are typically used for monitoring, configuration, and so forth.

  - Admin applications are deployed separately from the main application. If the application is deployed on the admin server, any application issue (say memory leak) may bring down the server on which the main application is deployed. If the admin server goes down, diagnosis is not possible.

Performance Optimization Recommendations

This section explains the steps and recommendations to improve the overall end-to-end performance in the request-processing pipeline. It includes recommendation categories based on the findings from the current performance assessment exercise.

Web Performance Optimization Recommendations

The analysis of key pages and web components in main applications identified problem patterns.

The Chrome Lighthouse tool performed the analysis. Table 9-6 features this information and web performance recommendations.

Table 9-6. Performance Recommendations

Problem Pattern	Brief Description	Suggested Remediation Step
Numerous JS and CSS files	Each of the pages has an average 20+ JS files, 18+ CSS files which are not minified	Merge and minify CSS and JS files to create a minimal number of files
Numerous images	Many pages have 50+ images	• Reduce image number through CSS Sprite • Compress images • Lazily load the images
The positioning of JS and CSS files	All JavaScript files are placed at the top of the page, which blocks the page load	Place CSS at the top and JS at the bottom to optimize perceived page load time
Non-caching of static assets	In almost all the pages, the caching headers are not set for static assets (images, JS, CSS files). On average, you found 10+ images have cache headers missing	Based on the update frequency, you need to set the cache headers for static assets for optimal performance.
Very high TTFB	Very high TTFB indicates a higher server response time	Implement the server-side recommendations
Large page size	Static assets contribute to high page size	Merging and minification and CSS sprite address this issue. Enable HTML compression at the web server level
Unused CSS files	On average, 3+ CSS pages per page are not used	Remove unused CSS files

Server-side Performance Optimization (Services and Database)

Table 9-7 features the main problem patterns and performance optimizations for the server side (database queries and service invocations).

Table 9-7. *Services and Database Performance Improvement Recommendations*

Problem Pattern	Brief Description	Suggested Remediation Step
Numerous database queries for each page	Sometimes a page results in the execution of numerous queries (for instance, home page results in 13 database queries)	• Minimize the number of database calls. One DB call per page is the best-case scenario • Move all DB logic into database stored procedure so that the database engine can do the heavy lifting • Fine-tune all slow performing queries. • Use the batch/bulk query call supported by hibernate
Database query in a loop	In some scenarios, the query is invoked within a loop	You should completely avoid database calls in a loop. To avoid this, you can create an Oracle-stored procedure to do all the heavy lifting operations and invoke the stored procedure only once from application passing all needed parameters.
Absence of caching	In a few pages, the common data is reused, and you make duplicate database calls to get common data (e.g., user profile data)	Leverage Redis, Memcached, or object cache to cache commonly used data and lookup values.
Optimize WSRP calls and heavyweight XML-based SOAP web service calls	Many pages are slow due to WSRP calls.	Avoid WSRP calls and heavy XML-based SOAP web service calls and fetch data asynchronously or using lightweight REST calls/microservice calls.
Absence of caching	The user profile page and account information page make multiple database calls in real time.	• Retrieve the account data and user profile data through cache instead of a REST call • Minimizes the performance overhead for account information and user profile calls

(continued)

CHAPTER 9 PERFORMANCE ENGINEERING CASE STUDY

Table 9-7. (*continued*)

Problem Pattern	Brief Description	Suggested Remediation Step
Absence of a centralized service layer	There is no centralized services layer. Numerous point-to-point service invocations	• Create a centralized middleware responsible for service orchestration, caching, and data transformation • Creates centralized middleware layer for services • Reduces multiple REST calls
Minimal reusability	Each page invokes a user profile service to create the user profile object leading to a real-time database call.	• Reuses the profile object for subsequent calls after the first call for validating the user • Eliminates duplicate user profile service calls in a single request pipeline
Absence of security tokens	The user profile service makes multiple database calls in real time.	• After the first successful authentication, use the access token with subsequent microservice calls • Eliminates the overhead caused by user profile service
Absence of asynchronous service invocation	All microservices are synchronous, leading to performance issues.	• Invoke all microservices asynchronously by removing any dependency on previous calls. • Asynchronous calls happen in parallel and improve the perceived load time.
Insufficient memory	The wait time and thread block time are high.	• Conduct performance testing to tune the JVM parameters. • XMS, XMX • NewSize, MaxNewSize • PermGen, MaxPermGen

Performance Roadmap

This section lays out the roadmap plan based on performance recommendations for the legacy application. This includes a short-term plan with immediate tactical gains, and the medium-term plan and long-term plan for strategic gains.

Short-Term Plan (30 Days)

A short-term plan targets quick wins that are easily achieved. Table 9-8 features the options to consider in a short-term plan.

Table 9-8. Short-Term Performance Plan

Category	Performance Recommendations
Web Layer	- Cache static assets such as JS, CSS, and Images. Set cache headers appropriately so that browser can cache these assets for an extended duration, improving the response times. - Remove all unnecessary and duplicate CSS, JS files, and broken pages/links. - Position the CSS and JS appropriately for improving the perceived load time. Place CSS at the top and JS at the bottom. - Wherever possible, remove or cache entitlements in themes. - Cache themes, headers, menus, and footers to speed up the page.
Services	- Initiate and fine-tune all service calls. - WSRP should be replaced with lightweight REST calls.
Database	- Initiate and fine-tune all database queries. Target simple fixes and easy to implement query tuning. - Enable the Hibernate L1 and L2 caching.
Infrastructure	- Infrastructure: Set up a robust monitoring infrastructure to alert on service availability and performance SLAs.

CHAPTER 9　PERFORMANCE ENGINEERING CASE STUDY

Medium-Term Plan (60 Days)

Medium-term plan targets to builds upon the optimizations started in a short-term plan. Table 9-9 features the options to consider for a medium-term plan.

Table 9-9. Medium-Term Performance Plan

Category	Performance Recommendations
Web Layer	• Reduce images in each of the pages and use CSS sprites. • Enable page compression and enable image compression.
Services	• Load page asynchronously by AJAX call. • Implement asynchronous pagination is implemented in the search result pages. • Implement user profile caching.
Database	• Fine-tune all database queries. • Avoid the database query in a loop and replace it with a database stored procedure.

Long-Term Plan (>60 Days)

You need to overhaul the overall design and architecture of the application. The design changes to the presentation layer, and the service layer are covered next.

Presentation Layer Rebuilt on Angular Platform

The proposed end-to-end flow is as follows and depicted in Figure 9-3.

- Rebuild the UI and migrate the portlets to the Angular platform.

- Integrate Angular with microservices. The Angular framework invokes the business microservices through gateway service.

- Business microservices are granular services that use databases or enterprise systems to get the required information.

- The business microservices layer caches the frequently fetched service result to improve the performance.

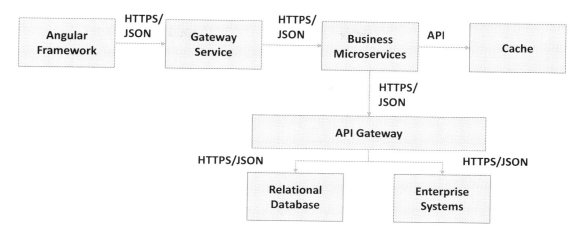

Figure 9-3. *Proposed Angular-based solution architecture*

Web Services Migrated to the Microservices Model

The main advantages of using a microservices-based integration model are as follows.

- Modular microservices bring in decoupled architecture allowing the layers to be changes in a flexible way.

- Enhances the reusability of microservices and provides independent scalability and extensibility.

- Lightweight micro services invoked in asynchronous mode improve the performance.

Hence the proposal is to migrate existing heavy SOAP-based web services and WSRP to lightweight REST-based services. Develop the microservices based on the business capability and UI requirements.

- Design the granularity of the business microservices aligned with the UI needs.

- Design the JSON to have a friendlier data format for the UI needs to reduce the conversion overhead.

The core integration patterns are discussed in Chapter 12. They can be used for microservices.

Chapter 9 Performance Engineering Case Study

Figure 9-4 depicts a reference architecture using cloud-based and container-based scalable microservices.

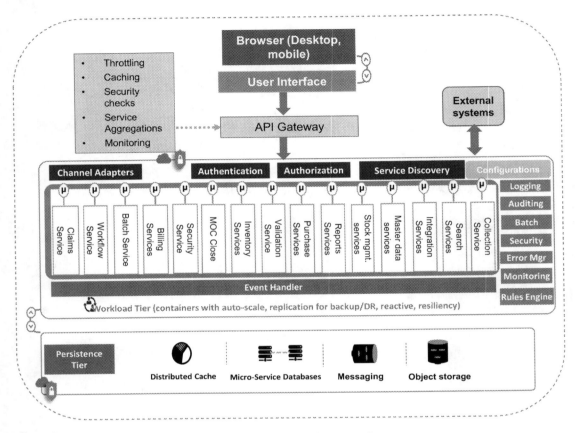

Figure 9-4. *Cloud-based microservices reference architecture*

Architecture Principles for Modern Solution Architecture

Architecture principles modernize the current architecture of the application, bringing in a microservices container-based approach with a cloud-integrated solution. Figure 9-5 depicts the core architecture principles for modern solutions.

CHAPTER 9 PERFORMANCE ENGINEERING CASE STUDY

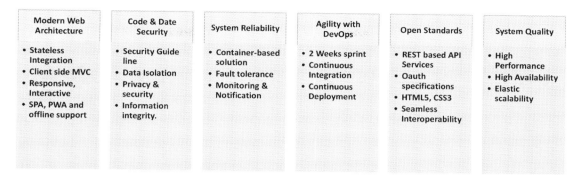

Figure 9-5. *Modern web architecture principles*

The key solution expectations and the design guidelines for modern web platforms are depicted in Table 9-10.

Table 9-10. *Core Solution Tenets*

Solution Expectations	Design Guidelines	Benefits
Fully leverage cloud services	Platform-based design	• Reduce the cost of running datacenters • Speed and agility in bringing up automation and DevOps practices with the usage of cloud services • Reduced build/deployment costs • Quicker go to market • Scalable and highly available, leveraging autoscaling features • High operational efficiency in bringing serverless and PaaS modules

(*continued*)

Table 9-10. (*continued*)

Solution Expectations	Design Guidelines	Benefits
Microservices containerized platform API-based integrations	Monolithic to microservices refactoring	• Independent business domain services bringing agile deployments and fewer downtimes that increases high operational efficiency • Services replicate along both the x and y axis of the scalability cube, autoscale by load • Built-in resiliency, hardened against failures • Versioning with consumer-specific contracts, the central registry for service discovery/lookup • Centralized monitoring, logging • Loosely coupled modules that make good maintainability with ease of use for troubleshooting • Portable across any platform as easily adaptable to containerized platform • API-based integrations that make highly extensible and adaptable across multiple systems • Standard and consistent user experience
Security, compliance with seamless user management	Highly secure, compliant	• Utilizing the benefits of cloud security standards • OAuth 2 for REST API–based authorizations • Deploying firewalls, network segregation, authentication, authorization, and selective encryption of datasets in transit and rest
Maintainability and monitoring as the solution scales up	Error log, performance KPI, ease of troubleshoot	• Cloud monitoring stack for generating notifications for high resource consumption usage • API audit mechanisms • Automations for resource optimizations • Capturing audit and error logs • Self-healing capabilities without much downtime

Summary

- The performance engineering exercise provides a holistic and end-to-end performance analysis of the application.

- Performance engineering is a holistic exercise to identify, test, analyze, and report performance issues and recommendations.

- The performance engineering process includes stages such as requirements and KPI definition, performance test strategy and design, iterative performance test execution, performance analysis, and recommendation and performance engineering report.

- As part of web performance analysis, you perform the web frameworks and JavaScript framework analysis, page load times, and page size analysis for key pages, presentation component analysis, and web analytics report analysis.

- During server-side analysis, you test the performance of the business components, services, database queries, and other server-side solution components. Infrastructure analysis includes capacity and network analysis, Server configuration analysis, cache configuration analysis, and Infrastructure recommendation.

- As part of performance testing, you conduct load testing and stress testing.

- Based on the insights from performance testing and bottleneck analysis, performance optimization recommendations are provided for web components and server components.

PART V

Performance Patterns

CHAPTER 10

Modern Web Performance Patterns

Modern web platforms need high performance to fulfill the expectations of Internet users, and elastic scalability to absorb increased user loads, data loads, and high availability. The presentation layer has seen maximum disruption in terms of challenges and technologies. The crucial success factors for the presentation layer are performance, interactivity, responsiveness, and availability. Web users expect seamless rendering of modern web platforms on various devices and channels with optimal performance. Modern web platforms should scale to a large volume of web users.

The patterns provide a proven best-practices approach for known problems. Each design pattern has a context and drivers that characterize the problem scenario. The design pattern–based solution provides repeatable, extensible, and scalable methods to address a problem with good performance. Each pattern defines several variations, advantages, best-fit scenarios, and tools that implement the solution.

This chapter discusses the best practices and proven performance patterns for modern web platforms. The performance patterns address commonly occurring and complex problems related to performance, scalability, and integration. The first section discusses common performance-related challenges, patterns, and best practices. Later sections dive into progressive web app–related patterns, cache-aside patterns, the PRPL pattern, and the isomorphic pattern. The final section discusses modern web scenarios and applicable patterns.

Performance engineers, web developers, digital architects, project managers, and program managers should find this chapter useful.

CHAPTER 10   MODERN WEB PERFORMANCE PATTERNS

Presentation Patterns and Best Practices

This section briefly explains the commonly used presentation patterns, antipatterns, and best practices.

Common Performance Antipatterns

Performance antipatterns are the known challenges that later become bottlenecks and issues. Mistakes in design and implementation lead to performance antipatterns.

As part of a performance engineering exercise, you identify performance antipatterns in an existing application, and then design best practices and a performance pattern to address the antipatterns.

First, let's look at common performance antipatterns.

Resource-Related Antipatterns

The following are resource-related antipatterns.

- Too many assets on the web page result in frequent server request impacting the page load time.

- Large-sized assets bloat the overall web page size, resulting in increased bandwidth consumption and slower page response times.

- Non-optimized images result in a heavy asset size on the page leading to higher first meaningful paint (FMP).

- Multiple versions of the same file or unnecessary files on the web page lead to unnecessary requests.

- Non-minified versions of scripts and stylesheets appear on the web page.

Testing-related Antipatterns

The following are testing-related antipatterns.

- The absence of compatibility testing on all supported browsers and mobile devices leads to user experience and performance challenges

- The absence of performance testing for various loads from various geographies and on various devices

CHAPTER 10   MODERN WEB PERFORMANCE PATTERNS

Other Antipatterns

The following are antipatterns for exception handling, usability, and other areas.

- Improper handling of errors (timeouts, application errors, connection errors) on the page results in usability issues on the page

- Suboptimal sizing of the infrastructure components such as CPU cores, memory, server nodes based on the performance and scalability requirements

- Absence of performance monitoring setup to monitor the response time in real time

Common Presentation Patterns

The following are some of the most widely used presentation patterns.

- **UI composition pattern**: A single web page is composed of multiple independently developed UI components or fragments. Different teams can independently develop the UI components in parallel that loads the content asynchronously. These independent UI components can be managed and deployed easily.

- **Page templates**: you can create a common page layout that defines the page structure. A template provides common elements such as navigations, header/footer, brand style, layout (grid, card, list, etc.). You can then reuse these page templates for rendering various pages by loading the data into the corresponding UI component.

- **Resource prefetching**: The client application prefetches the required resources, links to optimize the initial response time. Upon receiving the prefetch hint, the browser prefetches the specified documents, images in the background, and caches the resource. HTTP/2 protocol provides a push mechanism to optimize the server-side push.

- **Cloud-first approach**: In this approach, all fresh and reimagined solutions are built using cloud-native technologies. The cloud-first approach leverages the PaaS (platform as service), SaaS (software as service) model to minimize the IT maintenance cost. The cloud

275

CHAPTER 10   MODERN WEB PERFORMANCE PATTERNS

infrastructure is prioritized over the on-premise infrastructure. The approach advocates to migrate existing and legacy applications to the cloud iteratively.

- **Network independent design**: The design is applicable for mobile apps wherein you gracefully handle the network outages by providing offline user experience. You leverage the mobile's local storage and sync it with the remote server when the network connection is resumed.

- **Mobile-first approach**: The approach advocates to build user experiences primarily for mobile users. In the mobile-first approach, the user interface screens, data, navigation, information architecture, security, performance are designed for mobile devices and later expand it to tablets and desktop devices. Responsive web design (RWD), progressive web apps (PWA), graceful degradation, progressive advancement, offline experience are some of the core features of mobile-first design.

- **Minimalistic design**: Ensure that the design for the home pages and landing pages are simple and mobile-friendly. A minimalistic design includes only basic and needed UI components on the home page and landing page. The minimalistic design reduces the asset count, page size, network requests to improve the initial page load time. Instead of loading the complete JavaScript framework and CSS framework, conditionally load the required files on the page.

- **Separation of concerns**: In multi-layered enterprise architecture, each layer is responsible for handling single responsibility. Separation of concerns provides loose coupling and provides flexibility at each of the layers.

- **Single-page application (SPA)**: The SPA consists of a single page for the entire web site. The JavaScript framework loads the data dynamically based on events and user actions. The browser loads all the required JavaScript, CSS, and images on the initial page load. SPAs provide simple, intuitive, responsive, and native-mobile app-like features.

- **Micro frontends**: The web application is composed of independently developed frontend modules composed into a single view. The micro frontends address the frontend monolith problem, just like the way microservices address the monolith applications. In a micro frontend pattern, each module/app is self-contained, technology agnostic, and are developed by different teams independently using their favorite frontend technology.

Presentation Layer Best Practices

The following are key presentation layer best practices.

- You need to optimize the first meaningful paint (FMP) and time to interactive (TTI) for all the pages. You can use tools such as Chrome Lighthouse to identify the resources blocking the critical render path.

- Avoid any synchronous AJAX calls and synchronous service calls to third-party services and scripts.

- Optimize the content load times for the above-the-fold content.

- Identify the UI components that need huge data and optimize the data load for the same.
    - Introduce server-side pagination for large lists.
    - Load the data on demand for the lists with sliders.

- As the JavaScript frameworks are costly web resources that need to be downloaded, parsed, and compiled, optimize the load and execution of JavaScript.
    - Load and execute the JavaScript asynchronously.
    - Load and execute the JavaScript on-demand.
    - Use the single-page application (SPA) architecture only for appropriate scenarios. For simple static web sites such as blogs, campaigns, you can use traditional multi-page applications.

CHAPTER 10   MODERN WEB PERFORMANCE PATTERNS

- Identify the unnecessary files that cause potential performance overhead and block the critical render path in the default JavaScript frameworks and include only the needed JavaScript.
- Minify and merge the JavaScript to reduce the bandwidth consumed.

In subsequent sections, let's deep-dive into some of the most popular presentation patterns, such as progressive web architecture (PWA), cache-aside pattern, PRPL pattern, and isomorphic pattern.

Progressive Web Architecture (PWA) Patterns

A responsive web pattern is used in responsive web applications (RWA). They are gaining immense popularity. PWAs improve both mobile web and native mobile apps by providing enhanced user engagement. The following are some of the key features of progressive web applications.

- You can implement a native mobile app–like experience through PWAs and provide features such as push notifications, self-updates, and so forth. PWAs are discoverable by search engines, linkable/shareable, installable, and responsive.
- PWAs are built on progressive enhancement capabilities providing basic functionality to all and providing more sophisticated functionality for the modern browsers that support the underlying technologies.
- PWAs can be added to the home screen similar to the native mobile apps and seamlessly updated, providing a frictionless installation experience.
- PWAs are fast and enhance user engagement.
- PWAs are network independent, providing offline capabilities, network independence, and offers.
- PWAs can do a partial page refresh to render the updated content on the browser.
- PWAs are safe because they are rendered over HTTPS.

CHAPTER 10   MODERN WEB PERFORMANCE PATTERNS

PWAs include various patterns such as client-side rendering (CSR), server-side rendering (SSR), an app shell. Progressive web patterns are discussed next.

Context

The mobile web users expect high performance, responsive, and interactive web applications. Web users also expect frictionless installation and safe web platforms. The web platforms should leverage the strengths of partial updates to provide optimal render time and response time.

Drivers

The following are the main drivers of the PWA.

- The web platform should provide a fast-performing web application.
- The first meaningful paint and time to interactive for the web page should be minimum. The rest of the views are loaded based on user navigation and user interaction.
- The web platform should work on multiple desktop browsers and mobile browsers.
- The web user should be able to get native mobile app features such as push notifications.

Core Patterns

Progressive web architecture relies upon various patterns and technologies. The key patterns are server-side rendering, client-side rendering, app shell, and service worker. These core patterns are briefly discussed next.

Server-side Rendering (SSR)

In the SSR approach, the web page is fully rendered on the server. The server sends the entire DOM as a single document to the browser. Hence the browser can load the first page quickly based on the server capacity. When the user navigates across pages for downloading new DOM content, the browser must make the server call making the page navigations slower compared to that of client-side rendering.

CHAPTER 10   MODERN WEB PERFORMANCE PATTERNS

The following scenarios are best suited for SSR.

- The web platforms that have static page content such as news, blogs, product information, marketing information, campaigns can use the SSR.

- The web platforms that need to have a high level of compatibility across various browsers, devices, and the ones that need mature tools and technologies can use SSR.

Client-side Rendering (CSR)

The CSR renders completely on the client-side (browser) using the JavaScript framework for DOM manipulation and to render the HTML. As the complete rendering happens on the browser end, the user navigations, button clicks are very fast. CSR rerenders the portions of the page that have changed or updated based on user interaction.

The following scenarios are best suited for CSR.

- The web platforms that have static page layout can use the CSR.

- The web platforms with a high level of interactivity (drag and drop, zoom, slider, sorting, charts and graphs, etc.) can leverage the client-side rendering.

- E-commerce platforms, social media platforms that need frequent dynamic data can use CSR.

- The applications that can load the data asynchronously can leverage CSR.

Hybrid Option of Using Both CSR and SSR

You can combine both CSR and SSR to reap the benefits of both the technologies. For the initial page rendering, you can use the SSR and cache the app shell. For subsequent user navigations and user interactions, you can use CSR.

Service Worker

The service worker is a JavaScript-based component that runs separately from the main UI thread. The service worker caches the page content and handles network requests and user interactions. After registration, the service worker acts as a data fetch proxy and automatically caches the requests based on the rules. The service worker runs in the background handling all the needed events. The service worker handles the following responsibilities.

- To provide offline capabilities, the service worker acts as a proxy by intercepting the network request. The service worker is responsible for handling push notifications. During offline mode, the service worker stores the user tasks and synchronizes the tasks with the server once the application is online.

- Based on the nature of the data, the service worker can adopt a suitable caching strategy. If the data (e.g., image or CSS) rarely changes, the service worker can adopt the cache first and use a network fallback strategy. When the data frequently changes or if the user expects fresh data, the service worker could use the network first with cache as the fallback option.

App Shell

The app shell consists of the minimal resources (e.g., CSS, JavaScript, and HTML) required to load the skeleton of the application without the actual content. The app shell loads the minimal user interface (the shell or the application skeleton) almost instantly. For instance, an e-commerce platform loads the basic view layouts, fonts, marquee images to render the basic first page. The JavaScript dynamically updates the page view content based on user actions such as navigation, button clicks, and so forth.

The service worker delivers the shell quickly and caches the content making the application available in offline mode. The key features of the app shell are as follows.

- The app shell should include only the minimal UI so that it can load fast.

- The app shell should be able to cache the static assets from the local cache.

- The app content should separate the dynamic page content from the page navigation.

An example of an app shell with minimal UI, including a top header, fonts, and associated CSS, is depicted in Figure 10-1. The page with only the words Books and Recommendations form the app shell. The content for the Books and Recommendations sections are loaded dynamically using client-side loading through JavaScript.

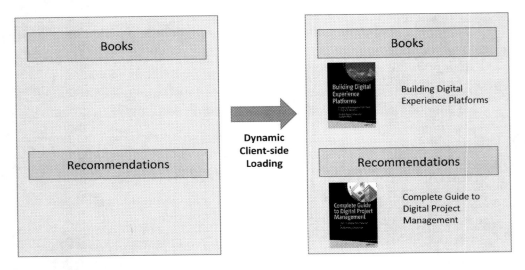

Figure 10-1. App shell example

High-Level Flow

The main solution components for progressive web architecture include service workers and app shells, as depicted in Figure 10-2.

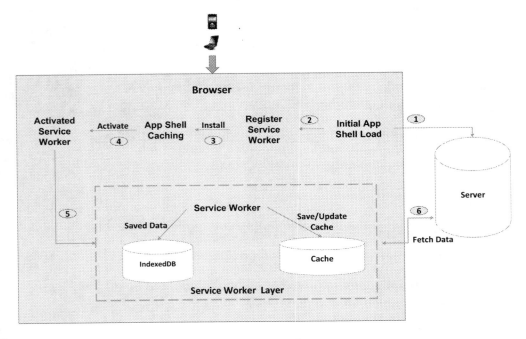

Figure 10-2. Progressive web application architecture

CHAPTER 10   MODERN WEB PERFORMANCE PATTERNS

The high-level steps of the rendering of the PWA are as follows.

- Only service workers supporting browsers register the service worker. If the service worker is not supported, the browser directly invokes the server APIs to fetch the data.

- Once the service worker is registered, the service worker handles the install event. The service worker then renders the app shell (consisting of core HTML template, CSS, fonts, JavaScript), caches it, and handles all future site navigations. After the app shell is rendered, the web app loads the content dynamically using the AJAX calls (XMLHTTPRequest). The service worker handles the fetch events that are triggered by the page requests.

- The Service worker can use the cached data if the application is offline or can get the data from the server. The service worker uses Cache API to manage the application cache. The service worker stores the previous session data in IndexedDB.

- If the application needs dynamic data, the service worker gets the data from the server. The server worker can get the data to partially rerender the page.

Considerations

The following are the main considerations for the progressive web application patterns.

- You can develop the progressive web app based using server-side rendering, client-side rendering, and app shell. Based on the application needs, you need to select a suitable combination of PWA patterns.

- The web platforms, such as publishing platforms with static content, can use app shell and SSR for initial page rendering. For subsequent page navigations and user interactions, you can use CSR.

CHAPTER 10   MODERN WEB PERFORMANCE PATTERNS

- Web platforms that have a high degree of dynamic data, such as e-commerce platforms or social media platforms, can use the app shell and CSR for delivering dynamic data.

- PWAs provide the perfect opportunity to migrate existing mobile web sites.

Variations

The following are the variations of the progressive web application patterns.

- Initial page rendering handled by SSR along with the app shell. Subsequent updates are done through CSR.

- Handle all the dynamic updates through CSR.

Advantages

The main advantages of progressive web apps are as follows.

- You can implement the mobile-first strategy using PWAs, which provide fast initial render time by leveraging the app shell and SSR. You can optimize the subsequent page navigations and event handling through CSR.

- PWAs provide offline capabilities and other features, such as push notifications and background synchronization.

- PWAs provide platform-agnostic web experience.

- Leverage PWAs as an alternative to native mobile apps for slower network and lesser bandwidth scenarios.

Table 10-1 highlights the core solution tenets for modern web applications.

CHAPTER 10 MODERN WEB PERFORMANCE PATTERNS

Table 10-1. Core Solution Tenets

Solution Tenets	Solution
Easy Discoverability	• Since PWAs are web applications at the core, they are discoverable by search engines. They are accessible on the browsers and can install on the home screen on the mobile device to provide an app-like experience. • An automatic prompt is available for Android devices. For iOS, a prompt to show the installation link can help users with the installation.
Enhanced Engagement	• Push notifications enable to reengage the users on to the application. In-app notifications, SMS, or email notifications can engage mobile users.
Quick to Market	• MVP/phase approach to releasing quickly to market • PWA is developed using a headless approach on top of an existing ecosystem with content authoring and publishing is handled in existing CMS • Content authoring and publishing is handled in existing CMS • Minimal development or modification at backend services
Connectivity Independent	• PWAs provide the option to cache the data in the browser and use it when there is poor or no connectivity. • The best of caching strategy is based on the outcome of the discovery to provide an effective offline experience.
Robust Performance	• Service workers are JavaScript files that run separately from the main browser thread allowing caching of assets, enabling good performance compared to the traditional web. • The application is lightweight due to decoupled architecture with headless content, with a lightweight frontend façade, which improves performance.
Cost-Effective	• PWAs are platform-agnostic, be it desktop, tablet, or mobile devices. The same application performs well on the web and mobile devices, including Android and iOS. Develop once and use across browsers and devices.

CHAPTER 10 MODERN WEB PERFORMANCE PATTERNS

Relevant Use Cases

The following scenarios are ideal for using progressive web app patterns.

- You can use a combination of app shell and CSR/SSR for building e-commerce platforms and social media platforms.

- You can use CSR for developing highly interactive web applications that need complex features such as drag and drop and client-side animations.

- You can use a combination of CSR and SSR for publishing platforms such as news, blogs, and wikis.

Tools and Technologies

You can implement the PWAs using Angular tools such as ahead-of-time (AoT) compilation, service worker, service worker precache. Ionic 2 framework based on Angular can be used for the development of the PWAs.

Cache-Aside Pattern

The cache-aside pattern improves data access performance. The data is stored close to the access layer to improve performance.

Context

The presentation layer depends on the data (database data, web content, service data). The web pages predominantly have static content.

Drivers

The following are the main challenges.

- The presentation layer makes frequent chatty calls to the data sources to fetch the data.

- Frequent resource invocations impact page performance and the user experience.

CHAPTER 10   MODERN WEB PERFORMANCE PATTERNS

Solution

A cache system stores the frequently accessed data to improve data access performance. The cache system stores the values in memory as a key-value pair.

The following is the high-level flow of the caching system, and it is depicted in Figure 10-3.

- For the first-time read, the client loads the data from the data source, such as a database.

- The client loads the cache with the data with appropriate expiration time. The cache expiration time is set up based on the update frequency of the data. For instance, the lookup list of countries change rarely and hence can be cached for an extended duration, whereas a project list changes frequently and must be cached only for a minimal duration.

- For subsequent reads, the client checks the cache for the requested data; if the data is not cached, the client reads the data from the data source and caches the new data. If the data is cached, the client uses the cached data.

- For write operations, the client uses the persistence manager to insert, update, or delete the data. The persistence manager refreshes/updates the cache for relevant data and updates the data source.

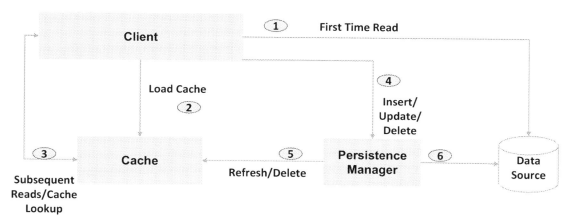

Figure 10-3. High-level flow of a caching system

Considerations

The following are the main considerations for the cache-aside pattern.

- The cache size should be configured based on the cached data.

- The cache eviction algorithm (e.g., eviction policies based on least frequently accessed, first in first out) should be fine-tuned based on the cache access patterns.

- Heavy-duty one-time computations, responses from costly queries and resource calls, static lookup data are ideal cache candidates.

- You can preload the cache during the application startup, called *cache priming*, to improve the application performance.

- The cache monitoring system should be set up to monitor the key cache metrics (cache hit ratio, cache miss ratio, cache size, etc.).

- The read-through and write-through cache system should synchronize the data with the underlying database to maintain data consistency.

- The cached data should be replicated across all cache nodes in the cluster for a distributed caching system.

- The lifetime of the cached items should be based on the frequency of the data change. For example, the country list data does not often change; hence you can cache it for a week.

- Some of the read-through and write-through caching systems use the asynchronous pattern to read/write the data from the data source. This potentially creates a time lag to reflect the latest data.

- The cached data can be offloaded to a disk to extend the cache capacity.

- A clustered cache provides high availability, and it should support cache replication across cluster nodes.

CHAPTER 10 MODERN WEB PERFORMANCE PATTERNS

Variations

An enhancement to the normal cache-aside system provides the read-through and write-through capabilities, as depicted in Figure 10-4.

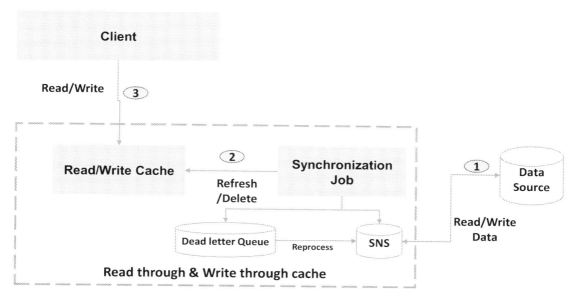

Figure 10-4. Read-through and write-through cache

The following are brief steps of read-through and write-through caches.

- The client sends all the read and writes requests to the cache system. The cache system is responsible for ensuring the reading and writing the latest requested data from the data source.

- The synchronization job uses the subscription pattern (simple notification service) to update the data source asynchronously.

- The synchronization job logs the errors in the centralized system (e.g., dead letter queue) so that you can retry the failed transactions.

The following are variants of caching.

- You can leverage the caching headers (max-age, cache-controls, expires) to cache the static assets at the browser end. Images, scripts and stylesheets, and other static resources that rarely change can leverage browser caching.

CHAPTER 10   MODERN WEB PERFORMANCE PATTERNS

- A content delivery network (CDN) provides edge-side caching to serve the assets and resources from the nearest possible location (also known as an *edge*) to the requested client. Static web pages, images, videos, media files, binary files are best suited for CDN-layer caching.

Advantages

The main advantages of the cache-aside pattern is that you can improve overall page performance and solution scalability. In a read-through and write-through caching solution, the solution design is simple because the cache system abstracts the read and write operations.

Relevant Use Cases

The following scenarios are ideal for using a cache-aside pattern.

- Applications that predominantly use static data.
- Applications that frequently fetch the data from the database or service.
- Applications have more reads than write operations. If the read/write ratio is 60:40 or more, the application can greatly benefit from the cache-aside pattern.

Tools and Technologies

You can use multiple elegant caching frameworks such as Redis, Oracle Coherence, and Memcached.

PRPL Pattern

The PRPL (push, render, precache, and lazy load) pattern helps deliver progressive web apps (PWA), making them interactive and faster. The key components of the PRPL pattern are given below:

CHAPTER 10   MODERN WEB PERFORMANCE PATTERNS

- **Push** the critical resources.
- **Render** the initial route quickly.
- **Precache** the remaining assets.
- **Lazily load** the remaining routes and data.

The PRPL pattern optimizes the load time for the resources (images, CSS, and JavaScript) needed for the current page. The PRPL pattern reduces the initial page load time and optimizes the FMP and TTI. The browser need not load and execute the unnecessary resources, and the bandwidth consumed is reduced.

Context

The progressive web apps (PWA) need to deliver the pages quickly to optimize the first-time page load. You need to optimize the FMP and TTI to the smallest extent possible to make the page interactive at the earliest. The pattern is useful for mobile devices to provide high performance and offline capability.

Drivers

The following are the main drivers of the PRPL pattern.

- The PWA apps download and execute numerous stylesheets, images, and CSS files, adding performance overhead.
- The initial page loads potentially unnecessary resources consuming larger bandwidth impacting page size.
- The mobile users demand lower FMP and TTI for the PWA apps on mobile devices.

Solution

The PRPL pattern essentially loads the critical resources optimally. The core idea is to load the critical resources needed for the above-the-fold content (the content in the visible range of the user) is loaded quickly. PRPL pattern ensures that the PWA applications are loaded with minimal TTI as the amount of data loaded is less.

CHAPTER 10   MODERN WEB PERFORMANCE PATTERNS

The various steps of the PRPL pattern are shown in Figure 10-5.

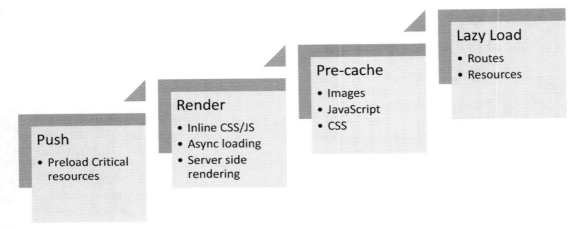

Figure 10-5. PRPL pattern steps

Push

Identify the critical resources that are in the critical path that loads the above-the-fold content. You can use tools such as Google Chrome Lighthouse to audit the critical resources (fonts, scripts, styles, images, XHR requests, etc.) that are blocking the load of above-the-fold content. Once you identify the critical content, you can proactively preload it as follows in the <head> element.

```
<link rel="preload" as="style" href="js/app.css">
<link rel="preload" as="script" href="js/app.js">
```

You can also leverage the HTTP/2 server push using the Link: rel=preload HTTP header. The HTTP/2 enabled web servers to push the corresponding resources to the browser-based on these headers.

Render

Identify all the render-blocking resources required for the FMP and improve the render time as follows.

- Use inline scripts or inline CSS for the render-blocking content to improve the initial load time.
- Defer the non-essential resources and load the content asynchronously.

Render the completed HTML to the browser using server-side caching.

292

CHAPTER 10　MODERN WEB PERFORMANCE PATTERNS

Precache

The service worker caches the required resources such as JavaScripts and CSS files in the background. The service worker proxy can use the cached assets to provide offline experience and to improve the performance.

Essentially the service worker fetches all the essential resources needed for the application shell. Once the resources are cached, it is faster for the browser to retrieve the resources for the subsequent requests.

Lazy Load

Delay the loading of non-critical resources until they are needed. Identify the resources that satisfy the following criteria.

- The assets that are below the fold or outside the viewport of the device
- The assets that need numerous network calls

Use code-splitting to create chunks of the bundles and lazily load the chunks on demand.

Considerations

The following are the main considerations for a PRPL pattern.

- You should only preload only the needed critical resources for the page.
- For the HTTP/2 server push, the server should not push too many assets or unused assets or cached assets.

Variations

You can also use the PRPL methods in SPA and regular JavaScript-based applications.

Advantages

The following are the main advantages of the PRPL pattern.

- The PRPL pattern improves the initial page load time, first meaningful paint, and time to interactive.
- The PRPL pattern reduces the payload size for the initial page load.

CHAPTER 10   MODERN WEB PERFORMANCE PATTERNS

- The PRPL pattern enables the offline capability for web applications.
- The PRPL pattern complements the PWA to improve the mobile web experience.

Relevant Use Cases

The following are scenarios that are ideal for using a PRPL pattern.

- PWA and SPA applications development
- JavaScript-based web applications.
- Mobile web applications.

Tools and Technologies

For Angular Framework, you can use the built-in service workers, lazy loading feature, and bundling features for implementing the PRPL pattern. You can use blazy.js and LazyLoad modules for lazy loading.

Google Chrome Lighthouse tool can be reused to analyze the critical render path and render-blocking resources.

Isomorphic Pattern

Isomorphic applications execute on both the server-side and client-side, which maintains better code, is SEO-friendly, and engages user experience. Isomorphic applications also provide faster rendering of first-page loads.

Context

The web applications need to deliver the pages in quick time to optimize the first-time page load. You need to optimize the FMP and TTI to the smallest extent possible to make the page interactive at the earliest. The pattern is useful for mobile devices to provide high performance and offline capability.

CHAPTER 10   MODERN WEB PERFORMANCE PATTERNS

Drivers

The following are the main drivers.

- Have a single code base for both client and server.
- The web platform should be SEO-friendly.
- The web platform should provide good performance with reduced maintainability.
- The web platform should render on non-JS enabled clients.

Solution

The isomorphic application provides a single code base that runs on both the client end and the server end. Figure 10-6 depicts the various components of an isomorphic application.

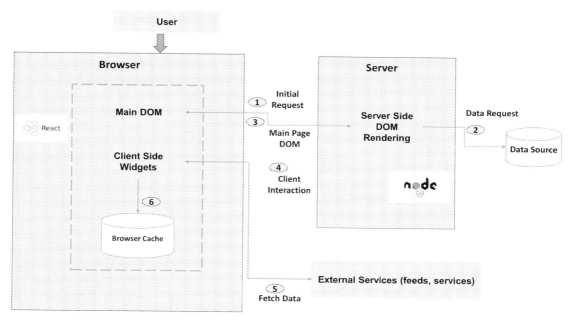

Figure 10-6. Isomorphic application flow

CHAPTER 10 MODERN WEB PERFORMANCE PATTERNS

The high-level steps of the isomorphic application are as follows.

- The user requests a SPA application that contains data (i.e., product data), client-side widgets, and third-party plugins (Twitter feeds, stock price widget, etc.). The client-side widgets should be placed below the fold to improve the FMP and TTI.

- When the user requests for the web page, the isomorphic application invokes the server API for the page DOM.

- The server identifies the data that needs to be rendered. The server component gets the product data from the main data source. For the client-side widgets (that are only rendered on browser end), the server component renders the placeholder layout.

- Upon receiving the page DOM, the browser parses and renders the page. Users can view the above-the-fold page content so that the user can interact with the page.

- The client-side widgets, such as the feed widget, uses AJAX/XHR calls to get the required feed data.

- For each of the user interaction (navigation, button clicks, etc.), the SPA application uses the client-side rendering to update the page partially.

Considerations

The following are the main considerations for an isomorphic application.

- Testing and debugging isomorphic applications are challenging, and hence the unit testing must be designed to handle the server-only and common scenarios.

- Identify the SEO requirements and its criticality of the application.

- The SPA applications that don't have strict performance requirements and strict SEO requirements, isomorphic architecture are overhead.

Advantages

The main advantages of the isomorphic applications are as follows.

- The first-time page load is highly optimized, and the application improves the perceived performance, TTI, and FMP.
- You can overcome the initial page load delays associated with SPA.
- You can enable SEO easily with better search engine indexability.
- The isomorphic applications use a single code base that is easy to maintain and reduces the cost.
- A uniform data model can be used for both client-side rendering and server-side rendering. As the main portion of the page uses server-side rendering, you can render the main page without JavaScript support.

Relevant Use Cases

The following scenarios are ideal for using an isomorphic application.

- Web applications such as e-commerce applications that have strong SEO requirements
- Development teams that need a single code base for server and client end.
- Web platforms that need optimal TTI and FMP.

Tools and Technologies

Node JS server executes code on the server end. You can use JavaScript libraries such as Rendr, Meteor, Derby, Lazo.js, and React.js for implementing the isomorphic applications.

CHAPTER 10　MODERN WEB PERFORMANCE PATTERNS

Modern Web Scenarios

This section describes the common applications of presentation patterns for the core scenarios of a modern web platform.

Table 10-2 identifies the scenarios, significant use cases, and suitable data patterns.

Table 10-2. *Patterns for Modern Web Scenarios*

Modern Web Platform Scenario	Considerations	Suitable Data Patterns
E-commerce web platforms	High performance with minimal FMP Cater to desktop browsers and mobile devices Provide native app-like experience Increase user engagement Complement the native mobile app	Use PWA with client-side rendering (CSR) Use the PRPL pattern to complement the PWA pattern PWA with CSR
Social media platforms (content sharing, feeds)	Enable multi-channel access Fast initial response time Provide information sharing	
Mobile Web Platforms (providing lite versions)	Enable push notifications Enable offline browsing Provide a lighter alternative for native apps	
Collaboration platforms (blogs, wikis)	Handle large content volume Provide content search feature	Use PWA with server-side rendering (SSR) Enable on-demand content prefetching
Static web platforms (Product information web platforms, campaign platforms, marketing platforms)	High response times for static content Enable SEO for the pages	Use traditional multi-page web applications with the cache-aside pattern.

CHAPTER 10　MODERN WEB PERFORMANCE PATTERNS

Summary

- The most common antipatterns are high asset count, large size asset, duplicate and unnecessary assets, including unminified scripts, absence of compatibility testing and performance testing, improper error handling, improper infra sizing, Absence of performance monitoring.

- The key presentation layer best practices are optimization of key page metrics, avoiding synchronous calls, optimization of content load time, and optimization of JavaScript.

- The common presentation patterns are page templates, UI composition patterns, resource prefetching, cloud-first approach, network-independent design, mobile-first approach, minimalistic design, separation of concerns.

- PWAs provide the best of both the worlds of mobile web and native mobile apps for providing enhanced user engagement.

- The main drivers of the PWA are high performance, multi-device compatibility, native-app like user engagement.

- The SSR approach renders the complete web page

- The CSR renders completely on the client-side (browser) using the JavaScript framework for DOM manipulation and to render the HTML.

- The service worker is responsible for handling network requests and caching. The app shell consists of the minimal resources (CSS, JavaScript, HTML) required to load the skeleton of the application without the actual content.

- The key steps in the PWA flow are service worker registration, app shell rendition, dynamic content load, and session data caching.

- The cache-aside pattern using a cache system stores the frequent access data to improve the data access performance.

- In read-through and write-through cache, the client sends all the requests primarily to the cache system. The PRPL pattern uses push, render, precache, and lazy loading to optimize the initial page delivery.

- Isomorphic applications execute on both the server and on the client-side, which maintains better code, is SEO-friendly, and engages user experience.

CHAPTER 11

Modern Web Data Patterns

Efficient data management is one of the key responsibilities for modern web platforms. Modern web platforms handle large volumes of data to render intuitive interfaces. Analytics and reporting web platforms aggregate and process data from distributed data sources and handle multiple data formats. Social media platforms and collaboration platforms deal with large volumes of hierarchical data and efficiently share and store the data. E-commerce platforms are interested in real-time data updates from multiple data sources. Analytics applications need to do data-crunching for forecasting and calculations. The integration involves the exchange of various formats of data.

The increasing use of Big Data for enterprises requires efficient methods for handling data. The volume, variety, and velocity of the data pose new challenges in maintaining application performance, scalability, and data integrity. As large-scale enterprise data is distributed, you need proven best practices to maintain consistency.

Essentially, modern web platforms need to deal with multiple data-related concerns, such as managing large volumes of data, distributed data processing, data consistency and transaction management, and real-time data handling. Modern web platforms should be designed to address these data-related concerns and scale to handle large volumes of data with optimal performance.

This chapter discusses the patterns that address data-related concerns. These data-related patterns can be effectively used in combination. Most data patterns compliment others to solve a complex problem.

Data-related antipatterns, best practices, and common patterns are explained first. The key rules and data patterns are covered next. Then there is a discussion on the saga pattern, CQRS pattern, data lakes pattern, and NoSQL pattern. In the end, modern web scenarios and applicable data patterns are discussed.

CHAPTER 11 MODERN WEB DATA PATTERNS

Performance engineers, data architects, DBAs, web developers, digital architects, project managers, and program managers should find this chapter useful.

Common Data-related Antipatterns and Best Practices

This section discusses common data-related challenges/antipatterns and best practices for modern web platforms.

Data-related Antipatterns

The following are data-related antipatterns.

- The application uses a real-time complex table to retrieve data from multiple tables, impacting performance and scalability.
- The read and write operations happen on the same database, further impacting performance and scalability.
- The database calls are done synchronously, blocking further processing steps.
- Strict consistency or two-phase commit (2PC) is enforced on distributed data.
- The applications make too many database calls.
- The database sends large amounts of data to the application in the response.

Data-related Best Practices

The following are data-related best practices.

- Use a separate database for read and write operations. The CQRS pattern and event sourcing pattern efficiently handle this.
- Cache the static data in a centralized cache to improve the performance of the database retrieval. Set the cache expiry based on the data update frequency.

- The database calls should happen asynchronously to reduce the performance overhead on the application.

- Batch the data to minimize the back and forth between client and server.

- If the data needs to be retrieved from multiple tables that require a complex join, it is recommended that you create denormalized views or a materialized view, or a NoSQL database to optimize the data retrieval operation.

- For modern web platforms that need a large amount of data on a page, you should fetch lazily only on demand. For instance, you can use pagination to fetch page-wise data when the user selects a page. Similarly, you can load the data for a given slider view instead of the entire list.

- For reporting applications, prepare required report data beforehand in a materialized view and refresh the materialized view frequently.

- For analytical calculations, run frequent jobs to calculate data and store the calculated results in a summary table to avoid real-time complex joins.

Common Data Patterns

Common data patterns are used regularly for modern web platforms. The following are some of the most widely used data patterns.

- **Materialized view pattern**: The data store often persists the data across various tables that may not be suitable for complex real-time queries. This complicates the query and adds a performance overhead to join the data from multiple tables in real-time. As a solution, you can prepopulate the required data in a denormalized view to ease the query and improve performance. The materialized view provides ready-to-use data to improve query performance. Materialized views can be refreshed from source tables periodically. Materialized views provide an efficient solution for reporting and data warehousing applications.

CHAPTER 11   MODERN WEB DATA PATTERNS

- **Index table pattern**: Popular application queries use fewer tables more often than others. Based on the popular and costly queries, define the index tables or lookup tables for the query conditions. The columns used in the "where clause" of the queries becomes the "key" of the index tables. Index tables speed up the query retrieval. If the database supports additional secondary indexes or unique keys, you can leverage those features to speed up the query performance.

- **Data partitioning**: To improve the scalability, security, availability, and performance of the data, you can logically partition the data based on logical categories. You can identify the logical categories based on the analysis of the application domain, complex queries, performance requirements, and data consistency requirements. Business domain, operation type (read or write), geography, or language-based partitioned can be implemented. For maintaining the eventual consistency, you can use data partitioning with event sourcing and CQRS patterns.

- **Idempotent transactions**: Idempotent transactions can be repeatedly executed without impacting the system state. The idempotent transactions can be used to retry the failed transactions.

- **Eventual consistency pattern**: Large-scale distributed databases use horizontally distributed database replicas for high availability and high performance. In such cases, strict consistency is difficult to achieve. The data changes to any of the replicas are asynchronously propagated to other replicas eventually to achieve the eventual consistency. The saga pattern, data lake pattern, and CQRS patterns achieve eventual consistency.

- **Change data capture (CDC) pattern**: The database changes since the last snapshot are converted into an event stream. You can use the row-level timestamp to indicate the updated time. The database changes then trigger the change events to propagate or communicate the changes or can be logged into a system.

- **Data streaming pattern**: In the data streaming architecture, the systems are designed to ingest and process large volumes of continuously streamed raw data in real time. A stream constitutes continuous events flowing from one system to another. Systems such as IoT devices, logs, and real-time analytics generate a huge volume of data. As the streamed data is large and unstructured, the system also provides data processing and data visualization capabilities to identify the patterns in the data. Apache Kafka and AWS Kinesis Data streams are some of the popular stream processing tools.

- **In-memory database (IMDB)**: The IMDB databases primarily uses the system memory/RAM for database storage instead of disk. IMDB uses transaction logs to record the data changes and enable rollback in the future. Real-time and mission-critical applications, data warehouse applications, and analytics platforms use IMDB.

The next few sections discuss the saga pattern, CQRS pattern, data lakes pattern, and NoSQL pattern, which are useful for high scalability and high performance in a distributed database scenario.

Saga Pattern

There are normally multiple systems of record (SORs) in an enterprise scenario for managing enterprise data. In such cases, a complex business transaction is distributed across various databases. You need to maintain consistency and data integrity across all the databases involved in the transaction.

Drivers

The following are the drivers for the saga pattern.

- Maintain the data consistency in a distributed transaction that spans across various databases.
- Ensure eventual consistency for a long-running transaction without using two-phase commit (or long duration locks).
- Provide a rollback mechanism for handling failed transactions.
- The performance of the business transaction should be optimal.
- Eliminate single point of failure.
- Provide a scalable and asynchronous way of data operations.

Solution

In the saga pattern, you define a centralized orchestrator or a choreographer to manage the distributed transaction spanning multiple databases. The saga pattern uses a sequence of compensatory operations to execute rollback operations.

Variations

There are two variations to the saga pattern - Orchestration and Choreography.

Orchestration

In the orchestration model, a centralized orchestrator invokes a sequence of services. The orchestrator can also use a message broker to asynchronously invoke the services using event-based communication. For each event, there is a compensating event to handle the fallback transaction. Figure 11-1 depicts the orchestrator.

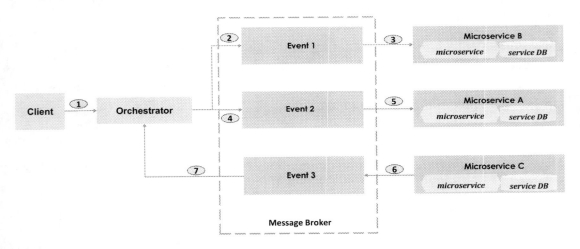

Figure 11-1. Saga orchestrator

Choreography

Each of the services publishes events and subscribes to the events of an event broker. Each of the services takes action based on the received event. If the transaction fails, the corresponding service publishes a new event to the message broker so that the subscribed services can roll back and take appropriate action. Figure 11-2 depicts the choreographer.

CHAPTER 11   MODERN WEB DATA PATTERNS

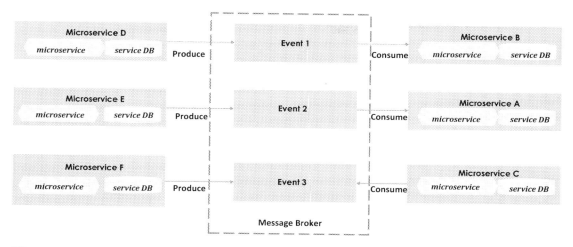

Figure 11-2. Choreography model

Considerations

The following are the considerations for the saga pattern.

- Ensure that there are no cyclic dependencies for a single transaction. You need to design compensatory operations for handling the rollback.

- Use the asynchronous invocations to publish the events and invoke services.

- Use a common unique ID to identify the transaction.

- You can leverage the saga pattern for executing the complex workflows.

Advantages

The following are the main advantages of the saga pattern.

- You can handle the distributed transactions efficiently with high scalability and high performance.

- Ensure the eventual consistency for long-running transactions.

CHAPTER 11 MODERN WEB DATA PATTERNS

Relevant Use Cases

The following are scenarios that are ideal for using the saga pattern.

- Distributed transactions involving multiple database servers. Ensure data consistency, scalability, and performance for distributed transactions.

- Perform rollback through compensatory transactions and events.

Tools and Frameworks

You can use message brokers such as RabbitMQ, Solace, TIBCO, and Apache Kafka to implement the choreography model or event-based model. You can use ESBs such as Mulesoft and API gateways to implement the orchestration.

CQRS Pattern and Event Sourcing Pattern

In a regular enterprise scenario, web platforms need data that is spanning across multiple databases and database schemas. The microservice pattern with database-per-service needs a separate database for each microservice. A complex enterprise scenario that has distributed database transactions spanning multiple databases enforces the data query and data persistence operations that are spread across multiple databases. The complex query and persistence operations should not incur any performance overhead on modern web platforms. A web page needing multiple services ends up querying and posting data to multiple databases without causing performance overhead.

The CQRS pattern provides an efficient way to handle the data retrieval and data persistence across multiple databases.

Drivers

The key drivers for the CQRS pattern are as follows.

- The business transaction involves a sequence of process steps in a task-oriented user interface.

- Query data from multiple databases that need complex joins impacting the real-time performance.

- Create, update, or delete the data from multiple databases efficiently.
- Provide a scalable data query and data persistence methods.
- Ensure data consistency and integrity during data query and data persistence operations.
- Provide high-performance data query and persistence methods.

Solution

To maintain eventual consistency, you use the CQRS pattern with event sourcing pattern. We discuss these two patterns next.

CQRS Pattern

The CQRS consists of two main components: the *command part* and the *query part*. The command part handles the data persistence concern and is used for data insert, update, and delete operations. The query part is responsible for data retrieval.

The CQRS pattern neatly decouples the data retrieval process from the data persistence process providing high performance and scalability. CQRS pattern can be easily implemented in an event-based programming model to provide eventual consistency across query and persistence processes.

Event Sourcing Pattern

Event sourcing pattern uses message publish and subscribe methods to maintain the consistency across multiple data sources providing high scalability and high performance. In the event sourcing model, you define the state of a business entity as an immutable sequence of state-changing events and publish the state changing events to an event store. You can use a queue service or a message broker (such as Apache Kafka topic) to implement the event store. The event store provides APIs to publish and subscribe to the events. The services that are interested in the event can subscribe to the event store and can update based on the events.

As events are immutable, the event model ensures the atomicity of the transaction. Event sourcing also enables a loosely-coupled architecture, where you can easily onboard the new applications.

CHAPTER 11 MODERN WEB DATA PATTERNS

By replaying the event sequence, you can reconstruct the entity state. The event store provides a convenient mechanism for storing the historical data and for auditing purposes.

Since the event store has all events related to the entity state changes, to reprocess the transaction or to roll back the transaction, you can rewind the events in the event store.

Compensating Transaction Pattern

To update an event or to roll back the transaction in an error, the business entity produces a compensatory event to the event store. The transaction in a typical distributed environment spans multiple databases. Hence, to maintain eventual consistency, the compensating transactions involve a sequence of transactions to roll back and undo each of the events.

Handling Failures

If regular transactions fail or a compensating transaction fails, you can log the failures to a centralized location (e.g., a dead-letter queue) and reprocess/retry the transaction. If the first retry fails, analyze the cause for failure; if the failure is permanent (e.g., HTTP 404), cancel the transaction. If the failure is temporary (e.g., HTTP 500), the process can retry after some delay.

Solution Description

The CQRS pattern is used along with event sourcing pattern. Figure 11-3 depicts the main components of the event sourcing pattern.

CHAPTER 11 MODERN WEB DATA PATTERNS

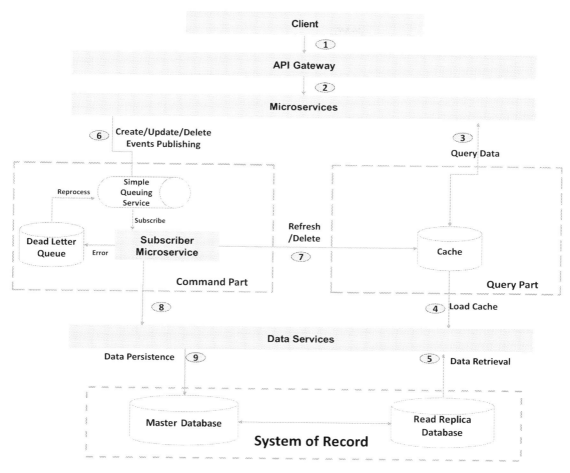

Figure 11-3. *CQRS pattern with event sourcing pattern*

API gateway acts as the single-entry point for all incoming requests. The API gateway routes the requests to the microservice layer. The microservices layer abstracts all the database CRUD (create, read, update, and delete) operations.

Query Part

You are leveraging the cache or a materialized view for optimizing the data retrieval operation. As a prerequisite, you need to prepopulate the cache by loading the cache values (often called a *cache warming*). You can use the read replica of the master database to load the cache. The read replica of the database further optimizes the data retrieval operation. Similarly, you can create a materialized view that provides the denormalized view of the aggregate data.

Once the cache is loaded, or the materialized view is ready, the microservices layer can start executing the data retrieval operations.

Command Part

The create, update, delete events are posted asynchronously to the event store or message broker (such as Amazon Simple Queue Service (SQS) that acts as an event store); you can use Apache Kafka topic as an event store. The subscriber microservice subscribes to the SQS to listen to the CRUD events. Upon receiving the events-related to create/update/delete events, the subscriber microservice orchestrates multiple APIs to update, delete and create database operations asynchronously. The subscriber microservice also updates and refreshes the cache with the data updates.

If there are any errors in the subscriber microservice operation, the errors are stored in the dead-letter queue so that you can use that to reprocess the failed transactions.

Considerations

The following are the main considerations for the pattern.

- The query part relies on eventual consistency. You need to refresh the read replica of the cache from the master database frequently. Similarly, you need to refresh the materialized view or the cache regularly. If the cache/materialized view is not updated, the application gets stale data.

- The event store for handling the original event or compensating transaction should be resilient and not lose the transaction.

Variations

The following are variations of the pattern.

- For the query part, you can use a cache or a denormalized table or a materialized view to get the data.

- For the query part, you can also use the NoSQL-based denormalized database, such as DynamoDB.

Advantages

The main advantages of the CQRS pattern and event sourcing pattern are as follows.

- The solution provides a high performance, fault-tolerant system.
- Provide a loosely coupled interface for query interface and command interface.
- The database read and write operations can scale independently.
- Event sourcing can handle atomic operations efficiently.
- The queries are simplified, and the query operation is optimized for performance.
- Query data from multiple databases that need complex joins impacting the real-time performance.
- Create, update, or delete the data from multiple databases efficiently.
- Provide a scalable data query and persistence methods.
- Ensure data consistency and integrity during data query and data persistence operations.
- Provide high-performance data query and persistence methods.

Relevant Use Cases

The following scenarios are ideal for using the CQRS pattern and event sourcing pattern.

- Applications that need high-performance data queries and persistence operations for transactions spanning multiple database tables, ensuring data consistency and data integrity
- Applications that need highly scalable data queries and persistence operations across multiple databases
- Applications that have complex queries that need to be scaled independently

CHAPTER 11   MODERN WEB DATA PATTERNS

- Applications that tolerate eventual consistency for a data query operation
- Applications in which the screens need the data from multiple databases and require complex table joins quickly in real-time

Tools and Frameworks

You can use messaging systems like Apache Kafka, Solace, and RabbitMQ for implementing a messaging system and an event store. You can use Apache Kafka to implement the event sourcing pattern. For implementing the cache, you can use Redis caching system. Alternatively, you can also use DynamoDB, a NoSQL database, for providing the read interface.

Data Lake Design Pattern

An enterprise data lake centrally stores a vast amount of raw enterprise data in structured, semistructured, and unstructured formats. Since a data lake handles a large volume of data, the key challenges of big data (volume, variety, and velocity) are applicable for data lake scenarios.

Drivers

The following are key drivers for the data lake design pattern.

- Create a centralized repository of all the raw data for the organization.
- Enable data-driven decisions by drawing insights from the holistic organization data.
- Enable self-service for critical business functions.
- Provide high scalability and durability for the organization's data.
- Support heterogeneous data from various data sources.
- Decouple the enterprise computation from the enterprise data storage providing independent scalability.
- Enable layer-wise security for various consumers.

Solution

The data lake architecture has various layers that are built on top of the core raw data. The additional layers add the structure, process the data, enforce security, standardize data to ease the data consumption, and enable various use cases for the organization. The data lake architecture is depicted in Figure 11-4.

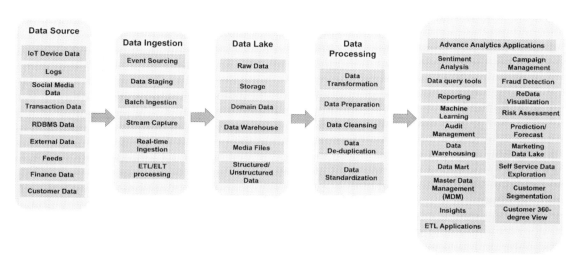

Figure 11-4. Sample data lake architecture

Data Sources

An organization can feed raw data from multiple sources such as IoT sensor data, customer data, finance data, log data, social channel data, e-commerce transaction data, finance data, and operations. The structure and format of the data vary for each of the data sources. When enterprise data lake is integrated with existing data warehouse systems, the raw data can be pushed to the data lake to optimize the scalability and maintenance cost.

Data Ingestion

The raw data is ingested for processing and reporting. The data lake uses a schema-on-read pattern, where the original schema for the data is preserved. The data can be ingested in real time or batch mode. Extract, transform, load (ETL) processing is used in data ingestion.

CHAPTER 11 MODERN WEB DATA PATTERNS

Data Lake

The data lake stores the raw enterprise data in centralized storage independent of the schema. The data is in various formats, standards, and structures. Data lakes store domain and department-specific data (e.g., marketing department or sales department data). You can enrich the enterprise data with metadata and other information.

The raw data can be repurposed for a variety of applications. The Apache Hadoop platform implements a scalable data lake at an optimized cost.

Data Processing

The data processing layer of the data lake performs various activities such as data deduplication, cleansing, normalization, standardization, data aggregation, data processing, remodeling, and data transformation.

Data processing transforms the raw data stored in the data lake into a specific data format suitable for consuming applications.

Applications

Many different enterprise applications can use the data lake. The most popular utility of the data lake is developing advanced analytics applications such as customer segmentation, predicting/forecasting data trends, fraud detection, and risk assessment. Marketing data lake analyzes the data to understand customer behavior across various channels to explore the cross-selling and upselling opportunities. Enterprises can build other applications such as master data management (MDM) solutions, data warehousing applications, and self-service data exploration.

Considerations

The following describes key considerations for data lakes.

- Establish data governance practices to define the processes related to data security, data integrity, data accessibility, and metadata.

- You need to streamline the data ingestion process and data integration tools with the data lakes.

CHAPTER 11   MODERN WEB DATA PATTERNS

- Enforce the security and compliance restrictions while ingesting, storing, and accessing sensitive information (personally identifiable information, credit card information, social security numbers, etc.).

- Identify the strategic use cases and business scenarios for a data lake. This helps in streamlining and optimizing the data lake processes.

Advantages

The following are the advantages of data lakes.

- A data lake provides an opportunity for enterprises to store raw data.

- Enterprises can look at the data holistically to identify trends and patterns and develop business intelligence applications.

- Enterprises can use the data lake to develop advanced analytics applications, AI/machine learning applications.

- Enterprises can get a 360-degree view of the customer data across various channels and enterprise applications.

Relevant Use Cases

The following are relevant use cases that are best suited for data lakes.

- Enable marketing team to understand the user behavior across various channels (mobile app, web site, call center, kiosk, etc.) using the analytics built on the data lake. The insights mined from the data can improve user engagement and explore cross-sell and up-sell opportunities.

- Get a 360-degree view of customer transactions across all the organization applications.

- Develop data-driven advanced analytical applications to get data-driven insights. You can leverage various analytics for applications such as customer segmentation, fraud detection, risk calculation, targeted selling, personalization, and campaign management.

CHAPTER 11   MODERN WEB DATA PATTERNS

- Store vast amounts of sensor data generated by devices to optimize the resources. For instance, a logistics management company can use real-time sensor data to optimize the delivery route and delivery time.

- Use the data from the data lake to predict, forecast, and identify data patterns that help in inventory planning, campaign management, and so forth.

- Use the data lake to train the machine learning applications in pattern identification. Build various applications such as sentiment analysis, master data management (MDM), data archival, data visualization application, and ETL applications.

- Explore and analyze data across various organization departments and categories using data query tools.

- Enable self-service model for the business through data exploration.

Tools and Technologies

You can use Apache Spark for implementing the data processing layer, to implement business intelligence, for data warehousing applications, and real-time streaming solutions. For ingesting big data from the data lake, you can use tools like Amazon Redshift, Google BigQuery, and other data tools. A data lake can be built and managed by Apache Hadoop. Apache Hadoop provides storage, runtime environment, and data integration capability needed for data lakes. Tools like Apache Hive create structured schemas on top of data lakes.

NoSQL Pattern

When the enterprises must deal with large-scale data (such as social media data, logs, transaction data, event data, etc.), methods used for traditional RDBMS systems are not easily scalable. NoSQL provides an efficient alternative for managing big data consisting of structured and non-structured data types.

Drivers

The following are key drivers for the NoSQL pattern.

- Handle the storage, performance, and scalability of large-scale data efficiently.

- Maintain eventual data consistency when strong consistency and two-phase commit (2PC) is not feasible for large distributed data.

- Scale large unstructured data (e.g., documents, logs) efficiently.

- Manage time-series, log data, and stream data efficiently.

- Handle the data records that don't need an intertable relationship.

Solution

NoSQL provides flexible storage and flexible schema for managing a large volume of data. NoSQL databases can be designed to run on many commodity machines for high scalability. The data can be partitioned and replicated on these machines for high reliability and high performance. NoSQL databases provide horizontal scaling for handling a large volume of data. NoSQL databases provide eventual consistency, high availability, high scalability, and partition tolerance. NoSQL databases don't achieve the ACID (Atomicity, Consistency, Isolation, and Durability) properties of a transaction, but it achieves availability and partition tolerance support by providing eventual consistency. NoSQL provides eventual consistency and provides high availability and partition tolerance as per the CAP theorem.

The key features of NoSQL databases are as follows.

- Denormalized data to flatten the data representation and don't need costly real-time table joins for a query response.

- Embedded document part of the column value

- Provides flexible schema structure

- Supports database sharding for distributed queries

NoSQL database consists of four main types of architecture patterns.

CHAPTER 11   MODERN WEB DATA PATTERNS

Key-Value Store Pattern

The data is stored as a key-value pair similar to a hash map. The key is used as an identifier for fetching the value. The value object can be a JSON file or a blob object or any other document. The key-value store pattern is used in e-commerce applications, lookup tables, query caches, and so forth. DynamoDB, Berkley DB, and Redis are some of the examples of key-value store databases.

Column Store Pattern

The data value is stored in a column. The column store can efficiently store the sparsely populated matrix. Each column stores a different format and structure of the data. Computations can be easily done at the column level. HBase, Cassandra, Google BigTable are some of the examples of the column store databases.

Document Store Pattern

The document stores are essentially the key-value databases where the documents such as JSON, XML, and text are stored as values. Document stores manage hierarchical information efficiently. You can store structured or unstructured documents as values, and hence document stores are efficient in managing the documents (e.g., purchase orders, invoices, forms, product information, brochures). MongoDB and Couchbase are examples of document store databases.

Graph Store Pattern

The database stores graph entities that manage connections across various entities. Graph stores efficiently represent the nodes and edges of a graph. Graph stores are ideal candidates for managing social media data, entity connections, rules system, pattern matching, path traversal, and degree of similarity, and spatial data. Neo4J and FlockDB are examples of graph databases.

Considerations

The following are considerations for using a NoSQL database.

- Understand the unstructured data (document, time series, key-value pair, and node to node relationship). Based on the data characteristics, you can select the most appropriate NoSQL database.
- Select the appropriate unique key for indexing the NoSQL data.
- Design the NoSQL denormalized entities based on the queries.

Advantages

The following are the advantages of using NoSQL databases.

- Provide a scalable data management for large-scale distributed databases.
- Maintain eventual consistency for the distributed database.
- Provide flexible schema for storing various data formats.

Relevant Use Cases

The following are use cases fit for NoSQL patterns.

- The need for handling a large amount of data and providing high performance, high availability, and high scalability
- The need to store a large amount of unstructured data, such as documents, files, videos, and images; for example, social media platforms that deal with a large amount of unstructured data can leverage NoSQL
- Eventual consistency is tolerable for transactions
- There is no need to strict joins across tables

For the systems that need constant consistency, such as financial transactions, real-time approval systems, and so forth, it is better to use traditional RDBMS due to the strong consistency needs.

CHAPTER 11 MODERN WEB DATA PATTERNS

Tools and Frameworks

There are many popular NoSQL databases such as MongoDB, CouchDB, Cassandra, DynamoDB, and Neo4J.

Modern Web Scenarios

This section describes the common applications of data patterns for the core scenarios of a modern web platform.

Table 11-1 identifies the scenarios, significant use cases, and suitable data patterns.

Table 11-1. Data Patterns for the Modern Web

Modern Web Platform Scenario	Considerations	Suitable Data Patterns
E-commerce order management	Store the order files for efficient retrieval Guarantee high availability Provide real-time integration	Leverage NoSQL document database such a MongoDB Provide eventual consistency and high availability Denormalized data view with minimum relations across entities
Social media content management	Scalable system for storing images, videos, and documents Ensure eventual consistency Provide scalable content management	
Product data management	Manage a large volume of product catalogs Provide flexible and dynamic schema Scale for higher data volume	
Analytics application	Enable image classification, machine learning, text analytics on large-scale unstructured data	

(continued)

Table 11-1. (*continued*)

Modern Web Platform Scenario	Considerations	Suitable Data Patterns
IoT Device Data management in domains, such as the oil and gas industry, life sciences, and logistics industry	Manage a high volume of device data, telemetry data, and sensor data Scale to the volume, variety, and velocity of the data Build real-time analytics and business intelligence applications Build predictive and forecasting applications based on real-time data	Manage the device data in a suitable NoSQL database. Ingest the data into the enterprise data lake to enable advanced analytics
Marketing and customer data management	Provides a 360-degree view of all customer activities across all channels (web, mobile, stores, call center, etc.) Provides scalable profile management Provides real-time personalization based on customer transaction data, contextual data, and customer behavior data	
Distributed enterprise systems (order management, inventory management, reservation system, booking system, distributed banking transaction management)	Implemented using database-per-microservice pattern Provide eventual consistency for transactions spanning multiple services and multiple databases Provide a rollback feature using compensatory transactions Support long-running transactions and task-based workflows	Apply the orchestrator model of the saga pattern if you have a centralized ESB or API gateway. If not, you can use the choreographer model of the saga pattern using event publishing and event subscription.

(*continued*)

CHAPTER 11   MODERN WEB DATA PATTERNS

Table 11-1. (*continued*)

Modern Web Platform Scenario	Considerations	Suitable Data Patterns
Large-scale complex applications that read and update multiple systems or record (e.g., master data management)	Provide high-performance database read operations Decouple and scale database read operations from database write operations Enable eventual consistency for the database write operations	Apply the CQRS pattern that provides decoupled read and write operations.

Summary

- Some common data-related antipatterns are complex real-time table joins, performing read and write operations to the same table, synchronous database calls blocking other operations, and implementing strict consistency for distributed transactions.

- The common data-related best practices are using a separate database for read and write operations, static data caching, asynchronous database calls, using denormalized views, lazy/on-demand data loading, and using materialized views for reporting scenarios.

- Some of the common data patterns are materialized view pattern, index table pattern, data partitioning, idempotent transactions, eventual consistency pattern, and change data capture (CDC) pattern, data streaming pattern.

- The saga pattern manages the distributed transaction spanning multiple databases using a centralized orchestrator or a choreographer. In the orchestration model, a centralized orchestrator invokes a sequence of services.

CHAPTER 11 MODERN WEB DATA PATTERNS

- The saga pattern manages the distributed transaction spanning multiple databases using a centralized orchestrator or a choreographer. In the orchestration model, a centralized orchestrator invokes a sequence of services. In choreography, each of the services publishes and subscribes to the events of the event broker.

- The CQRS consists of two main components: the command part and the query part. The command part handles the data persistence concern and is used for data insert, update, and delete operations. The query part is responsible for data retrieval.

- Event sourcing pattern uses message publish and subscribe patterns to maintain the consistency across multiple data sources.

- In the compensating transaction pattern, the compensating transactions involve a sequence of transactions to roll back and undo each of the events.

- An enterprise data lake is a centralized storage repository that holds a vast amount of enterprise data in a raw format, including structured, unstructured, and semistructured.

- Enterprise data lake consists of layers such as data source, data ingestion, data lake, data processing, and applications. The data source layer consists of various internal and external sources that feed raw data into the data lake. The data ingestion layer consists of various methods to ingest the raw data into the data lake. The central data lake is responsible for providing scalable storage for the raw data. The data processing layer is responsible for processing the data to enable the applications. The applications can range from data visualizations, AI/ML applications, analytics applications, and so on.

- NoSQL provides flexible storage and flexible schema for managing a large volume of data and hierarchical data.

- NoSQL database consists of four types of architecture patterns: the key-value store pattern, the column store pattern, the document store pattern, and the graph store pattern.

CHAPTER 12

Modern Web Integration Patterns

Enterprise integrations are a quintessential part of modern web platforms. They form the backbone of enterprise platforms. API-based integrations fetch dynamic data from various data sources for modern web platforms. Integrations extend existing capabilities and help onboard new capabilities. Modern web platforms are integrated with internal and external interfaces and typically use stateless APIs. Some of the integrations are at the client end, and some are integrated at the server end. The integrations should be optimal to ensure that integrated interfaces do not introduce additional performance overhead. A few integrations become chatty, leading to frequent server calls, and in some other scenarios, the synchronous nature of the integrations block the subsequent flows.

There are other integration-related concerns, including security, scalability of the upstream systems, error handling, monitoring, and deployment. Modern web platforms need optimal integration design for a better user experience. Headless integration, token-based security, and GraphQL, stateless and asynchronous services are key trends in the integration space.

This chapter starts by discussing common integration-related performance challenges and antipatterns. It also looks at some of the core integration-related patterns and best practices commonly used in modern web solutions. Later sections talk about microservices-related patterns, event-driven architecture, and GraphQL patterns.

Performance engineers, integration architects, digital architects, project managers, and program managers should find this chapter useful.

CHAPTER 12   MODERN WEB INTEGRATION PATTERNS

Common Integration Antipatterns and Best Practices

Integration antipatterns identify commonly known issues that may potentially become serious performance challenges in the future. Identifying the integration antipatterns early in the development stage helps you fix identified issues.

This section discusses network-related antipatterns since it is closely related to integrations. Common integration best practices are also discussed. Both integration antipatterns and integration best practices can be part of a checklist during code review.

Network-related Antipatterns

The following are network-related antipatterns.

- Higher download times of assets are caused due to network latency, or asset size, or synchronous downloads.
- There is a high asset count on the key pages such as landing page and home page.
- Chatty call issues occur when a single web page invokes multiple server calls to complete a task. This adds to the performance overhead for the pages.
- Absence of caching leads to frequent calls to the data source.
- The absence of CDN leads to higher asset load times.
- A non-optimized critical render path leads to higher initial page load times.

Integration-related Antipatterns

The following are integration-related antipatterns.

- Inefficient interface design without proper well-defined contracts and UI-friendly data leads to multiple calls.
- Heavy request and response payloads such as XML-based payload result in unnecessary data processing, reduced throughput, reduced scalability, impacting the performance.

CHAPTER 12 MODERN WEB INTEGRATION PATTERNS

- Synchronous calls block the page and impact the overall render time.

- Heavy-duty data processing adds additional overhead to the client.

- Resource intensive computation happening in the main UI thread instead of performing it in a separate background thread.

- Improper handling of errors (e.g., timeouts, application errors, and connection errors) on the page results in usability issues.

- Improperly sized infrastructure components such as CPU cores, memory, server nodes based on the performance and scalability requirements.

- Absence of performance monitoring setup to monitor the response time in real time.

Integration-related Best Practices and Common Patterns

This section goes over common best practices and integration-related patterns. Integration architects can apply these best practices during integration design.

- **Canonical data model**: In an enterprise ecosystem, multiple systems are interdependent and exchange the data. Each interface has its own data structure, protocol, and data standards resulting in multiple data-related translations at various layers. *A canonical data model pattern defines a common data structure with uniform protocol and standards that you can use for data exchange.* The canonical data model also includes a superset of the data that reduces the integration, translation, and maintenance overhead and decouples the interfaces.

- **Retry pattern**: The applications involving multiple interfaces face transient failures (connection errors, application errors, etc.). In some scenarios, the database update operations fail. In such cases, you need to log the failures to the error log and retry the failed transaction after some delay. Alternatively, you can schedule a job to periodically check the error log and retry the failed transactions. The retry pattern brings in the resilience for the application. The CQRS pattern uses a dead letter queue to log the error scenarios.

CHAPTER 12   MODERN WEB INTEGRATION PATTERNS

- **Domain-driven design (DDD)**: In this design pattern, the model objects are closely modeled on the core business domain. The development team closely collaborates with the domain experts to design the business logic, interfaces, and payload contracts across layers based on the business domain needs. The DDD defines the domain, context for the domain models, and the ubiquitous language for the development team. The core building blocks of DDD are entities, value objects, domain events, services, repositories, and factories. The domain-focused DDD provides flexibility and improves communication among the team members.

- **Asynchronous invocation**: Modern web platforms heavily use the asynchronous invocation to improve the perceived response time. Client applications use AJAX requests to fetch the resources asynchronously without blocking the page load. The callbacks associated with the asynchronous requests handle the response. Modern web platforms use the AJAX-based asynchronous requests for loading the content, invoking the server API, and so forth.

- **Lazy loading**: To optimize the page response time, you can lazily load the requested responses on demand. During the initial page load, you can only load the content above the fold and load the content below the fold upon user access.

- **Façade pattern**: The service façade acts as a single point of entry for the consumers and abstracts the server API information. The service façade provides a contract-based communication with the clients and handle the data aggregation, call sequencing, routing, exception handling, and caching. Web platforms can leverage the service façade to reduce the chatty server calls.

- **WebSockets**: You can achieve full-duplex communication between client and server with WebSockets. Browser clients can use the WebSocket protocol to do real-time and synchronous communication with the server. WebSockets effectively avoid costly polling. Real-time applications such as stock quote API, chats can use WebSocket.

CHAPTER 12   MODERN WEB INTEGRATION PATTERNS

- **Web real-time communication (WebRTC)**: You can use WebRTC APIs to provide audio/video conferencing, screen sharing, file exchange, and stream multimedia content. WebRTC is a W3C standards-compliant protocol that establishes direct and peer-to-peer communication.

- **API first approach**: Modern web platforms heavily depend on the APIs for information aggregation and onboarding new features. The API first approach proposes that APIs are prioritized and built first to provide the business capabilities. The APIs expose well-defined contracts and the description for the consumers. Web platforms and mobile platforms consume these APIs.

- **Backend for frontend**: In the backend for a frontend pattern, the API layer provides channel-specific variants to provide the response payload in a channel-friendly manner. Additionally, the backend API also aggregates the information from multiple services and do the data transformation, protocol translation required for providing the response. For instance, the mobile APIs provide the data specific for mobile screens, whereas the desktop browser-specific APIs provide the detailed data needed for browser views.

- **Mini service design**: In database-per-service, each microservice having its own database causes chatty calls, mini services provide a pragmatic alternative. The miniservices group the features of logically related microservices in a single service, reducing the number of service calls. As the miniservices provide multiple features, the code is heavier and complex than microservices. You can use miniservice for handling logically-related complex business logic using a single database or a single data source.

- **Data load on demand**: Design the views to fetch the data only when needed. For the large dataset, load only the data needed for the first page (or above-the-fold content). You can leverage the pagination UI component that initially loads the data only the first page, and when the user accesses the next page, you load the data specific for the second page. Similarly, in the slide UI component, you load the data only for the current view. When the user slides up or slides down, you load the data needed for the view.

331

- **Contract-first approach**: In this approach, you primarily define the interface contract on priority. The contract defines the request and response payload structure, authorization information, and URL information. A well-defined contract enables the teams working on various layers to build in parallel and test the interfaces and consumers as per the defined contract.

- **Serverless Functions**: Most cloud platforms provide functions as a service (FaaS) that can be auto-scaled to handle the sudden increase in user requests or data volume. The serverless functions abstract the developers from underlying infrastructure, deployment, security, and monitoring. AWS Lambda, Azure Functions, and Google Cloud Functions are examples of the serverless functions.

- **Multispeed services:** The enterprises using legacy systems can leverage multispeed IT architecture. In multispeed IT, microservices are designed to cater to the fast-changing consumer-facing digital platforms. The microservices internally use mature legacy services such as SOA services. The multispeed IT decouples the modern web platforms from legacy systems with each of these platforms have different release cycles.

- **Offline-first approach:** The applications that need to work with a limited connection can use the offline-first approach. You use the local storage (browser cache or device cache or local database) to store the frequently accessed data, and the application uses local storage when the network is not available. The application stores the user actions during offline mode and synchronizes it with the server when the network is available.

Microservice Patterns

The microservices framework is the most popular service framework in modern web platforms. Microservices are granular and lightweight services that encapsulate logically independent business capability. Microservices are modular, independently deployable, and independently scalable services that are an integral part of modern web platforms.

CHAPTER 12 MODERN WEB INTEGRATION PATTERNS

Most modern web platforms provide features such as asynchronous loading, partial page refresh, on-demand lazy data loading, and microservices fits perfectly into these use cases.

Microservices use stateless communication mode to communicate with the server. Modern web platforms use REST-based stateless and asynchronous services and use JSON as the payload structure. You can build layered and decoupled applications based on well-defined contracts. Microservices are also used in the headless integration model. Microservices are easily deployed on popular cloud platforms and containers.

This section goes over various patterns that implement scalable and secure microservices.

Context

The microservices model offers key benefits for modern web platforms. The following are the core features of the microservices.

- Independent business domain services bringing agile deployment model with fewer downtimes and increased operational efficiency.

- Services replicate along both the x and y axis of the scalability cube and provide load-based autoscaling.

- Built-in resiliency, hardened against failures

- Versioning with consumer-specific contracts, the central registry for service discovery/lookup.

- Centralized monitoring and logging.

- Loosely coupled modules with low maintenance

- Ease of use for troubleshooting.

- Portable across any platform as easily adaptable to a containerized platform.

- API-based integrations that make highly extensible and adaptable across multiple systems.

CHAPTER 12 MODERN WEB INTEGRATION PATTERNS

Drivers

The following are the main drivers for microservices.

- Develop contract-based decoupling across various layers.
- Develop services models that have intrinsic cohesiveness and loose coupling, among other services.
- Develop headless integration with systems such as CMS, ERP, and RDBMS.
- Implement a multispeed IT model to integrate with legacy systems.
- Develop a lightweight and asynchronous services model.
- Provide flexibility to develop services using various programming languages and tools.
- Implement fault tolerance, resilience, security, modularity, and scalable services in the model.
- Develop a testable services model.
- Develop services that can be independently developed and deployed.
- Continuously deliver the services with faster release cycles.

Core Patterns

The microservices model is popular due to its flexibility and scalability. This section discusses the core design patterns that are modeled around microservices to various enterprise scenarios.

Service Discovery Pattern

In a distributed microservice environment, you can implement the service discovery pattern to dynamically discover the service instance.

Figure 12-1 depicts the flow for the service discovery pattern.

CHAPTER 12 MODERN WEB INTEGRATION PATTERNS

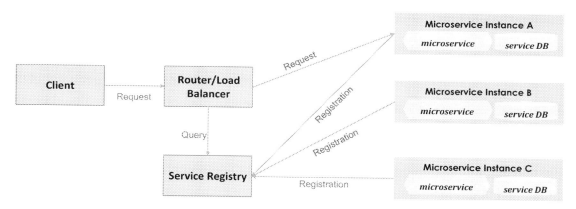

Figure 12-1. *Service discovery pattern*

- The router/load balancer routes the request from the service client to the corresponding microservice. The service registry has information on all registered microservices. The service registry has the location information (e.g., dynamic IP, port, and protocol) of all the dynamic services.

- Once the service client makes the request, the router uses the location information in the service registry and forwards the request to the corresponding microservice instance.

- On the server-side service discovery, you deploy the service registry at the server layer, and in client-side service discovery, along with the service client, you deploy registry.

Circuit Breaker

The circuit breaker handles the service failures and service timeouts. The circuit breaker pattern prevents the cascading of the errors across various layers. The following is a summary of the circuit breaker.

- The service client invokes the microservices through a proxy that acts as a circuit breaker.

- If the consecutive service calls fail or the consecutive service calls time-out, the circuit breaker trips, disconnecting the client and microservice for a preconfigured timeout duration.

- After the time-out duration, the circuit breaker starts allowing the requests to the microservice.

Chapter 12 Modern Web Integration Patterns

API Gateway Pattern

The clients are abstracted from the location information of the underlying microservice. The API gateway serves as the single-entry point for the requests for the microservices. The following explains concerns handled by the API gateway.

- The API gateway abstracts the client from the microservices' granularity. The API gateway exposes API that acts as a service façade by aggregating all the required granular microservices.

- The API gateway secures the APIs by providing role-based access or token-based access. You can also enforce further security rules such as IP based filtering and channel-based filtering.

- The API gateway also translates the protocol to invoke back-end microservices.

- The API gateway handles the routing of the request to the corresponding back-end microservice. The API gateway exposes channel-specific API; for instance, the API gateway provides a different API for mobile devices and a full-fledged API for desktop browsers. This pattern is often referred to as a *backend for frontend*.

- The API gateway also performs the API composition role by aggregating data from various services and combining the data in the memory.

Figure 12-2 depicts the API gateway pattern.

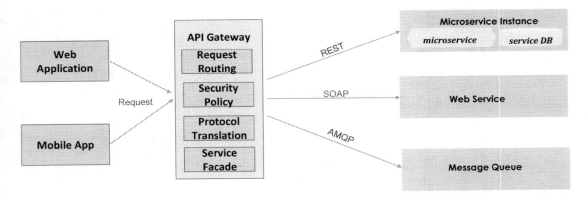

Figure 12-2. *API gateway pattern*

Access Token

For the stateless microservices, the server secures the request through access tokens (i.e., JSON Web Token, also known as JWT). API gateway authorizes the incoming requests through access tokens. You can encode the user identity, issued time, role information as part of the access token payload. You can also specify the encoding algorithm as part of the header and provide an encoded signature.

Decomposition Patterns

Microservices are decomposed based on various criteria. The following are various criteria based on which you can decompose microservices.

- Decomposition based on **business capabilities** (such as sales management, inventory management. for a retail domain) for a functional domain.

- Decomposition based on **services needed by UI components.**

- Decomposition based on **business transactions** such as checkout, search, product save, and so forth.

- Decomposition is based on **resources** (also known as *nouns* for a business domain).

- Decomposition based on **business subdomains** (product promotion management, product catalog management, etc.). The bounded context defines the scope of the subdomain. This is often referred to as **domain-driven development (DDD).**

Database Patterns

Normally, microservices use a dedicated database to enable independent scalability and independent deployment. The following are the database-related patterns for microservices.

- **Database per service**: Each microservice has its own database. The pattern enforces a private database or database schema exclusively for a microservice. The pattern provides loose coupling and independent scalability across services.

CHAPTER 12   MODERN WEB INTEGRATION PATTERNS

- **Shared database**: The database is shared across multiple microservices.

- **Event sourcing pattern**: A sequence of events defines the application state. The event sequence reconstructs the application state. Chapter 11 discusses the event sourcing pattern.

- **CQRS pattern**: It decouples the data retrieval flow from the data persistence flow. Chapter 11 discusses the CQRS pattern.

Other Patterns Related to Microservice Ecosystems

The following patterns are regularly used in a microservice ecosystem.

- **Log aggregation** in which you aggregate the log information from all application instances with minimal overhead. You can query the aggregated log to get insights into the errors, performance, and others.

- **Health check API pattern**: Each microservice provides a health check endpoint that publishes the overall service health (including the status code, connection information, specific application health information). The monitoring setup can use the health check API to get the overall health status of the microservice.

- **Service monitoring**: Each of the microservice endpoints are actively monitored. The monitoring infrastructure notifies any failures or errors.

- **Externalized configuration**: The service reads the environment-specific configurations (such as database connection) from an external source.

- **Saga pattern**: It is designed to handle the transactions that involve multiple services and private databases. The distributed transaction uses orchestration (a centralized orchestrator managing multiple transactions) or choreography (each service publishes events to other service) to maintain transaction integrity and handle failovers.

- **Exception tracking pattern**: It provides a centralized service exception management system to log, report, and notify exceptions.

- **Application metrics**: It provides a centralized metrics management service to aggregate, report, and notify the metrics.

CHAPTER 12   MODERN WEB INTEGRATION PATTERNS

- **Service integration contract test** pattern: It verifies if the service fulfills the specified contracts for its consumers.

- **Server-side page fragment composition pattern**: It defines multiple page fragments composed to form a single page. Each page fragment gets the data from corresponding microservices.

- **Blue-green deployment model:** It defines two production environments (blue and green), one of which serves the live production traffic at any point in time. During production deployment, other instance is brought up to minimize production downtime.

Solution

Figure 12-3 depicts the high-level components of the microservice ecosystem.

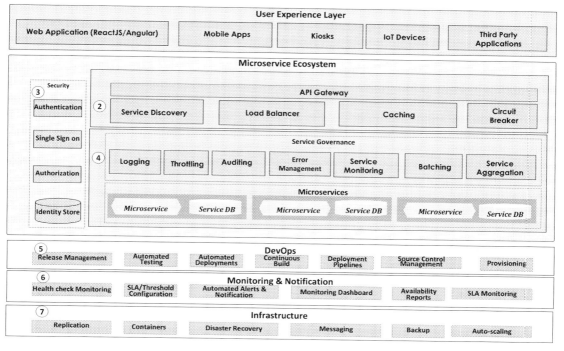

Figure 12-3. Microservice solution ecosystem

339

CHAPTER 12   MODERN WEB INTEGRATION PATTERNS

User Experience Layer

The modern web platform's user experience layer consists of web applications, mobile app, kiosks, IVR, and third-party applications. These web platforms fetch dynamic data through microservices.

Microservice Ecosystem

The API gateway routes the request to the corresponding microservice. You can leverage other patterns such as service discovery (to enable routing to the registered instances), load balancing (to equally distribute the traffic), circuit breaker (to block the traffic to the unavailable service), caching, and others.

The service governance layer manages the cross-cutting concerns of the microservices such as logging (of the main events), throttling (limiting number of requests), auditing (of security events), error management, service monitoring (to monitor the availability and performance), batching (sending multiple requests in a single batch) and service composition (retrieving data from multiple services).

The core microservices are deployed across various container pods or virtual machine instances. Each microservice has its own database.

The security layer handles concerns such as authentication, single sign-on, authorization, and the identity store.

The DevOps layer streamlines release management activities. It includes automated release management (through continuous integration and continuous deployment, also known as CICD), automated testing (by plugging in the testing in the CICD pipeline), source code management processes (check-in/checkout process, approval process, etc.).

The monitoring and notification infrastructure continuously monitors the health and heartbeat of the microservices. You can configure the threshold values for performance, availability, and error rate. If the performance or the availability of the microservices exceed the configured threshold, the notification infrastructure triggers the notification.

The infrastructure layer consists of on-premise systems or cloud-based containers to host the microservices. The container orchestration system (such as Kubernetes) provides on-demand scalability of the microservice instances.

Figure 12-4 depicts a sample of AWS-based microservice architecture.

CHAPTER 12 MODERN WEB INTEGRATION PATTERNS

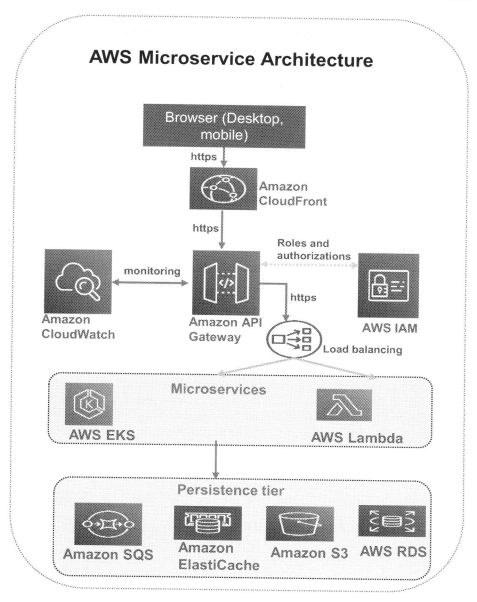

Figure 12-4. *AWS microservice architecture*

The AWS CloudFront CDN provides static assets for the clients. The server requests are routed through AWS API gateway that distributes the requests to various server components such as AWS EKS and AWS Lambda (that provide serverless functions). The AWS API gateway handles other concerns such as load balancing, request routing, and so forth. AWS EKS (Elastic Kubernetes Server) manages the infrastructure nodes/pods

341

CHAPTER 12 MODERN WEB INTEGRATION PATTERNS

that run the microservice instances. EKS auto-scales the pods based on the configured rules. For data persistence, you can use AWS services such as AWS SQS (Simple Queuing Service), Amazon ElastiCache, Amazon S3 (for storing the static assets, and hosting the Angular/React modules), and AWS RDS (for relational database objects).

Amazon CloudWatch monitors cloud systems and resources. You can configure the alerts and notifications in Amazon CloudWatch. AWS IAM enforces many access policies, such as role-based access.

Figure 12-5 depicts a sample Spring Boot–based reference architecture.

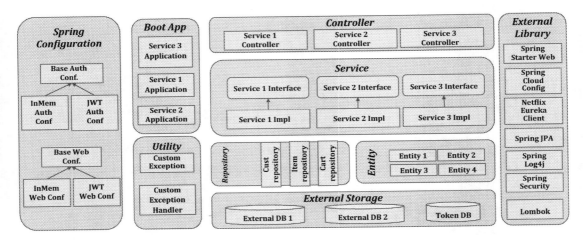

Figure 12-5. *Spring Boot–based microservice architecture*

Spring Boot is one of the most popular frameworks for implementing microservices in the Java world. The main solution components of the Spring Boot–based microservice framework are boot applications, controllers, and services. Each service uses an entity object for data retrieval and data persistence into the repository. Spring framework also provides additional libraries such as starter web application, cloud configuration, Spring JPA, Spring log4j, and Spring Security.

Considerations

The following are the main considerations for microservices related patterns.

- Design the granularity of the microservice-based on the appropriate decomposition pattern. A microservice that is too granular leads to chatty calls, and a coarse-grained service leads to high coupling, increased complexity, and reduced reusability.

CHAPTER 12 MODERN WEB INTEGRATION PATTERNS

- Use the single responsibility principle (SRP) to design the microservice so that they have high cohesiveness.

- Implement the resiliency through horizontal scaling and using the circuit breaker pattern. Test the application resiliency through "chaos monkey.", a resiliency testing tool.

- Implement the twelve-factor methodology in microservices architecture by providing the solution components for each of the twelve factors (code base, dependencies, config, backing services, build, release, run, processes, port binding, concurrency, disability, dev/prod parity, logs, and admin processes).

Variations

The following are the microservices variations.

- Coarse graining microservices that use a shared database are called *miniservices*.

- Serverless microservices use cloud-native services (such as AWS Lambda or Azure Functions) to provide on-demand scalability.

Advantages

The following are the main advantages of microservices-based applications.

- You can implement the agile delivery model using scalable, modular services, and by leveraging the DevOps processes.

- You can adopt various programming languages and distributed teams to develop contract-based microservices.

- Microservices implements most modern web architecture principles, such as headless integration, token-based security, asynchronous integration, modularity, and multispeed IT.

- As most of the cloud platforms provide managed services for microservices, you can build a cloud-native application.

- You can build a loosely coupled and decoupled solution model using microservices.

343

CHAPTER 12 MODERN WEB INTEGRATION PATTERNS

Relevant Use Cases

The following scenarios are ideal for using microservices.

- Modern single-page applications (SPA) that need asynchronous and granular services to render various UI modules
- Mobile apps need to get dynamic data from data sources.

Tools and Frameworks

Spring Boot is one of the most popular microservices frameworks. JWT is a popular mechanism to build access tokens. Spring Security, OAuth2, OpenID connect are other options for implementing the security features. Docker Swarm, Kubernetes are popular container ecosystems. You can use tools such as Prometheus, Splunk, ELK (Elasticsearch, Logstash, and Kibana) for implementing the monitoring infrastructure.

Technology Choices

Table 12-1 features various technology choices for implementing the microservice ecosystem for various stacks (Java, Node.js, Microsoft, and cloud-native).

Table 12-1. Microservice Technology Ecosystem Tools

Responsibility	Java Stack	Node.js	Microsoft Stack	Cloud Platform (AWS and Azure)
Core implementation Services	Spring Boot	ExpressJS	.NET, WCF	Azure Web Apps/ Azure Kubernetes Services Azure Functions AWS EKS
Service Contracts	Swagger			
Data/message formats	JSON			

(continued)

CHAPTER 12 MODERN WEB INTEGRATION PATTERNS

Table 12-1. (*continued*)

Responsibility	Java Stack	Node.js	Microsoft Stack	Cloud Platform (AWS and Azure)
Service Discovery, Configuration	Consul, Netflix OSS- Eureka, Apache Zookeeper	SWIM + Mesh	Consul / Microphone	AWS API Gateway
Event Subscription, Notifications	Vert.X + Spring Boot		.Net, WCF in Azure Web Apps/AKS	Azure Web Apps/ Azure Kubernetes Services Azure Functions AWS Lambda
Persistence Store	Oracle, SQL Server, MongoDB, DynamoDB			Azure SQL, Azure Blob Storage (file storage), AWS RDS
Cache	Redis, Memcached			Azure Cache for Redis AWS Elasticache
Application Container	Tomcat	Node, Process Manager	Windows Server, IIS	
Core implementation – Presentation Layer	RWD with Bootstrap, ReactJS/Angular, Vue, Templating Engine			
Enterprise Bus/ Middleware	Apache Camel/Spring Integration or MuleSoft		Microsoft BizTalk	
Provisioning, containers	Kubernetes/Docker			Azure Kubernetes Services AWS EKS
Logging, Tracing	Elk, Splunk			Application Insights/ELK

(*continued*)

345

CHAPTER 12   MODERN WEB INTEGRATION PATTERNS

Table 12-1. (*continued*)

Responsibility	Java Stack	Node.js	Microsoft Stack	Cloud Platform (AWS and Azure)
Metering, Monitoring	Micrometer, Prometheus, Grafana Netflix OSS-Turbine, Prometheus, Splunk, ELK (Elasticsearch, Logstash, Kibana), cAdvisor Visualization – Grafana, Kibana		Circonus	Azure Monitor AWS CloudWatch
Continuous Integration, Deployment	Git, Jenkins, SonarQube	Git, Jenkins	VSO	Azure DevOps
Workflow Engine	Spring core services executed in Azure Functions	Node custom services executed in Azure Functions	.NET services executed in Azure Functions	Azure Logic Apps integrated with Azure Functions
Security – OAuth authorizations	Spring Security + OAuth 2 + JWT OpenID connect	OAuth 2 libraries for Node.js	.NET libraries for OAuth 2, JWT	Azure Key Vault for password store + SSO (AD Integration)+ Java/Node/.NET OAuth 2 AWS IAM
Unit testing	Mockito for Java Enzyme and Jest for ReactJS or Karma and Jasmine, Protractor for AngularJS, Wiremock for microservices	Mocha for Node Enzyme and Jest for ReactJS or Karma and Jasmine, Protractor for AngularJS	NUnit for .NET Enzyme and Jest for ReactJS or Karma and Jasmine, Protractor for AngularJS	

(*continued*)

Table 12-1. (*continued*)

Responsibility	Java Stack	Node.js	Microsoft Stack	Cloud Platform (AWS and Azure)
Messaging Engine	Apache RabbitMQ			Azure Service Bus
API Gateway	Netflix OSS: Zuul			Azure API Management AWS API Gateway
WAF + Layer 7 load balancing				Azure Application Gateway
Rule Engine	Drools	JSON-rules-engine	NRules	

Event-Driven Architecture

Event-driven architecture (EDA) is fast becoming the mainstream integration phenomenon to support agile enterprises. EDA enables heterogeneous systems to communicate with each other through loosely coupled architecture.

EDA handles application state changes as events that are recognized, produced, transmitted, processed, and consumed in real time for distributed systems.

Event-driven architecture (EDA) provides loose-coupled architecture comprising event products, event consumers, and event routers. The event producers publish events to event router; event router filters; and routes the events to event consumers and event consumers consume the events. In the EDA paradigm, any change in state triggers an event that is detected and consumed by loosely coupled systems. Due to the loose coupling nature of the EDA, the producers, the consumers, can be scaled independently.

Context

The context for event-driven architecture is as follows.

- Enable choreography of the services
- Provide a scalable solution for handling a mix of on-premise components and cloud-native components.

CHAPTER 12　MODERN WEB INTEGRATION PATTERNS

Solution

The event-driven architecture uses event producer, event broker, and event consumer that creates loosely coupled components. The event-driven architecture compliments the microservices and service-oriented architecture (SOA).

In the SOA architecture, a centralized ESB orchestrates various services. The ESB invokes the corresponding services in a particular sequence. For high volume transactions, ESB can become the bottleneck.

EDA uses choreography or self-orchestration wherein each microservice subscribes to a topic where events are published.

Table 12-2 highlights some basic differences between the traditional SOA model and the EDA model.

Table 12-2. SOA vs. EDA

Consideration	SOA	EDA
Main execution-style	Orchestration–ESB invoking the services in sequence	Choreography—each service subscribes to a topic/event and processes the payload
Scalability	Limited by ESB scalability and poses burst handling challenges	Elastic scalability
Reusability	Complex services are less reusable	Multiple consumers can subscribe the topics
Extensibility	Adding new services need changes and adaptors	Easy to add new publishers, consumers
Communication type	Services and messages	Events
Interaction model	Request and response model	Publish and subscription model
Communication type	Synchronous communication Serial communications	Asynchronous Parallel execution

CHAPTER 12 MODERN WEB INTEGRATION PATTERNS

Event Mesh Architecture

Event mesh is one of the efficient ways to implement event-driven architecture. The event mesh architecture provides a scalable and reliable infrastructure that dynamically routes the events from producers to consumers across distributed environments (on-premise, public cloud, hybrid cloud, etc.). The event mesh provides a network of interconnected event handlers distributed across cloud, on-premise, and hybrid cloud.

Event mesh connects various producers and consumers, such as microservices, web services, legacy applications, cloud-based services, ERP, PaaS, IaaS, and IoT devices across heterogeneous platforms (on-premise and cloud). Event mesh enforces security through the ACLs (access control lists) and enables event-based interactions across heterogeneous systems.

Figure 12-6 depicts the event mesh architecture.

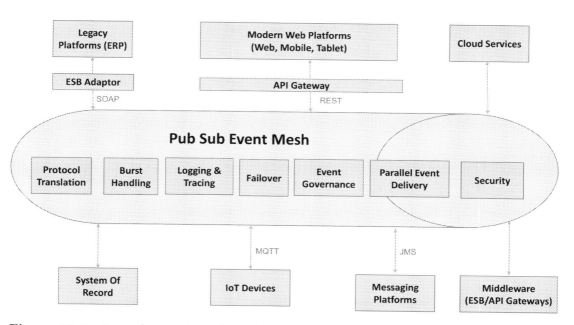

Figure 12-6. *Sample event mesh architecture*

CHAPTER 12   MODERN WEB INTEGRATION PATTERNS

Event Producers

The producers can publish the state changes to the corresponding topics using various protocols such as REST, MQTT, JMS, and AMQP. For instance, in an e-commerce domain, an order event can be published over REST to a topic (https://host:port/api/v1/order/request) with the appropriate payload in various formats (JSON, XML, etc.).

Event Consumers

The event consumers subscribe to a topic of interest and listen to the published events. For instance, the order management microservice can subscribe to the "api/v1/order/request" topic. Once a new order event is published, the order management microservice receives the payload and processes the event payload data.

Event Broker

The event broker is primarily responsible for event routing and reliable event delivery. The event broker enriches the event with metadata (timestamp, event source, etc.).

Considerations

The following are the main considerations for event-driven architecture.

- To event enable the legacy systems, use the event adaptors to publish the state change events.
- The event mesh provides a reliable and guaranteed delivery of the messages.
- The producer and consumer applications produce and consume events that are triggered by state changes. If native event generation or consumption is not available, you should use event adaptors for the same.
- The producer and consumer applications produce and consume messages asynchronously.
- The applications provide eventual consistency and provide compensatory transactions to handle the rollback.

Advantages

The following are the advantages of event-driven architecture.

- Complete decoupling of the producer systems and consumer systems.
- Independent scalability of producers and consumers
- Low latency of the transactions due to the event router.
- Provide features such as high availability, multiple protocol support, zero data loss, burst handling, event auditing, graceful failover, automatic retries, and throttling.
- Event-based architecture provides high throughput.
- Support multiple payload formats such as JSON, XML, text, and so forth.
- Cost optimization due to on-demand event handling instead of a continuous poll.
- Supports distributed transactions and eventual consistency.
- Event-driven systems are resilient for failures due to horizontal scaling and replication.
- Easier to add new channels as new publishers and subscribers
- Enables agile integration model by avoiding the costly adaptors.
- Provides eventual consistency and real-time analytics.

Relevant Use Cases

The following are relevant use cases for event-driven architecture.

- As part of legacy modernization, EDA integrates heterogeneous systems, including legacy platforms, with various data formats, protocols, and various environments.
- Use the EDA for providing real-time, low latency data integration models.
- You can implement long-running task workflows that accept eventual consistency.

CHAPTER 12   MODERN WEB INTEGRATION PATTERNS

Tools and Frameworks

Various tools such as Apache Kafka, Apache RabbitMQ, and KubeMQ. You can use Solace to implement event mesh architecture.

GraphQL

GraphQL is an alternative to the REST architecture pattern for querying complex hierarchy of data. GraphQL exposes a single endpoint providing all the functionality.

Drivers

The following are the key drivers for NoSQL pattern

- The client needs hierarchical data that often need multiple API calls.
- The client needs to avoid multiple server API calls to reduce the consumed bandwidth.

Solution

GraphQL pattern provides a single endpoint to execute a complex query and fetch only the required response attributes. GraphQL APIs are client-driven and expose a POST method for the clients.

- Expose all the API features over a single endpoint.
- GraphQL provides an object representation of the response data.
- GraphQL serves only the requested data in the structured format.
- The single GraphQL endpoint abstracts the underlying operations form the client.

Considerations

The following are the key considerations for the GraphQL pattern.

- The client must manage the response caching.
- Monitor the GraphQL and log the failures, response times, availability, and other key metrics.

Advantages

The following are the advantages of the GraphQL pattern.

- As the GraphQL provides only the required fields, the consumed bandwidth is less compared to REST APIs.
- The number of API calls with GraphQL is reduced when compared to REST APIs
- GraphQL communicates over various protocols, such as HTTP, HTTPS, TCP, WebSockets, FTP, and UDP.

Relevant Use Cases

The following are the use cases fit for the GraphQL pattern.

- Expose a single GraphQL endpoint that acts as a façade to the consumer and internally fans out to multiple back-end services (REST, SOAP, JDBC, etc.) to aggregate the response.
- A client needing a large amount of data or hierarchical data that needs multiple server calls can leverage GraphQL to minimize the server calls.
- Use GraphQL as a proxy to provide an additional layer of security for existing APIs.

Tools and Frameworks

Frameworks such as NodeJS, Apollo, Prisma, and Relay to build a GraphQL ecosystem.

CHAPTER 12 MODERN WEB INTEGRATION PATTERNS

Modern Web Scenarios

This section describes the common applications of integration patterns for the core scenarios of a modern web platform.

Table 12-3 identifies the scenarios, significant use cases, and suitable data patterns.

Table 12-3. *Data Patterns for Modern Web Platforms*

Modern Web Platform Scenario	Considerations	Suitable Data Patterns
Digital Experience Platform dashboards and UI for retail, finance, e-commerce, and telecommunication	Enable stateless services. Handle a large volume of data. Provide independent scaling of services. Enable multiple teams to work on different services in parallel. Enable service development in heterogeneous languages and heterogeneous databases. Enable multiple channels for consuming the services. Provide high scalability and high availability.	Design the microservice architecture. Decompose the microservice and design the granularity based on the business capability or UI needs. Use the backend for frontend pattern to support multiple channels. Manage microservices through API gateway for service governance. Containerize the microservices for independent scalability. Provide continuous integration to bring in agility.
Legacy modernization Migration of legacy service architecture to modern web architecture	Enable multispeed IT. Service enable existing legacy services. Support different release cycles for matured legacy services and modern microservices. Adapt to the fast-changing UI requirements.	Decompose the monolith service into granular microservices. Or Build a multispeed service architecture on top of existing legacy services. Use a service adaptor like ESB to service enable the existing legacy systems.

(continued)

CHAPTER 12   MODERN WEB INTEGRATION PATTERNS

Table 12-3. (*continued*)

Modern Web Platform Scenario	Considerations	Suitable Data Patterns
Offline jobs such as scheduled batch processing, image processing, continuous integration	Provide on-demand scalability. Provide high performance.	Use the serverless functions on cloud platforms.
Real-time communication such as IoT sensor data processing, real-time web page analytics, stream processing, pattern detection, fraud detection	Provide low latency. Provide on-demand scalability. Provide a resilient and high available system. Provide eventual consistency.	Use event-driven architecture. Design a distributed event mesh with event brokers for handling a large volume of events.
Heterogeneous data integration	Ingest data from various producers. Support multiple protocols and payload structure. Provide auditing and analytics.	

Summary

- The common network-related antipatterns are high asset count, high asset download time, chatty calls, absence of caching and CDN, and non-optimized critical render path.

- The common integration-related antipatterns are inefficient interface design, heavy request and response payloads, synchronous calls, heavy-duty data processing, resource intensive computation in the main UI thread, improper handling of errors, improperly sized infrastructure components, and absence of performance monitoring.

CHAPTER 12 MODERN WEB INTEGRATION PATTERNS

- The common integration best practices are the canonical data model, domain-driven design (DDD), asynchronous invocation, lazy loading, the façade pattern, WebSockets, web real-time communication (WebRTC), API-first approach, back end for front end, miniservice design, data load on demand, serverless functions, and multispeed services.

- A canonical data model pattern defines a common data structure with uniform protocol and standards that you can for data exchange.

- Microservices are granular and lightweight service methodology that encapsulates logically independent business capability

- The main drivers for microservices are contract-based decoupling, intrinsic cohesiveness, headless integration, support for multispeed IT model, support for lightweight and asynchronous model, programming language flexibility, fault tolerance, resilience, security, modularity, scalability, testability, and continuous deliverability.

- The service discovery pattern to dynamically discovers and routes the request to the corresponding service instance.

- The circuit breaker handles the service failures and service timeouts.

- The API gateway provides a single point of contact for routing to the microservices.

- Access token encodes user identity, issued time, role information, and other information.

- Microservices are decomposed based on business capabilities, services needed by UI components, business transactions, resources, and business subdomains.

- The database patterns for microservices are database per service, shared database, event sourcing pattern, and CQRS pattern.

- Microservice ecosystem handles concerns such as API gateway routing, service discovery, load balancing, caching, service governance (logging, auditing, throttling, error management, service aggregation), and core microservices. The microservice ecosystem is supported by DevOps processes, monitoring, and notification setup and infrastructure components.

- The main considerations for microservices are granularity design, separation of concerns, loose coupling, resiliency, and implementing the twelve-factor methodology.

- Event-driven architecture handles application state changes as events that are recognized, produced, transmitted, processed, and consumed in real time for distributed systems.

- The event-driven architecture defines three main components; event producer, event router, and event consumer that creates loosely coupled components.

- The event mesh architecture provides a scalable and reliable infrastructure that dynamically routes the events from producers to consumers across distributed environments (on-premise, public cloud, hybrid cloud, etc.).

- The GraphQL pattern provides a single endpoint to execute a complex query and fetch only the required response attributes

APPENDIX A

Performance Optimization Checklist

This appendix goes over the most common performance checklist items. It covers checklists for performance testing, Java code, memory leaks, JDBC, and application servers. The following is a brief summary.

- **Performance testing checklist:** The checklist for performance testing an enterprise application
- **Java performance checklist:** The performance best practices in Java
- **JDBC performance checklist:** A sample performance checklist for JDBC modules
- **Memory leak analysis checklist:** A sample checklist for analyzing memory leaks
- **Application server configuration**: Sample application server configurations that impact performance

These checklists can be used for review and as delivery acceptance criteria.

Performance Testing Checklist

The following is a sample performance testing checklist.

Checklist for Performance Test Scripting

This section provides the checklist for scripting performance test scenarios under various categories.

APPENDIX A   PERFORMANCE OPTIMIZATION CHECKLIST

Scripting Web Transactions

- Identify the most critical transactions (business-critical and resource critical) and document the workflow for those transactions.
- Make sure that the data that you are using does not cause a bottleneck because of concurrent access to the same data.
- Come up with a workload model, transaction mix, as discussed in Chapter 6.
- Script the identified transactions with the identified tool (such as Selenium, Apache JMeter).
- Use a uniform naming convention for all the scripts.
- Modify the scripts as needed, such as inserting transactions, rendezvous points, and user think times.
- Parameterize the variables.
- Correlate the dynamic values in the script (comparing the snapshots/autocorrelation, etc.).

Scripting Batch Transactions

- Determine the batch jobs that can run during business hours, those that process very large volumes of data, those that are known to take a long time or known to be resource-intensive, those that run frequently, those that must complete within a fixed window, and those that have strict SLA requirements.
- Determine how each batch job is executed and which input parameters the batch job needs when executed.
- Create custom scripts that start/schedule batch jobs. These scripts provide flexibility to start and stop batch jobs as required.
- Identify a list of other components that could potentially impact system performance.
- Do data conditioning and check if the test data is ready.

APPENDIX A   PERFORMANCE OPTIMIZATION CHECKLIST

Checklist for Performance Test Pre-Execution

- Perform a sanity test of the system to ensure the core flows are working as expected.

- Decide on the type of the tests to be conducted, duration of the test, no of virtual users.

- Decide if stubs are needed to simulate background activities of servers which impact the performance of the system under test or to provide data.

- Restart OS; hard boot all servers involved in the performance test.

- Restart the application; bounce the various processes, servers.

- Warm the system up, wait until the system stabilizes.

- Decide which servers need to be monitored: application server, database, web server, and so forth.

- Decide which monitors need to capture the metrics.

- Decide which metrics need to be monitored on each of the servers.

    - Generic parameters

    - CPU utilization: User, system, and idle

    - Memory utilization: Committed bytes, available bytes, and so forth

    - Paging rate: Page reads/sec, page writes/sec

    - Page file usage (VM usage)

    - Physical disk: Read, write and total

    - Disk queue length

    - Instrument code with timers for method/code-level timing

    - Server-side parameters, such as connection pool metrics, thread pool metrics for various application servers

    - Client-side parameters, such as response time, throughput, page response time, asset count, asset load time, page size, and asset size

APPENDIX A PERFORMANCE OPTIMIZATION CHECKLIST

- Network monitors
- Profiling, code coverage, and memory debuggers

* Decide whether the monitoring is performed using a tool, manually, or both.
* Decide on the sampling frequency—the rate at which the various metrics are gathered.
* Note the time on the server and the client; this should go into the report. If there is a significant time difference between the server and the client, it needs to be adjusted to a common scale.

Checklist for Performance Test Execution

* Configure the performance monitors and start the monitors if required.
* Run the stubs/batch jobs to simulate the background noises.
* Execute the tests based on the workload model designed.
* Provide real-time monitoring of all the defined parameters and metrics.
* Periodically check for failed transactions, the reason for the failure, the criticality, and what needs to be done (stop, continue, or ignore).
* Periodically check the health of the servers.
* Monitor the metrics that are being captured; have an idea of the average values.

Checklist for Performance Test Reporting

* Decide on a common and uniform format for reporting across iterations/cycles of execution.
* Use a uniform naming convention for all the reports.

APPENDIX A   PERFORMANCE OPTIMIZATION CHECKLIST

- Make sure you include generic information.
    - Name of the test
    - Start time and end time of the test
    - Number of users
    - Server configuration (CPU core, memory, etc.)
    - Servers monitored
- Plot the graphs manually if you have done manual monitoring. The following are some of the common graphs.
    - Response times vs. the number of users
    - Throughput vs. the number of users
    - Transactions per second
    - Hits per second
    - Users vs. time
    - Error rate
    - CPU utilization vs. Number of users/time
    - Memory utilization vs. Number of users/time
    - Throughput achieved

Java Performance Checklist

The following is a sample Java performance checklist.

- Whether instantiation of objects is done outside `for` loop or `while` loops? If so, you need to avoid object instantiation within a loop. This reduces memory allocation.
- If you are iterating through any list and assigning the list item to a variable inside the loop, please check that all the reference objects are moved outside iterators/loops.

APPENDIX A PERFORMANCE OPTIMIZATION CHECKLIST

- While building SQLs, whether "StringBuffer" or a single String object is used instead of using multiple string constants using the + operator. It is recommended to use StringBuffer for string concatenation operation.
- Check if correct data types are defined in the method input arguments, return value, and accessor methods. Avoid any unnecessary data conversions.
- Check whether unnecessary database calls are made for retrieving information that is already available.
- Check if there are any database calls in a loop. If so, remove them as it impacts the performance.
- Check whether there is any piece of code that needs to be executed conditionally; please put an appropriate condition before it.
- Check for unnecessary object instantiation. Are all the code blocks appropriately structured/split into various methods based on the functionality?
- Check if there are any reusable code blocks, and if so, move them to Utility classes
- Does the code contain a "Null/Empty" check, list size check while accessing any value from a hash map or an array list?
- Are all the line breaks between HTML tags removed?
- Check whether the web pages and the JS files were analyzed for 404 errors—pre- and post-deployment.
- Ensure that you have not added any unnecessary blank lines in your web pages.
- Check if there are any "System Out" statements in your codebase. If so, replace them with the logger statements with appropriate logger levels.
- Are all the new queries analyzed using database access plans?

- Is your code/page being analyzed by the performance tuning tool?
- Is your query analyzed for SQL query performance using SQL/JDBC Profiler?
- Ensure that you have analyzed the code for memory leaks using memory leak tools.

Performance Fine-Tuning Measures

The following are sample performance fine-tuning measures.

JSP-based Web Page Performance Optimization

The following are JSP-based web page performance optimization measures.

- Remove unnecessary comments from the web page. These comments create additional white lines in an HTML page.
- When you make the code changes, ensure that you do not add unnecessary blank lines in your code base.
- Pack JavaScript files into combined files wherever possible.
- Avoid using carriage returns in your code. Every carriage return adds additional download time for your page.
- Use the script tags as less as possible by consolidating the code in different script tags into a single script tag.
- Isolate embedded JavaScript code into a separate file and include the file in the web page. This helps better organize the JavaScript, promotes reuse of the code as it can be included in multiple web pages, and facilitates browser caching of the JavaScript file (to improve performance).
- For better performance, all data retrieving AJAX calls should be GET. Use POST methods only for the data update scenario.

APPENDIX A   PERFORMANCE OPTIMIZATION CHECKLIST

JDBC Performance Checklist

- Building SQLs using multiple string constants using + operator: Creates multiple string objects, and then concatenation operation is performed to create the resultant SQL String. Instead, you can use StringBuffer or use a single string object.

- Use param markers with PreparedStatements instead of static SQL with hardcoded values for better utilization of PreparedStatements cache on the database side.

- Review the query using database access plans/explain plans for the following points.

  - Usage of indexes wherever applicable
  - Costly joins
  - Possibility of costly full table scans
  - Cost of the query at various join conditions
  - Unnecessary sort conditions

- Avoid unnecessary DB calls by querying the database once and pass the data objects from one method to another as parameters.

- Avoid using 'select *' while fetching from tables. Instead, do a select 1 or another small bit of data.

Memory Leak Analysis Checklist

The following is a memory leak analysis checklist.

- Avoid the use of cyclic references, such as DOM elements that call methods on themselves.
- Nullify variables/elements after completing their usage.
- Use the latest version of the JavaScript library always.

APPENDIX A   PERFORMANCE OPTIMIZATION CHECKLIST

- Reduce the usage of unnecessary variables/methods in JavaScript. Minimize global variables. Try and use maximum local variables to reduce memory usage.

- Use tools to refactor JavaScript as they reduce the memory space used by the code and restructure the code to use proper coding standards.

- Conduct endurance testing for an extended duration to uncover any code related memory leak.

Application Server Configuration Checklist

Application server-level fine-tuning parameters are as follows.

- **JVM heap size**: Fine-tune the initial and maximum heap size to appropriate values. The values can range from 2 GB to 8 GB based on the application requirements.

- **Container thread pool**: You can set the minimum and maximum size values.

- **Data source connection pool**: You can set the connection pool settings such as initial pool size, maximum pool size, and so forth.

- **Cache settings**: You can set the cache size, cache flush algorithms, default time to live (TTL) values, and so forth.

- **Server infrastructure**: Fine-tune the server infrastructure, including CPU cores, disk size, and memory based on the application load requirements.

- **Server monitoring**: Monitor the server resources (CPU, memory, disk) and garbage collector (GC) activity during the load testing and fine-tune the server capacity accordingly.

APPENDIX B

Database Performance Optimization

This appendix covers some of the key performance-related considerations for the Oracle database and DB2 database engines. The checklist items cover the common best practices followed for database development.

> **Note** The checklist only provides sample recommendations for the database engines. The specific performance optimizations can vary based on the version of the database product.

Oracle Performance-Tuning Checklist

This covers the common best practices for Oracle database engines. The best practices are relevant for most versions of the product.

Select Query Optimization

- In the WHERE clauses, use ROWID whenever possible. The ROWID of the record is the single fastest method of record retrieval. This is useful when you select a row from a table in a cursor and update the same table.

- Ensure INDEXES are present on appropriate columns of tables on which select is being performed.

APPENDIX B   DATABASE PERFORMANCE OPTIMIZATION

- Whenever you have a series of columns used in the WHERE clause, it is better to use a COMPOSITE INDEX on all the columns in the WHERE clause, instead of having a separate index for each of the columns.
- AVOID USING FUNCTIONS, concatenation, data conversions, and calculations in the WHERE condition with indexed columns, as an index might not be used in these cases.
- If the usage of functions is unavoidable, use FUNCTION-BASED INDEXES on the respective columns. If the varchar2 column is indexed and is compared against a number, the index is discarded. Instead, compare the column after converting the number to a character using the TO_CHAR function for the number value.
- An index is an overhead on an insert, update and delete operations. Determine how many business transactions will use them. If there is an index that is seldom used, rethink if you need it. Finalize your index requirements at the detailed design stage.
- Disable indexes during batch updates or data migration to speed up the process. You can rebuild the table index post the batch process or migration process is completed.
- Consider using HINTS, which can improve performance.
    - In batch jobs, the use of /*+ ALL_ROWS */ optimizes the statement execution to retrieve the entire result-set in fast mode.
    - Use /*+ ORDERED */ process tables in the order they appear in where clause.
- In WHERE clauses, AVOID using
    - Inequality (!= or <>) conditions
    - Conditions like '%x' (static value beginning with the wildcard '%'); instead use 'x%', which enables usage of index

APPENDIX B   DATABASE PERFORMANCE OPTIMIZATION

- Use count (INDEXED COLUMN) instead of count (*)
- Use count (row id), count (1) if the indexed column is not there.
- Using count (*) might lead to a full-table scan.
- Run EXPLAIN PLAN and ensure
  - usage of index
  - the driving table is appropriate
  - table joins
  - join operations (SORT-MERGE, NESTED LOOPS)
- ANALYZE TABLES
  - For transaction tables
  - ANALYZE whenever bulk insert/update/delete is performed on the table.
  - ANALYZE regularly with a 30% row estimate. This provides reasonably good statistics for the optimizer.
  - For master tables
  - ANALYZE whenever bulk insert/update/delete is performed on the table.
  - The ANALYZE table analyzes its indexes.
- DBMS_STATS
  - For transaction tables, run the DBMS_STATS when the creation of indices is done on the table for improvement of performance
- Use AUTOTRACE from SQL*Plus to find execution statistics of the statement. This executes the statement and gives information on disk reads, sorts, and so forth.

APPENDIX B   DATABASE PERFORMANCE OPTIMIZATION

Insert Statement Optimization

- AVOID INDEXES on destination table during insert. If a bulk insert is planned, drop indexes before insert and recreate them after the insert is complete.

- Use BULK INSERTS for voluminous inserts. This involves fetching the data from the cursor in batches and using a FORALL statement instead of FOR statement while inserting/updating. The usage of FORALL makes the Inserts/Updates fast and provides a framework to SAVE EXCEPTIONS, instead of raising the same immediately.

- For conditional insert into multiple tables, use the 'Multi-Insert' feature using INSERT ALL, and INSERT FIRST statements.

- The usage of commits must be optimized. Committing within a loop must be avoided, as it increases the write to the database. If there is a large volume of data updated/inserted, use conditional commits after every 500 to 2000 records. The commit limit depends on the volume of data modified.

Update Statement Optimization

- ENSURE INDEXES are present on columns constituting the 'Where' clause of the update statement.

- For voluminous updates, consider either of the following.
  - Bulk updates
  - Inserts into temporary tables and achieving functionality

- Please ensure that indexes are avoided on columns (which are manipulated by the DML), which are a part of the insert/update/delete statement. Create indexes on columns used in the query filters (such as "where" clause of the query).

APPENDIX B   DATABASE PERFORMANCE OPTIMIZATION

Delete Statement Optimization

- Use TRUNCATE for full table delete. If using truncate is not possible (deadlock, etc.), delete multiples of 1000 records at a time, and commit to avoiding the overflow of a rollback segment.

- Please ensure that indexes are avoided on columns (which are manipulated by the DML), which are a part of the insert/update/delete statement.

Optimization of Joins

- When you compare values through join, always use the table with the fewest number of records (least expensive) on the left-hand side of the join.

- When you want to check for the existence of a record, do not use joins, instead use EXISTS. The EXISTS and NOT EXISTS clause can also be used as a substitute for IN and NOT IN.

- If more than one table always use alias even though the column name is unique in both the tables. This avoids the unnecessary scanning of the other tables.

- Whenever a query takes a long time, despite creating all the prerequisite indexes, explore the possibility of defining a MATERIALIZED VIEW on the query. The materialized views work on the principle of refresh. The query fetches data only the first time it is executed. Subsequently, the data is just refreshed, and the re-execution of the same query is avoided.

- Do not refresh the materialized view on commit.

APPENDIX B   DATABASE PERFORMANCE OPTIMIZATION

Generic Performance Optimizations

- Use CURSOR, in the FOR loop where ever possible. Avoid fetching the cursor each time if the number of records are more.
- Reference cursors streamline the structure of the cursor definition.
- Partitioned tables can be considered for parallel processing of records from the same table.
- PL/SQL tables (Index by Varchar2) are for scenarios requiring lookups.
- Frequently used lookup tables can be CACHED for faster access.
- Frequently accessed procedures/functions can be kept in memory for faster access, using DBMS_SHARED_POOL.KEEP procedure. But, ensure that keeping very large procedures might adversely affect the performance.
- The MULTISET feature for combining cursors wherever there is a master-detail relationship between the entities involved. This is faster than writing a separate cursor for fetching elements from the Master table and passing the foreign key column to another cursor, which fetches elements pertaining to the Detail table.
- Check whether the Cursors opened in your code are closed at the end of the program. Ensure the cursors are closed if they are not referred later.
- The Kill/Trace session monitors the performance of the code.
- If a wait for a certain period is required, DO NOT use the FOR loop with the NULL operation.
- All PL/SQL tables must be flushed at the end of the loop.

DB2 Performance Tuning Checklist

This section discusses sample performance tuning for the DB2 database.

Performance-Tuning Considerations

The following are factors that affect DB2 performance.

- Poor application design
- Poor system and database design
- System resource shortage
- Insufficient CPU capacity
- Insufficient memory capacity
- Too much disk I/O
- Insufficient network

Special scenarios for tuning are as follows.

- Large databases
- Databases that normally service large numbers of concurrent connections
- One or more special applications that have high-performance requirements
- A special hardware configuration
- Unique query or transaction loads
- Unique query or transaction types

Key DB2 Performance-Tuning Parameters

The key DB2 performance tuning parameters are depicted in Figure B-1.

APPENDIX B   DATABASE PERFORMANCE OPTIMIZATION

Bufferpools	Extent Size		
• Number of bufferpools • Memory allocation for bufferpools • Block based bufferpools • Table spaces • Type of table space • Page size • Number of table spaces • Container lay out • Disk array and Storage	• Pre fetch Size • Table design • Multidimensional clustering(MDC) • Materialized query table(MQT) • VARCHAR column, Identity, PCTFREE • NOT Logged initially • Index design • Clustered • Allow reverse scans • Cardinality • Include column • Type 1/ type 2 index • Profile registry configurations • Configurations to avoid runtime error	• Rows read • Total execution time • Buffer pool sizing/hit ratio • DB and DBM configuration parameters update • avg_appls • scatalogcache_sz • chngpgs_thresh • dft_degree • locklist • logbufsz • maxlocks • Dynamic Sql • Number of executions • DB2 SQL explain with query tuning and access path	• mincommit • min_dec_div_3 • num_iocleaners • dft_degree • pckcachesz • seqdetect • dft_sheapthres_shrdegree • Sortheap • DB2 event monitoring • Deadlocks/SQLs • DB2 utilities • Reorg/Reorgchk • Runstats/Rebind • Db2top/distribute • Memory/CPU/paging space/network utilization • Database partitioning feature (DPF) • Snapshot monitoring

Figure B-1. Key DB2 performance tuning parameters

DB2 Monitoring Configurations

Key snapshot monitor configurations are given as follows.

- Snapshot monitor levels
- Database manager
- Database
- Application
- Snapshot functional group levels
- Buffer pool activity
- Locks
- Sorts
- SQL statements
- Table activity
- Unit of work

APPENDIX B DATABASE PERFORMANCE OPTIMIZATION

The health center, activity monitor, and memory visualizer configurations are as follows.

- Monitor the database using a health monitor and health center.
- Use the activity monitor to analyze various performance problems.
- Set thresholds and actions to perform when those thresholds are reached.
- Monitor memory utilization using memory visualizer and db2mtrk.
- Display database and application status using db2pd.
- Manage storage with a storage management tool.

APPENDIX C

Performance Test Report Template

Executive Summary

Provide a summary (e.g., requirements, process, execution, results, achievements, outstanding issues, etc.) The following is an example.

The performance test report is based on the exhaustive performance testing carried out for the e-commerce platform. The non-functional requirement document is used for load testing. As part of performance testing, the performance testing team carried out load testing, stress testing, and endurance testing with 150 concurrent user loads. We found that 80% of pages loaded within 2 seconds; however, a few pages and transactions took more than 10 seconds, requiring further investigation.

Introduction

Introduce the document, briefly describing the scope and outcome of the report. The following is an example.

The performance test report details the findings of the e-commerce application and the dependent systems.

APPENDIX C   PERFORMANCE TEST REPORT TEMPLATE

Objective

Define the objectives of the performance test.
   The following are a few examples.

- Conduct performance testing and measure performance characteristics (Response time and CPU consumption of online transactions, throughput, and CPU time for the batch processes)
- Identify and tune performance bottlenecks and locking scenarios in the application and implement changes wherever necessary and possible within the constraints of time and effort
- Publish a report of the performance testing results summary.

Performance Testing Scope

In Scope

Define the scope of the test. The following is an example.
   The performance test report covers the landing pages, home page, and a product information page of the e-commerce application.

Out of Scope

Define what is beyond the scope of the test. The following is an example.
   The performance test does not include multi-geo testing across various geographies.

Performance Testing Environment

Define the details of the test environment.
   The details of the performance testing environment are as follows.

Environment Name	Application Server	Data Volume	OS	Web Server	DBMS
Pre-prod	Apache Tomcat	15 GB	Linux	Apache	Oracle 10g

APPENDIX C   PERFORMANCE TEST REPORT TEMPLATE

Automation Tools

Define all the automation tools used in the exercise.

Tool	Platform	Version
Apache JMeter	Linux	5.3
Selenium	Linux	3.1

Performance Monitoring tools

Define all the performance monitoring tools used in the exercise.

Monitoring tool	Platform	Brief Details
AppDynamics	Linux	Application monitoring
Splunk	Linux	Log monitoring

Performance Testing Dependencies\Assumptions

Define dependencies and assumptions. The following is an example.

The dependencies for the performance test are the availability of the environment and the readiness of all the interfaces.

Architectural Model

Provide an architectural model. The following is an example.

The e-commerce platform is built on the MVC architecture pattern. The front-end application uses the JSP with JavaScript. The server components are built using servlets that use an Oracle database.

381

APPENDIX C   PERFORMANCE TEST REPORT TEMPLATE

Approach to Performance Testing

Define the performance testing approach. The following is an example.

During performance testing we carry out activities such as Input validation, test data identification, performance test strategy, performance test execution, and recording the performance test results.

Performance Test Results and Observations

Provide results using important parameters like CPU time, throughput, response time, memory consumption, concurrency data, peak time performance, bottlenecks, key outstanding issues, recommendations, and achievements. All the exit criteria should be met and showcased here. Utilize graphs and charts for better representation.

Tuning Implementation Between Execution Cycles

Database/SQL Tuning

Summarize here and include a link to the detailed report in the appendix. For example, the following is the database analysis.

- Home page queries are performing slowly.
- The bulk data in the report page is taking more than 40 seconds

Detailed information on slowly performing queries is in the Appendix section of this report.

Application Design Tuning Opportunities

Summarize here and include a link to the detailed report in the appendix. For example, the following are application design tuning opportunities.

- The performance of the home page and landing page needs to be improved.
- All the pages do the complete page refresh to fetch the data; we need to implement asynchronous partial page refresh.

Recommendations

List all the recommendations, reasons, and benefits. For example, the following features recommendations and benefits.

Recommendation	Reason	Benefits
Increase the CPU and memory capacity for the server.	The memory consumption and CPU utilization increased with an increase in load with reduced performance.	The application can handle heavy loads with good performance.
Implement caching.	Repeated page visits make repeated server calls though the data has not changed.	Improve the performance of the repeated visits for the same page.

Open Items

List all the open items, reasons for closure, and the next steps, as follows.

Open Items	Reason for Closure	Next Steps
The performance test was not conducted from multiple geographies.	The first release targets only one geography.	In the next release, carry out the performance test from multiple geographies.

Conclusion

Conclude and summarize the overall improvements: online, batch, database, CPU, and so forth. Include all the key achievements.

APPENDIX C   PERFORMANCE TEST REPORT TEMPLATE

Other Information

This section can include additional sections, such as the following.

- CPU usage guidelines: Detailed information behind the recommendation for CPU sizing
- Response time—online/batch: Detailed information on response times at various loads
- Data used for performance testing: Detailed information about the simulated user data, content volume, and data volume for testing
- Tools used: Detailed information on all the performance testing tools
- SQL tuning recommendations: Recommendations for SQL tuning
- Application tuning opportunities: Recommendations for fine-tuning application performance
- Synopsis: Recommendation approach
- Architectural model: Detailed information on the existing architecture model

APPENDIX D

Performance Test Strategy Template

Introduction

This section provides a brief introduction of the document, what is covered, background, and so forth. The following is an example.

The document details the performance test strategy and details the performance testing steps, deliverables, risks, assumptions, and other information. You start by defining the entry and exit criteria for performance testing. You then list all the needed dependencies. You then detail the testing steps, including the requirement gathering, performance test design, performance test execution, monitoring, and other activities for performance testing of this application. Broadly the performance test phases align with the steps explained in Chapter 6; wherever needed, I have made changes to suit the application needs.

Objective

Define the core objectives of the performance testing phase. The following is an example.

The performance testing for the scope of this document ensures that the following Go Live objectives are met.

- Identify and select business scenarios and corresponding application transactions.

- Have maximum coverage of the application from a transaction coverage perspective.

APPENDIX D PERFORMANCE TEST STRATEGY TEMPLATE

- Capture the following characteristics for different components
    - Response time, CPU time, and memory consumption for online transaction
    - Elapsed time, CPU time, and memory consumption for batch process
- Identify, tune, and implement performance bottlenecks in the application wherever necessary and possible.
- Report the performance testing results summary.
- Conduct performance tests, and establish baseline numbers for critical new functionalities in applications.
- Measure and validate the response times and transaction throughput specified under expected peak load conditions for regression functionalities.
- Document CPU and memory utilization of the test systems under peak load.
- Evaluate whether the system (including physical infrastructure) supports the transaction volumes expected in production.
- Use methodical processes to objectively assess the ability of the system to perform certain functions within a prescribed time.
- Ensure that the status of the application performance test is transparent.
- Enforce the use of the defect management process through the life cycle of application performance testing. This ensures verification and validation of defect remediation actions.

All response times are the end-to-end response times for synchronous real-time interfaces calculated from respective applications and transactions within each application. The main test objectives are presented in Table D-1.

APPENDIX D PERFORMANCE TEST STRATEGY TEMPLATE

Table D-1. *The Main Test Objectives*

Test Objectives	Detailed Questions
Implementation Acceptance	Does the system have the stability to go into production?
Regression Acceptance	Does the new system impact the specified response times?
	If specific changes are being incorporated in this release to address performance or changes in the code base cause overall concern for performance, list those explicitly.
Bottleneck Identification	What is the cause of the current performance issue(s)?
Reliability	How stable is the system under heavy load?
Capacity Planning	At what point does performance degradation occur?
Configuration Sizing	What is the best performing configuration?
Product Evaluation	What is the most optimal infrastructure configuration (CPU, memory, disk) to support 100 concurrent users?
New Environment	Does the new environment perform equivalently to or better than the old environment?

Assumptions

List all the assumptions here. The following is an example.

The following are the key assumptions.

- The application is accessible only on desktop browsers.
- The maximum number of concurrent users is 100.
- The application is only accessible in Europe.

Entry and Exit Criterion

Define clear entry and exit criteria. The following is an example.

Examples of the entry criteria and exit criteria are as follows.

APPENDIX D   PERFORMANCE TEST STRATEGY TEMPLATE

Entry Criterion (Examples)

- Integration tested code is available
- Signed-off performance SLAs and NFR specifications
- Completed DBA review of SQL queries
- Fulfillment of external dependencies

Exit Criterion (Examples)

- All test scripts are executed
- Publish result summary report (CPU time, memory utilization, response time)
- Deliver performance-tested code
- Explain/reasons for the modules in which performance can't be tuned
- Performance optimization recommendations

Scope

Define the scope (inclusions). The following is an example.

The scope of performance testing includes complete application performance testing of enterprise applications.

- Enterprise application: Load testing of an identified list of critical scenarios/transactions from all modules to emulate a real-world scenario.
    - Performance critical transactions in enterprise application
    - Performance critical scenarios which cover real-time interfaces of enterprise application

The response times of all transactions of enterprise service measured is baselined after consultation with the technical team and business.

Out of Scope

Define all exclusions of the application. The following is an example.

Performance testing from different geographies is beyond the scope of the report.

Performance Testing Dependencies and Execution Support

List all the points where support is required. Table D-2 is an example.

Table D-2. *Performance Testing Dependencies*

Dependency	Description	Owner
Environment setup	Web server configuration, application server configuration, integration setup	Infrastructure team
Infrastructure setup	Server setup, database creation, monitoring setup	Infrastructure team
Performance data Capture and Performance report Generation support	Performance execution data collection	Performance testing team
Test data set	Creation of tables and their population	Enterprise DBA
DBA involvement for mass load\backup\refresh of data	Support required from the DBA for database load, backup, and refresh to do the performance run	Enterprise DBA
Database tuning support	DBA to review the SQL and provide inputs and create index and table changes wherever necessary	Enterprise DBA
Integration tested code	Baseline code after QA Drop and at the end of Integration testing	Performance testing team
Data setup	Set up the test data (such as user data, application data) needed for performance testing	Performance testing team
Other support areas	Code availability, infrastructure availability	Development team, Infrastructure team

APPENDIX D   PERFORMANCE TEST STRATEGY TEMPLATE

Performance Testing Steps/Activities
Approach

Application Performance Testing (APT) ensures that specific application under test meets the desired level of performance and throughput.

The following is the overall approach for how testing is planned and executed.

- APT of the application Go Live is divided into three phases
    - The **planning phase** includes all planning activities to produce a detailed test plan and an appropriate test strategy. It also explains future activities.
    - The **preparation phase** includes test environment setup activities, load testing tool customizations, test execution plan, test script generation, and a test readiness review.
    - The **execution phase** includes APT test execution and produces a formal test summary report describing the outcome of the test phase and the status of the test scenarios executed during the phase.
- The planning phase includes liaison with technical teams, business consultants, and businesses to finalize a list of transactions/business processes and expected volume in production.
- There are load runner scripts for end-user transactions; total transaction time for any transaction is emulated as transaction time between request leaving the client and the last response received by the client for the corresponding request.
- The test results from the execution phase are shared with the technical team, business consultants, and business stakeholders for analysis and to define acceptable criteria for all transactions. The problem areas identified are targeted for tuning/improvement through the test-and-tune cycle of performance testing.

APPENDIX D   PERFORMANCE TEST STRATEGY TEMPLATE

- Note that the tests described in this document do not measure the response time/throughput time for individual subcomponents in the application. The tests only measure the end-to-end response times (i.e., request sent to web service and the response received from web service and real-time interfaces).

- It is expected that environment tuning and defect resolution occur during the APT execution phase.

- The performance tests examine any errors occurring during the APT testing, including the following.
    - System failure during the test
    - Queue lengths to determine if there have been any failed asynchronous transactions (i.e., poison queue lengths)

- Clean run of application Go Live APT to include a 100% load test.

- The system monitoring is performed using PERFMON-enabled on the servers to collect system and application performance statistics during APT execution.

- The performance center/load runner is a load generation tool for APT and is supported by other in-house test harness/stubs.

- All test results and test artifacts are stored in the HP performance center.

Requirement Gathering

Define the baseline and the details. For example, gather performance metrics and transaction information.

Online Application

- Get the CPU time, response time, and other important parameters for each transaction.
- Get the volume for each transaction, workload distribution on a peak day; for example

APPENDIX D   PERFORMANCE TEST STRATEGY TEMPLATE

No.	Percentage Workload (in a peak hour of a peak day)	Volume (in a peak hour of a peak day)
1	70%	200 transactions per second

- Get the expected baseline results.

Batch Application

Get the CPU time, elapsed time, throughput, and other important parameters for each batch report/job.

Design

This is the design approach for the performance testing phase. The following is an example.

- Identify test data for each of the scenarios mentioned in the inclusion section
- Environment preparation
- Identify the number of concurrent users
- Write test scripts to cover various business scenarios and to simulate concurrency

Performance Testing Tools to Be Utilized

The tools in Table D-3 are utilized to perform the performance testing of this application.

Table D-3. *Performance Testing Tools*

Tool	Purpose
Jira	Defect management
HP Load Runner Virtual User Generator 9.5	Test script creation
HP Performance Center 9.5	Test case execution
HP Load Runner Load Generator Agent 9.5	
HP Load Runner Analysis 9.5	Results analysis

Monitoring

Application Monitoring Tools

The monitoring tools in Table D-4 are utilized during the performance testing of this application.

Table D-4. *Monitoring Tools*

Component/System	Tool
Transaction throughput	HP LoadRunner
System-level utilization of Network, CPU, Memory, and Hard Drive	Windows PERFMON correlated into LoadRunner Analysis

Application Monitoring Parameters

In addition to test execution, the performance testing tool can capture Web, application, database, server, and network resource utilization. Monitoring data is correlated with response time data to identify overall system thresholds related to the success criteria. Please list all systems in the AUT and the monitoring included for each in the performance test (see Table D-5).

APPENDIX D   PERFORMANCE TEST STRATEGY TEMPLATE

Table D-5. Application Monitors

System	Monitoring *What* and *How*
Windows (Application Server, Web Server, Load Generators)	LogicalDisk (disk writes/second and reads/second)
	Memory (available memory, utilized memory)
	Physical disk (disk writes/second and disk reads/second)
	Process (thread count)
	CPU utilization
Network	Network interface packets/second

Test Scenarios Execution Methodology

Define execution methodology here. The following is an example.

Execution Cycles

Execution cycles are test cycles designed for a targeted workload with expected results. Each cycle requires several test iterations to complete. The Table D-6 lists the available execution cycles and describes each type.

There are two cycles of execution, and each cycle includes the following steps.

1. Set up the environment.
2. Load the production quality and volume test data.
3. Simulate transaction scenario with a predefined number of concurrent users (for scalability test).
4. Capture the response time for the transaction.
5. Repeat the test and take the average value.

Table D-6. *Execution Cycles*

Execution Cycle	Description
Single User Cycle	Single user response times for all transactions. This is executed and measured under a No Load condition.
20% Load Cycle	This performance test cycle is designed to identify long-running transactions without executing heavy load against a system. This test is executed with 20% of peak load conditions. It is typically executed early in the performance testing life cycle to detect problematic transactions that may impact the entire system under larger user-volumes.
Peak Load Cycle	This performance test cycle emulates a "day in the life" scenario and validates system performance under peak load conditions of 1 to 2 hours. This test is intended to confirm end-user response times, and system resource utilization as consistent peak user-volumes are executed against the system.
Stress Threshold Cycle	This performance test cycle determines the maximum user activity that an application can sustain and is described as a "destructive" test. User activity is incrementally increased to a load equivalent to 150%–200% of current peak usage, expecting that a point of unacceptable degradation of response time and reliability is reached.
Endurance Cycle	This performance test cycle validates that the system functions over an extended period of average user load with no degradation of performance or reliability. A duration cycle is conducted by applying a substantial and constant (but less than maximum capacity) load for 12 to 24 hours. The endurance testing is done to discover memory leak issues.
Other	In multi-geo testing, you carry out performance testing from multiple geographies to understand response times, latency, and more.

APPENDIX D   PERFORMANCE TEST STRATEGY TEMPLATE

Test Execution Results Capturing

Define the test result capture guidelines. The following is an example.

- Request performance group to provide the run data based on the start time and end time for each of the transaction belonging to that thread
- Analyze the data and determine the need for another run for the same run number.

Post Execution Performance Tuning

Define the approach to tuning, the tools to be used, and so forth. The following is an example.

- Explain the analysis of the SQLs
- Design analysis of the application
- Performance recommendations discussion
- Change, re-execute, and capture

Performance Testing Success Criteria

Entry Criteria

For performance testing to commence or be considered valid, certain criteria needs to be met. The following items are entrance criteria for performance testing.

- The performance test plan/strategy is formally signed-off.
- The business and technical teams formally signed-off the NFR.
- The application areas to be tested should be considered functionally complete and stable from a manual testing perspective.
- The performance test environment is completely set up. This includes hardware, software, test IDs, and test data.
- All applications involved in performance testing are available with their latest code base.

- Automated test scripts are generated using the scripting tool.
- The load generators have been configured.
- The performance monitors are configured in different servers are responding as intended
- A defect management process is in place.

Test Execution Contingency Planning

Define a contingency plan. The following is an example.

- If the performance test data is available, export the existing test data dump from the QA environment for the testing.
- If the integration in the performance test environment is not ready, use the integration endpoint from the QA environment.

Deliverables

Define the deliverables, and attach a template for the final report. The following is an example.

- Performance model
- Test results

Performance Testing Risks

Provide a risk mitigation plan. The following is an example.

- The integration test is not expected to be 100% complete.
- Performance test timelines overlap with QA testing. All parallel tasks are executed on the same servers and use shared resources and may thus skew the performance results.
- Performance tuning changes may affect the QA domain functional test, and the QA functional test may affect performance-tuning changes.

APPENDIX D   PERFORMANCE TEST STRATEGY TEMPLATE

- Data model changes at a later stage (due to performance findings) may cause the need to retest most online transactions.
- External services are called multiple times in each scenario. The performance of the services is a key factor in deciding the overall performance of the application.

Glossary of Performance Terms

Define all the terms used in the document. Table D-7 is an example.

Table D-7. Glossary of Terms

Term	Explanation
Performance Testing	Automated testing is designed to emulate multiple users interacting with a system. This type of testing, comprised of multiple performance cycles, is executed to identify application performance bottlenecks before an application is released into production, mitigating the risk of system outages due to the high user and/or transaction volumes.
Virtual User	The virtual user mimics the real user's interaction in the real world. Virtual user scripts also measure the performance of application components by capturing transaction response times.
Business Process	The business process traces the web user path in performing a business function from process initiation to completion.
Transaction	A virtual user performs a single page request. In this context, the length of a transaction is measured from the time the client makes the request to the time of the last byte received. Response time is equal to this measurement.
Think Time	The average time user takes to go from one page to another.
User Profile	A matrix that illustrates application usage based on user role.
Concurrent Users	The users who access the application features simultaneously at the same point in time. Normally, you consider concurrent users per second.
AUT	An Application Under Test is the entire solution or system, including servers, workstations, data, and hardware/environment.

Bibliography

[1]. "Using site speed in web search ranking." (2010, April 09). Retrieved January 04, 2018, from http://googlewebmastercentral.blogspot.com/2010/04/using-site-speed-in-web-search-ranking.html

[2]. Galletta, D.F., Henry, R.M., McCoy, S., and Polak, P. (2004). "Web Site Delays: How Tolerant are Users?" *J. AIS*, 5, 1.

[3]. Apache JMeter. (n.d.). Retrieved January 07, 2018, from http://jmeter.apache.org

[4]. Pathan, A. M. K., and Buyya, R. (2007). *A Taxonomy and Survey of Content Delivery Networks*. Grid Computing and Distributed Systems Laboratory, University of Melbourne, Technical Report, 4.

[5]. Cardellini, V., Casalicchio, E., Colajanni, M., and Yu, P. S. (2002). "The state of the art in locally distributed Web-server systems." *ACM Computing Surveys (CSUR)*, 34(2), 263–311.

[6]. Gilly, K., Juiz, C., and Puigjaner, R. (2011). "An up-to-date survey in web load balancing." *World Wide Web*, 14(2), 105–131.

[7]. Kumar, D., Olshefski, D. P., and Zhang, L. (2009, September). "Connection and performance model driven optimization of pageview response time." *Modeling, Analysis and Simulation of Computer and Telecommunication Systems, 2009*. MASCOTS'09. IEEE International Symposium on (pp. 1–10). IEEE.

[8]. Nygren, E., Sitaraman, R. K., and Sun, J. (2010). "The akamai network: a platform for high-performance internet applications." *ACM SIGOPS Operating Systems Review*, 44(3), 2–19.

[9]. Yang, J., Wang, W., Muntz, R., and Wang, J. (1999). "Access driven Web caching." *UCLA Technical Report# 990007*.

[10]. Charland, A., and Leroux, B. (2011). "Mobile application development: web vs. native." *Communications of the ACM*, 54(5), 49–53.

BIBLIOGRAPHY

[11]. Cohen, E., Krishnamurthy, B., and Rexford, J. (1998, October). "Improving end-to-end performance of the Web using server volumes and proxy filters." *ACM SIGCOMM Computer Communication Review* (Vol. 28, No. 4, pp. 241-253). ACM.

[12]. Mesbah, A. (2009). *Analysis and Testing of Ajax-based Single-Page Web Applications.*

[13]. Palpanas, T., and Mendelzon, A. (1998). *Web Prefetching Using Partial Match Prediction.* University of Toronto, Department of Computer Science.

[14]. "Mobile Analysis in PageSpeed Insights | PageSpeed Insights | Google Developers." Retrieved December 17, 2016, from `https://developers.google.com/speed/docs/insights/mobile`

[15]. *Web Storage* (Second Edition). Retrieved December 17, 2016, from `http://dev.w3.org/html5/webstorage/`

[16]. Challenger, J., Iyengar, A., Witting, K., Ferstat, C., and Reed, P. (2000). "A publishing system for efficiently creating dynamic web content." *INFOCOM 2000. Nineteenth Annual Joint Conference of the IEEE Computer and Communications Societies. Proceedings. IEEE* (Vol. 2, pp. 844-853). IEEE.

[17]. Verma, D. C. (2003). *Content Distribution Networks: An Engineering Approach.* John Wiley & Sons.

[18]. Iyengar, A., Nahum, E., Shaikh, A., and Tewari, R. (2002). "Enhancing web performance." *Communication Systems* (pp. 95-126). Springer US.

[19]. Killelea, P. (2002). *Web Performance Tuning: Speeding Up the Web.* O'Reilly Media, Inc.

[20]. "Apache Performance Tuning." Retrieved November 21, 2016, from `http://httpd.apache.org/docs/current/misc/perf-tuning.html`

[21]. Podlipnig, S., and Böszörmenyi, L. (2003). A survey of web cache replacement strategies. *ACM Computing Surveys (CSUR),* 35(4), 374-398.

[22]. Acharjee, U. (2006). *Personalized and Artificial Intelligence Web Caching and Prefetching* (Doctoral dissertation, University of Ottawa (Canada)).

BIBLIOGRAPHY

[23]. "PMD." (n.d.). Retrieved January 07, 2018, from `http://pmd.sourceforge.net/`

[24]. Pallis, G., Vakali, A., and Pokorny, J. (2008). "A clustering-based prefetching scheme on a Web cache environment." *Computers and Electrical Engineering*, 34(4), 309–323.

[25]. Wong, K. Y. (2006). "Web cache replacement policies: a pragmatic approach." *IEEE Network*, 20(1), 28–34.

[26]. Chen, H. (2008). *Prefetching and Re-fetching in Web Caching systems: Algorithms and Simulation*. ProQuest.

[27]. Chen, T. (2007). "Obtaining the optimal cache document replacement policy for the caching system of an EC website." *European Journal of Operational Research*, 181(2), 828–841.

[28]. Kumar, C., and Norris, J. B. (2008). "A new approach for a proxy-level web caching mechanism." *Decision Support Systems*, 46(1), 52–60.

[29]. Kumar, C. (2009). "Performance evaluation for implementations of a network of proxy caches." *Decision Support Systems*, *46*(2), 492–500.

[30]. Domenech, J., Gil, J. A., Sahuquillo, J., and Pont, A. (2010). "Using current web page structure to improve prefetching performance. *Computer Networks*," 54(9), 1404–1417.

[31]. Domenech, J., Pont, A., Sahuquillo, J., and Gil, J. A. (2006). "A comparative study of web prefetching techniques focusing on user's perspective." *IFIP International Conference on Network and Parallel Computing (NPC 2006)*.

[32]. Cobb, J., and ElAarag, H. (2008). "Web proxy cache replacement scheme based on back-propagation neural network." *Journal of Systems and Software*, 81(9), 1539–1558.

[33]. Ali, W., and Shamsuddin, S. M. (2009, May). "Intelligent client-side web caching scheme based on least recently used algorithm and neuro-fuzzy system." *International Symposium on Neural Networks* (pp. 70–79). Springer, Berlin, Heidelberg.

[34]. ElAarag, H., and Romano, S. (2009, March). "Improvement of the neural network proxy cache replacement strategy." *Proceedings of the 2009 Spring Simulation Multiconference* (p. 90). Society for Computer Simulation International.

BIBLIOGRAPHY

[35]. Sulaiman, S., Shamsuddin, S. M., Forkan, F., and Abraham, A. (2008, May). "Intelligent Web caching using neurocomputing and particle swarm optimization algorithm." *Modeling and Simulation, 2008. AICMS 08. Second Asia International Conference on* (pp. 642-647). IEEE.

[36]. Tian, W., Choi, B., and Phoha, V. (2002). "An adaptive web cache access predictor using neural network." *Developments in Applied Artificial Intelligence*, 113-117.

[37]. Wong, K. Y. (2006). "Web cache replacement policies: a pragmatic approach." *IEEE Network*, 20(1), 28-34.

[38]. Jiang, Y., Wu, M. Y., and Shu, W. (2002, August). "Web prefetching: Costs, benefits and performance." *Proceedings of the 7th international workshop on web content caching and distribution (WCW2002)*. Boulder, Colorado.

[39]. Tang, N., and Vemuri, V. R. (2005, March). "An artificial immune system approach to document clustering." *Proceedings of the 2005 ACM Symposium on Applied Computing* (pp. 918-922). ACM.

[40]. Ali, W., Shamsuddin, S. M., and Ismail, A. S. (2011). "A survey of web caching and prefetching." *International Journal of Advances in Soft Computing and Its Applications*, 3(1), 18-44.

[41]. Liu, M., Wang, F. Y., Zeng, D., and Yang, L. (2001). "An overview of world wide web caching." *Systems, Man, and Cybernetics, 2001 IEEE International Conference on* (Vol. 5, pp. 3045-3050). IEEE.

[42]. Barish, G., and Obraczke, K. (2000). "World wide web caching: Trends and techniques." *IEEE Communications magazine*, 38(5), 178-184.

[43]. Pons, A. P. (2005). "Improving the performance of client web object retrieval." *Journal of Systems and Software*, 74(3), 303-311.

[44]. Shi, L., Han, Y. J., Ding, X. G., Wei, L., and Gu, Z. M. (2006). "An SPN-based integrated model for Web prefetching and caching." *Journal of Computer Science and Technology*, 21(4), 482-489.

[45]. Hussain, S., and McLeod, R. D. (2000). "Intelligent prefetching at a proxy server." *Electrical and Computer Engineering, 2000 Canadian Conference on* (Vol. 1, pp. 209-211). IEEE.

[46]. Wu, Y. H., and Chen, A. L. (2002). "Prediction of web page accesses by proxy server log." *World Wide Web*, 5(1), 67-88.

[47]. Xu, C. Z., and Ibrahim, T. I. (2003, January). "Towards semantics-based prefetching to reduce web access latency." *Applications and the Internet, 2003. Proceedings. 2003 Symposium on* (pp. 318–325). IEEE.

[48]. Xu, C. Z., and Ibrahim, T. I. (2000, April). "Semantics-Based personalized prefetching to improve Web performance." *Proceedings of the 20th IEEE Conference on Distributed Computing Systems* (pp. 636–643).

[49]. Kirchner, H., Krummenacher, R., Risse, T., and Edwards-May, D. (2004). "A location-aware prefetching mechanism." *4th International Network Conf. (INC'04)* (pp. 453–460).

[50]. Agababov, V., Buettner, M., Chudnovsky, V., Cogan, M., Greenstein, B., McDaniel, S., and Yin, B. (2015, May). "Flywheel: Google's Data Compression Proxy for the Mobile Web." *NSDI* (Vol. 15, pp. 367–380).

[51]. "SPDY: An experimental protocol for a faster web." Retrieved January 04, 2018, from `https://www.chromium.org/spdy/spdy-whitepaper`

[52]. "PageSpeed Examples Directory." (n.d.) January 04, 2018, from `http://www.modpagespeed.com/`

[53]. Zhou, W., Li, Q., Caesar, M., and Godfrey, P. (2011, December). "ASAP: A low-latency transport layer." *Proceedings of the Seventh Conference on emerging Networking Experiments and Technologies* (p. 20). ACM.

[54]. Mundwiler, R., and Gaffin, M. (2001). *U.S. Patent No. 6,178,173*. Washington, DC: U.S. Patent and Trademark Office.

[55]. Radhakrishnan, S., Cheng, Y., Chu, J., Jain, A., and Raghavan, B. (2011, December). "TCP fast open." *Proceedings of the Seventh Conference on emerging Networking Experiments and Technologies* (p. 21). ACM.

[56]. Lohr, S. (2012, February 29). "Impatient Web Users Flee Slow-Loading Sites." Retrieved January 04, 2018, from `http://www.nytimes.com/2012/03/01/technology/impatient-web-users-flee-slow-loading-sites.html`

[57]. S. (2014, May 25). "Velocity and the Bottom Line." Retrieved January 04, 2018, from `http://radar.oreilly.com/2009/07/velocity-making-your-site-fast.html`

[58]. Netravali, R., Goyal, A., Mickens, J., and Balakrishnan, H. (2016, March). "Polaris: Faster Page Loads Using Fine-grained Dependency Tracking." *NSDI* (pp. 123–136).

BIBLIOGRAPHY

[59]. Datta, A., Dutta, K., Thomas, H. M., VanderMeer, D. E., Ramamritham, K., and Fishman, D. (2001, September). "A comparative study of alternative middle tier caching solutions to support dynamic web content acceleration." *VLDB* (pp. 667–670).

[60]. Datta, A., Dutta, K., Ramamritham, K., Thomas, H., and VanderMeer, D. (2001, May). "Dynamic content acceleration: A caching solution to enable scalable dynamic web page generation." *SIGMOD Conference* (p. 616).

[61]. Katabi, D., Handley, M., and Rohrs, C. (2002). "Congestion control for high bandwidth-delay product networks." *ACM SIGCOMM Computer Communication Review*, 32(4), 89–102.

[62]. "High Speed TCP for Large Congestion Windows." (n.d.). Retrieved January 04, 2018, from http://www.ietf.org/rfc/rfc3649.txt

[63]. Zhu, H., and Yang, T. (2001). "Class-based cache management for dynamic web content." *INFOCOM 2001. Twentieth Annual Joint Conference of the IEEE Computer and Communications Societies. Proceedings. IEEE* (Vol. 3, pp. 1215–1224). IEEE.

[64]. Su, Z., Yang, Q., Lu, Y., and Zhang, H. (2000). "Whatnext: A prediction system for web requests using n-gram sequence models." *Web Information Systems Engineering, 2000. Proceedings of the First International Conference on* (Vol. 1, pp. 214–221). IEEE.

[65]. Domenech, J., Pont, A., Sahuquillo, J., and Gil, J. A. (2004, August). "An experimental framework for testing web prefetching techniques." *Euromicro Conference, 2004. Proceedings. 30th* (pp. 214–221). IEEE.

[66]. Souders, S. (2007). *High Performance Web Sites: Essential Knowledge for Front-End Engineers*. sl.

[67]. Souders, S. (2009). *Even Faster Web Sites: Performance Best Practices for Web Developers*. O'Reilly Media, Inc.

[68]. Sundaresan, S., Magharei, N., Feamster, N., and Teixeira, R. (2013). *Characterizing and Mitigating Web Performance Bottlenecks in Broadband Access Networks*. Georgia Institute of Technology.

[69]. Cohen, E., and Kaplan, H. (2003). "Proactive caching of DNS records: Addressing a performance bottleneck." *Computer Networks*, 41(6), 707–726.

BIBLIOGRAPHY

[70]. Ramu, K., Sugumar, D. R., and Shanmugasundaram, B. (2012). "A study on web prefetching techniques." *Journal of Advances in Computational Research: An International Journal*, 1(1–2), 200.

[71]. Palmer, J. W. (2002). "Web site usability, design, and performance metrics." *Information systems research*, 13(2), 151–167.

[72]. Valduriez, D. F. V. I. P., and Yagoub, K. (1999). *Caching Strategies for Data-Intensive Web Sites*.

[73]. "Build Better | Test Smarter." (n.d.). Retrieved January 07, 2018, from http://www.soapui.org/

[74]. Arun Iyengar and Daniela Rosu. 2002. "Architecting Websites for high performance." *Sci. Program*, 75–89.

[75]. Paulson, L. D. (2005). "Building rich web applications with Ajax." *Computer*, 38(10), 14–17.

[76]. Shi, W., Collins, E., and Karamcheti, V. (2003). "Modeling object characteristics of dynamic web content." *Journal of Parallel and Distributed Computing*, 63(10), 963–980.

[77]. Svedloff, G. (2006). *U.S. Patent No. 7,047,318*. Washington, DC: U.S. Patent and Trademark Office.

[78]. Schmiedl, G., Seidl, M., and Temper, K. (2009, September). "Mobile phone web browsing: a study on usage and usability of the mobile web." *Proceedings of the 11th international Conference on Human-Computer interaction with Mobile Devices and Services* (p. 70). ACM.

[79]. Vakali, A., and Pallis, G. (2003). "Content delivery networks: Status and trends. *IEEE Internet Computing*, 7(6), 68–74.

[80]. Ravi, J., Yu, Z., and Shi, W. (2009). "A survey on dynamic Web content generation and delivery techniques. *Journal of Network and Computer Applications*, 32(5), 943–960.

[81]. Sivasubramanian, S., Pierre, G., Van Steen, M., and Alonso, G. (2007). "Analysis of caching and replication strategies for web applications. *IEEE Internet Computing*, 11(1).

[82]. "HTTP Archive Trends." Retrieved November 21, 2016, from http://httparchive.org/trends.php

BIBLIOGRAPHY

[83]. Fortino, G., and Mastroianni, C. (2008). "Special section: Enhancing content networks with P2P, Grid and Agent technologies. *Future Generation Computer Systems*, 24(3), 177–179.

[84]. Candan, K. S., Li, W. S., Luo, Q., Hsiung, W. P., and Agrawal, D. (2001, May). "Enabling dynamic content caching for database-driven web sites." *ACM SIGMOD Record* (Vol. 30, No. 2, pp. 532–543). ACM.

[85]. "Best Practices for Speeding Up Your Website: Yahoo Developer Network." Retrieved November 21, 2016, from https://developer.yahoo.com/performance/rules.html

[86]. Schneider, F., Agarwal, S., Alpcan, T., and Feldmann, A. (2008, April). "The new web: characterizing AJAX traffic." *International Conference on Passive and Active Network Measurement* (pp. 31–40). Springer, Berlin, Heidelberg.

[87]. "Web performance optimization." Retrieved November 21, 2016, from https://en.wikipedia.org/wiki/Web_performance_optimization

[88]. "Optimizing the Critical Rendering Path | Web | Google Developers." Retrieved November 21, 2016, from https://developers.google.com/web/fundamentals/performance/critical-rendering-path/optimizing-critical-rendering-path

[89]. "PageSpeed Rules and Recommendations | Web | Google Developers." Retrieved November 21, 2016, from https://developers.google.com/web/fundamentals/performance/critical-rendering-path/page-speed-rules-and-recommendations

[90]. Rempel, G. (2015, January). "Defining Standards for Web Page Performance in Business Applications." *Proceedings of the 6th ACM/SPEC International Conference on Performance Engineering* (pp. 245–252). ACM.

[91]. Mineki, G., Uemura, S., and Hasegawa, T. (2013, January). "Spdy accelerator for improving web access speed." *Advanced Communication Technology (ICACT), 2013 15th International Conference on* (pp. 540–544). IEEE.

[92]. Hoxmeier, J. A., and DiCesare, C. (2000). "System response time and user satisfaction: An experimental study of browser-based applications. *AMCIS 2000 Proceedings*, 347.

[93]. "PageSpeed Insights Rules | PageSpeed Insights | Google Developers." Retrieved November 21, 2016, from https://developers.google.com/speed/docs/insights/rules

[94]. Kambhampaty, S., Modali, V. S., Bertoli, M., Casale, G., and Serazzi, G. (2005, October). "Performance modeling for web based J2EE and .NET Applications." *Proc. of world Academy of Science, Engineering and Technology* (Vol. 8).

[95]. Shivakumar, S. K. (2014). *Architecting High Performing, Scalable and Available Enterprise Web Applications*. Morgan Kaufmann.

[96]. Hinz, M., Fiala, Z., and Wehner, F. (2004, September). "Personalization-based optimization of web interfaces for mobile devices." *Mobile HCI* (pp. 204–215).

[97]. Gomes, P., Tostao, S., Goncalives, D., and Jorge, J. (2001). "Web Clipping: Compression Heuristics for Displaying Text on a PDA. *Mobile HCI'01*.

[98]. Milic-Frayling, N. (2002). "Smartview: Flexible viewing of web page contents." *Proc. World Wide Web Conference (WWW'02), May*.

[99]. Kohavi, R., Deng, A., Longbotham, R., and Xu, Y. (2014, August). "Seven rules of thumb for web site experimenters." *Proceedings of the 20th ACM SIGKDD international conference on Knowledge discovery and data mining* (pp. 1857–1866). ACM.

[100]. Brutlag, J., Abrams, Z., and Meenan, P. (2011). "Above the fold time: Measuring web page performance visually." *Velocity: Web Performance and Operations Conference*.

[101]. "Above the fold." (2017, December 09). Retrieved January 04, 2018, from http://en.wikipedia.org/wiki/Above_the_fold

[102]. Patrick Meenan, Chao (Ray) Feng, Mike Petrovich. (n.d.). "Going Beyond onload: How Fast Does It Feel?" *Velocity New York 2013*. Retrieved January 04, 2018, from http://velocityconf.com/velocityny2013/public/schedule/detail/31344

[103]. Jan, R. H., Lin, C. P., and Chern, M. S. (2006). "An optimization model for Web content adaptation." *Computer Networks*, 50(7), 953–965.

[104]. Noble, B. (2000). "System support for mobile, adaptive applications." *IEEE Personal Communications*, 7(1), 44–49.

BIBLIOGRAPHY

[105]. Singh, A., Trivedi, A., Ramamritham, K., and Shenoy, P. (2004). "PTC: Proxies that transcode and cache in heterogeneous Web client environments." *World Wide Web*, 7(1), 7-28.

[106]. "Optimizely." (n.d.). Retrieved January 04, 2018, from http://pages.optimizely.com/A-Blueprint-for-AB-Testing-and-Optimization-in-native-mobile-apps.html

[107]. "Rudy, G. Tidbits from the sites that made it work—School of Computing." Retrieved November 23, 2016, from http://www.cs.utah.edu/~grudy/Building Scalable Website s.pdf

[108]. Nagy, Z. S. O. L. T. (2013). "Improved speed on intelligent web sites." *Recent Advances in Computer Science*, 1(14), 215–220.

[109]. "Browser Automation." (n.d.). Retrieved January 07, 2018, from http://www.seleniumhq.org/

[110]. Leighton, T. (2009). "Improving performance on the internet." *Communications of the ACM*, 52(2), 44–51.

[111]. Palomäki, J. (2010). "Web Application Performance Testing."

[112]. Subraya, B. M. (ed.). (2006). *Integrated Approach to Web Performance Testing: A Practitioner's Guide: A Practitioner's Guide*. IGI Global.

[113]. Nederlof, A., Mesbah, A., and Deursen, A. V. (2014, May). "Software engineering for the web: the state of the practice." *Companion Proceedings of the 36th International Conference on Software Engineering* (pp. 4–13). ACM.

[114]. Nederlof, A. (2013). *Analyzing Web Applications: An Empirical Study*.

[115]. Butkiewicz, M., Madhyastha, H. V., and Sekar, V. (2011, November). "Understanding website complexity: measurements, metrics, and implications." *Proceedings of the 2011 ACM SIGCOMM conference on Internet measurement conference* (pp. 313–328). ACM.

[116]. Guinard, D. (2011). *A Web of Things Application Architecture*.

[117]. Bouch, A., Kuchinsky, A., and Bhatti, N. (2000, April). "Quality is in the eye of the beholder: meeting users' requirements for Internet quality of service." *Proceedings of the SIGCHI conference on Human Factors in Computing Systems* (pp. 297–304). ACM.

[118]. Ihm, S., and Pai, V. S. (2011, November). "Towards understanding modern web traffic." *Proceedings of the 2011 ACM SIGCOMM conference on Internet measurement conference* (pp. 295–312). ACM.

[119]. Rhea, S. C., Liang, K., and Brewer, E. (2003, May). "Value-based web caching." *Proceedings of the 12th international conference on World Wide Web* (pp. 619–628). ACM.

[120]. Mickens, J. (2010, June). "Silo: Exploiting JavaScript and DOM Storage for Faster Page Loads." *WebApps*.

[121]. Theurer, T. (2007). "Performance Research, Part 2: Browser Cache Usage-Exposed. *Yahoo User Interface Blog*.

[122]. Zhang, X., Wang, N., Vassilakis, V. G., and Howarth, M. P. (2015). "A distributed in-network caching scheme for P2P-like content chunk delivery. *Computer Networks*, 91, 577–592.

[123]. Jang, I., Suh, D., and Pack, S. (2014, June). "Minimizing content download time in mobile collaborative community." *2014 IEEE International Conference on Communications (ICC)* (pp. 2490–2495). IEEE.

[124]. Zhu, M., Li, D., Wang, F., Li, A., Ramakrishnan, K. K., Liu, Y., and Liu, X. (2016). "CCDN: Content-Centric Data Center Networks. *IEEE/ACM Transactions on Networking*, 24(6), 3537–3550.

[125]. Davis, P. E., Dean, S. E., Meliksetian, D. S., Milton, J., Weitzman, L., and Zhou, N. (2006). *U.S. Patent No. 7,076,728*. Washington, DC: U.S. Patent and Trademark Office.

[126]. Hackos, J. T. (2002). *Content Management for Dynamic Web Delivery*. John Wiley and Sons, Inc.

[127]. King, A. (2008). *Website Optimization*. O'Reilly Media, Inc.

[128]. Sundaresan, S., Magharei, N., Feamster, N., and Teixeira, R. (2013). *Characterizing and Mitigating Web Performance Bottlenecks in Broadband Access Networks*. Georgia Institute of Technology.

[129]. Brutlag, J. (2009). *Speed Matters for Google Web Search*.

[130]. "Continuous Code Quality." (n.d.). Retrieved January 07, 2018, from http://www.sonarsource.com/

BIBLIOGRAPHY

[131]. Chu, J., Cheng, Y., Dukkipati, N., and Mathis, M. (2013). "Increasing TCP's initial window."

[132]. Al-Fares, M., Elmeleegy, K., Reed, B., and Gashinsky, I. (2011, November). "Overclocking the Yahoo!: CDN for faster web page loads." *Proceedings of the 2011 ACM SIGCOMM conference on Internet measurement conference* (pp. 569–584). ACM.

[133]. Cohen, E., and Kaplan, H. (2002). "Prefetching the means for document transfer: A new approach for reducing Web latency." *Computer Networks*, 39(4), 437–455.

[134]. Jung, J., Sit, E., Balakrishnan, H., and Morris, R. (2002). "DNS performance and the effectiveness of caching." *IEEE/ACM Transactions on networking*, 10(5), 589–603.

[135]. Palazzi, C. E., Brunati, M., and Roccetti, M. (2010, July). "An OpenWRT solution for future wireless homes." *Multimedia and Expo (ICME), 2010 IEEE International Conference on* (pp. 1701–1706). IEEE.

[136]. Li, Z., Zhang, M., Zhu, Z., Chen, Y., Greenberg, A. G., and Wang, Y. M. (2010, April). "WebProphet: Automating Performance Prediction for Web Services." *NSDI* (Vol. 10, pp. 143–158).

[137]. Wang, X. S., Balasubramanian, A., Krishnamurthy, A., and Wetherall, D. (2013, April). "Demystifying Page Load Performance with WProf." *NSDI* (pp. 473–485).

I. "Internet Explorer 9 Network Performance Improvements." Retrieved November 25, 2016, from http://blogs.msdn.com/b/ie/archive/2011/03/17/internet-explorer-9-network-performance-improvements.aspx.

[138]. Zhou, W., Li, Q., Caesar, M., and Godfrey, P. (2011, December). "ASAP: A low-latency transport layer." *Proceedings of the Seventh Conference on Emerging Networking Experiments and Technologies* (p. 20). ACM.

[139]. Meyerovich, L. A., and Bodik, R. (2010, April). "Fast and parallel webpage layout." *Proceedings of the 19th International Conference on the World Wide Web* (pp. 711–720). ACM.

[140]. Badam, K. (n.d.). "Looking Beyond Page Load Times – How a relentless focus on Task Completion Times can benefit your users." *Velocity New York* 2013. Retrieved January 07, 2018, from http://velocityconf.com/velocityny2013/public/schedule/detail/32820

[141]. Kohavi, R., Deng, A., Frasca, B., Walker, T., Xu, Y., and Pohlmann, N. (2013, August). "Online controlled experiments at large scale." *Proceedings of the 19th ACM SIGKDD international conference on Knowledge discovery and data mining* (pp. 1168-1176). ACM.

[142]. Ash, T., Ginty, M., and Page, R. (2012). *Landing Page Optimization: The Definitive Guide to Testing and Tuning for Conversions.* John Wiley & Sons.

[143]. Stefanov, S. (2012). *Web Performance Daybook* (Vol. 2). O'Reilly Media, Inc.

[144]. Chung, S. (2007, February). "The investigation and classifying the web traffic delay and Solution plans presentation." *Advanced Communication Technology, The 9th International Conference on* (Vol. 2, pp. 1158-1161). IEEE.

[145]. Levering, R., and Cutler, M. (2006, October). "The portrait of a common HTML web page." *Proceedings of the 2006 ACM symposium on Document engineering* (pp. 198-204). ACM.

[146]. Krishnamurthy, B., and Wills, C. E. (2006, May). "Cat and mouse: content delivery tradeoffs in web access." *Proceedings of the 15th international conference on World Wide Web* (pp. 337-346). ACM.

[147]. Habib, M. A., and Abrams, M. (2000, October). "Analysis of Sources of Latency in Downloading Web Pages." *WebNet* (Vol. 227, p. 232).

[148]. Garrett, J. J. (2005). *Ajax: A New Approach To Web Applications.*

[149]. "WebSiteOptimization.com." Retrieved November 29, 2016, from http://www.websiteoptimization.com/speed/tweak/graphic-optimization/

[150]. "WebSiteOptimization.com." Retrieved November 29, 2016, from http://www.websiteoptimization.com/speed/tweak/time-to-first-byte/

[151]. Fan, L., Cao, P., Almeida, J., and Broder, A. Z. (2000). "Summary cache: a scalable wide-area web cache sharing protocol." *IEEE/ACM Transactions on Networking (TON)*, 8(3), 281-293.

[152]. Perkowitz, M., and Etzioni, O. (2000). "Towards adaptive web sites: Conceptual framework and case study." *Artificial intelligence*, 118(1-2), 245-275.

BIBLIOGRAPHY

[153]. Pradhan, R., and Claypool, M. (2001). "Adaptive content delivery for scalable web servers." *Proceedings of the Third International Network Conference (INC2002)* (p. 47). Lulu. com.

[154]. Nagase, F., Hiraguri, T., Nishimori, K., and Makino, H. (2012). *Web Acceleration by Prefetching in Extremely Large Latency Network.*

[155]. Henderson, C. (2006). *Building Scalable Websites.* O'Reilly Media, Inc.

[156]. Gopshtein, M., and Feitelson, D. G. (2010, May). "Empirical quantification of opportunities for content adaptation in web servers." *Proceedings of the 3rd Annual Haifa Experimental Systems Conference* (p. 5). ACM.

[157]. Baeza-Yates, R., and Jonassen, S. (2012, April). "Modeling static caching in web search engines." *European Conference on Information Retrieval* (pp. 436–446).

[158]. Cidon, A., Eisenman, A., Alizadeh, M., and Katti, S. (2015). "Dynacache: Dynamic cloud caching." *7th USENIX Workshop on Hot Topics in Cloud Computing.*

[159]. Desruelle, H., and Gielen, F. (2014). "Context-driven progressive enhancement of mobile web applications: A multi-criteria decision-making approach." *The Computer Journal.*

[160]. Pilgrim, M. (2010). *HTML5: Up and Running.* O'Reilly Media, Inc.

[161]. "Yahoo Developer Network." Retrieved December 11, 2016, from `http://developer.yahoo.com/yslow/`

[162]. "PageSpeed Tools | Google Developers." Retrieved December 11, 2016, from `https://developers.google.com/speed/pagespeed/`

[163]. "HttpWatch 10: HTTP Sniffer for IE, iPhone and iPad." Retrieved December 11, 2016, from `http://www.httpwatch.com/`

[164]. "Fiddler free web debugging proxy." Retrieved December 11, 2016, from `http://www.telerik.com/fiddler`

[165]. "HTTP Archive." Retrieved December 11, 2016, from `http://httparchive.org/`

[166]. "J. Test your JavaScript, CSS, HTML or CoffeeScript online with JSFiddle code editor." Retrieved December 11, 2016, from `https://jsfiddle.net/`

BIBLIOGRAPHY

[167]. "CSS LINT." Retrieved December 11, 2016, from http://csslint.net/

[168]. Crockford, D. "JSLint: The JavaScript Code Quality Tool." Retrieved December 11, 2016, from http://www.jslint.com/

[169]. "CSS Validation Service." Retrieved December 11, 2016, from http://jigsaw.w3.org/css-validator/

[170]. "Markup Validation Service." Retrieved December 11, 2016, from http://validator.w3.org/

[171]. "JavaScript Minify Tool." Retrieved December 11, 2016, from http://www.jsmini.com/

[172]. "JavaScript Compression Tool." Retrieved December 11, 2016, from http://www.jscompress.com/

[173]. "JPEGmini—Your photos on a diet!" Retrieved December 11, 2016, from http://www.jpegmini.com/

[174]. "Smush.it!" Retrieved December 11, 2016, from http://www.imgopt.com/

[175]. R. Rflynn/imgmin. Retrieved December 11, 2016, from https://git.com/rflynn/imgmin

[176]. "Pingdom Tools." Retrieved December 11, 2016, from http://tools.pingdom.com/fpt/

[177]. "Analyze your site's speed and make it faster." Retrieved December 11, 2016, from https://gtmetrix.com/

[178]. "WebPageTest." Retrieved December 11, 2016, from https://www.webpagetest.org/

[179]. "Dynatrace Synthetic Monitoring | Dynatrace." Retrieved December 11, 2016, from https://www.dynatrace.com/platform/offerings/synthetic-monitoring/

[180]. "CSS Sprites Generator v.0.0.2-alfa." Retrieved December 11, 2016, from http://www.csssprites.com/

[181]. "SpriteMe." Retrieved December 11, 2016, from http://www.spriteme.org/

[182]. "The easiest way to create your CSS sprites." Retrieved December 11, 2016, from http://wearekiss.com/spritepad

BIBLIOGRAPHY

[183]. "New Relic: Real User Monitoring (RUM). "Retrieved December 11, 2016, from https://newrelic.com/browser-monitoring

[184]. "Real user monitoring (RUM) | Dynatrace." Retrieved December 11, 2016, from https://www.dynatrace.com/capabilities/real-user-monitoring

[185]. Wireshark, Retrieved December 11, 2016, from https://www.wireshark.org/

[186]. Charles Proxy. Retrieved December 11, 2016, from https://www.charlesproxy.com/

[187]. "New Relic: Application Performance Monitoring." Retrieved December 11, 2016, from https://newrelic.com/application-monitoring

[188]. Schlossnagle, T. (2006). *Scalable Internet Architectures*. Pearson Education.

[189]. "Nagios: The Industry Standard in IT Infrastructure Monitoring." Retrieved December 11, 2016, from https://www.nagios.org/

[190]. Marcotte, E. (2017). *Responsive Web Design: A Book Apart n°4*. Editions Eyrolles.

[191]. "Speed Index: WebPagetest Documentation." Retrieved December 16, 2016, from https://sites.google.com/a/webpagetest.org/docs/using-webpagetest/metrics/speed-index

[192]. Li, M. et al. 2005. "Characteristics of Streaming Media Stored on the Web." *ACM Transactions on Internet Technology* 5(4): 601–626.

[193]. "Checkstyle – Checkstyle 8.7." (n.d.). Retrieved January 07, 2018, from http://checkstyle.sourceforge.net/

[194]. Johnson, D., White, A., and Charland, A. (2007). *Enterprise AJAX: Strategies for Building High Performance Web Applications*. Prentice Hall.

[195]. Bhatti, N., Bouch, A., and Kuchinsky, A. (2000). "Integrating user-perceived quality into web server design." *Computer Networks*, 33(1), 1–16.

[196]. Abbott, M. L., and Fisher, M. T. (2009). *The Art of Scalability: Scalable Web Architecture, Processes, And Organizations for the Modern Enterprise*. Pearson Education.

BIBLIOGRAPHY

[197]. "SteveSouders.com." High Performance Web Sites WPO Web Performance Optimization Comments, www.stevesouders.com/blog/2010/05/07/wpo-web-performance-optimization/

[198]. Iyengar, A., Challenger, J., Dias, D., and Dantzig, P. (2000). "High performance web site design techniques." *IEEE Internet Computing*, 4(2), 17-26.

[199]. Andresen, D., Yang, T., Egecioglu, O., Ibarra, O. H., and Smith, T. R. (1996, May). "Scalability issues for high performance digital libraries on the world wide web." *Digital Libraries, 1996. ADL'96., Proceedings of the Third Forum on Research and Technology Advances in* (pp. 139-148). IEEE.

[200]. Altman, E., Arnold, M., Bordawekar, R., Delmonico, R. M., Mitchell, N., and Sweeney, P. F. (2010). "Observations on tuning a Java enterprise application for performance and scalability." *IBM Journal of Research and Development*, 54(5), 2-1.

[201]. Cardellini, V., Colajanni, M., and Yu, P. S. (1999). "Dynamic load balancing on web-server systems." *IEEE Internet computing*, 3(3), 28-39.

[202]. Pinzger, M. (2008, September). "Automated web performance analysis." *Automated Software Engineering, 2008. ASE 2008. 23rd IEEE/ACM International Conference on* (pp. 513-516). IEEE.

[203]. Stolz, C., Viermetz, M., Skubacz, M., and Neuneier, R. (2005, September). "Guidance Performance Indicator Web Metrics for Information Driven Web Sites." *Proceedings of the 2005 IEEE/WIC/ACM International Conference on Web Intelligence* (pp. 186-192). IEEE Computer Society.

[204]. Ling, P. (2011, August). "Based on web application front-end performance optimization." *Electronic and Mechanical Engineering and Information Technology (EMEIT), 2011 International Conference on* (Vol. 1, pp. 234-237). IEEE.

[205]. Ray, E. T. (2011). *U.S. Patent No. 20130117298A1*. Washington, DC: U.S. Patent and Trademark Office.

[206]. Wei, C., Buffone, R., and Stata, R. (2010). *U.S. Patent No. 20110137973A1*. Washington, DC: U.S. Patent and Trademark Office.

[207]. Lepeska, P., and Sebastian, W. B. (2015). *U.S. Patent No. 9,106,607*. Washington, DC: U.S. Patent and Trademark Office.

BIBLIOGRAPHY

[208]. Coman, M. O., Berkeley, J. R., Guresh, E., Mut, O., Verlaan, A., Gao, Y., and Deshpande, R. R. (2014). *U.S. Patent No. 8,627,204*. Washington, DC: U.S. Patent and Trademark Office.

[209]. Wei, C., Buffone, R., and Stata, R. (2010). *U.S. Patent No. 20110137973A1*. Washington, DC: U.S. Patent and Trademark Office.

[210]. Zhang, X., Wang, N., Vassilakis, V. G., and Howarth, M. P. (2015). "A distributed in-network caching scheme for P2P-like content chunk delivery." *Computer Networks*.

[211]. Jang, I., Suh, D., and Pack, S. (2014). "Minimizing content download time in mobile collaborative community." *IEEE International Conference on Communications (ICC)*.

[212]. Zhu, M., Li, D., Wang, F., Li, A., Ramakrishnan, K. K., Liu, Y., Liu, X. (2016). "CCDN: Content-Centric Data Center Networks." *IEEE/ACM Transactions on Networking IEEE/ACM Trans. Networking*, 1–14.

[213]. Griffin, W. and Jones, B. and Lee, S.K., U.S. Patent No. 11/192,791. Washington, DC: U.S. Patent and Trademark Office.

[214]. Davis, P. E., Dean, S. E., Meliksetian, D. S., Milton, J., Weitzman, L., and Zhou, N. (2006). *U.S. Patent No. 7,076,728*. Washington, DC: U.S. Patent and Trademark Office.

[215]. Baldursson, S. (2004). *U.S. Patent No. 20050064852A1*. Washington, DC: U.S. Patent and Trademark Office.

[216]. Maghoul, F. and Yiu, P. and Davis, M. and Athsani, A. and Yi, J., *U.S. Patent No. 12/240,323*. (n.d.). Washington, DC: U.S. Patent and Trademark Office.

[217]. Douglis, F., Haro, A., and Rabinovich, M. (1997, December). "HPP: HTML Macro-Preprocessing to Support Dynamic Document Caching." *USENIX Symposium on Internet Technologies and Systems* (pp. 83–94).

[218]. Ramaswamy, L., Iyengar, A., Liu, L., and Douglis, F. (2004, May). "Automatic detection of fragments in dynamically generated web pages." *Proceedings of the 13th international conference on World Wide Web* (pp. 443–454). ACM.

[219]. Edge Side Includes. Retrieved January 05, 2018, from http://www.esi.org.

[220]. Gu, P., Wang, J., Zhu, Y., Jiang, H., and Shang, P. (2010). "A novel weighted-graph-based grouping algorithm for metadata prefetching." *IEEE Transactions on Computers*, 59(1), 1-15.

[221]. Bouras, C., Konidaris, A., and Kostoulas, D. (n.d.). "Predictive Prefetching on the Web and Its Potential Impact in the Wide Area." *World Wide Web*, 143-179.

[222]. Datta, A., Dutta, K., Thomas, H., VanderMeer, D., and Ramamritham, K. (2002, June). "Proxy-based acceleration of dynamically generated content on the World Wide Web: an approach and implementation." *Proceedings of the 2002 ACM SIGMOD international conference on Management of data* (pp. 97-108). ACM.

[223]. Mohapatra, P., and Chen, H. (2001). "A framework for managing QoS and improving performance of dynamic Web content." *Global Telecommunications Conference, 2001. GLOBECOM'01. IEEE* (Vol. 4, pp. 2460-2464). IEEE.

[224]. Cao, P., Zhang, J., and Beach, K. (1999). "Active cache: Caching dynamic contents on the web." *Distributed Systems Engineering*, 6(1), 43.

[225]. Christos, B., Vaggelis, K., and Ioannis, M. (2004, April). "Web page fragmentation for personalized portal construction." *Information Technology: Coding and Computing, 2004. Proceedings. ITCC 2004. International Conference on* (Vol. 1, pp. 332-336). IEEE.

[226]. "FindBugs: Find Bugs in Java Programs." (n.d.). Retrieved January 07, 2018, from http://findbugs.sourceforge.net/

[227]. Venkataramani, A., Yalagandula, P., Kokku, R., Sharif, S., and Dahlin, M. (2002). "The potential costs and benefits of long-term prefetching for content distribution." *Computer Communications*, 25(4), 367-375.

[228]. Fan, L., Cao, P., Lin, W., and Jacobson, Q. (1999, May). "Web prefetching between low-bandwidth clients and proxies: potential and performance." *ACM SIGMETRICS Performance Evaluation Review* (Vol. 27, No. 1, pp. 178-187). ACM.

[229]. Khaing, A. A., and Thein, N. L. (2005, November). "Efficiently creating dynamic web content: A fragment based approach." *Information and Telecommunication Technologies, 2005. APSITT 2005 Proceedings. 6th Asia-Pacific Symposium on* (pp. 154-159). IEEE.

BIBLIOGRAPHY

[230]. Brodie, D., Gupta, A., and Shi, W. (2004, May). "Keyword-based fragment detection for dynamic web content delivery." *Proceedings of the 13th international World Wide Web conference on Alternate track papers and posters* (pp. 298–299). ACM.

[231]. Bruck, P. A., Motiwalla, L., and Foerster, F. (2012, June). "Mobile Learning with Micro-content: A Framework and Evaluation." *Bled eConference* (p. 2).

[232]. Nagler, W., Ebner, M., and Sherbakov, N. (2007). "Flexible teaching with structured micro-content-How to structure content for sustainable multiple usage with recombinable character." *Conference ICL2007*, September 26–28, 2007 (pp. 8–pages). Kassel University Press.

[233]. Candan, K. S., Agrawal, D., Li, W. S., Po, O., and Hsiung, W. P. (2002, August). "View invalidation for dynamic content caching in multitiered architectures." *Proceedings of the 28th international conference on Very Large Data Bases* (pp. 562–573). VLDB Endowment.

[234]. "Eclipse." (n.d.). Retrieved January 07, 2018, from `https://www.eclipse.org/`

[235]. Chan, M. C., and Woo, T. Y. (1999, March). "Cache-based compaction: A new technique for optimizing web transfer." INFOCOM'99. Eighteenth Annual Joint Conference of the IEEE Computer and Communications Societies. Proceedings. IEEE (Vol. 1, pp. 117–125). IEEE.

[236]. Naaman, M., Garcia-Molina, H., and Paepcke, A. (2004). "Evaluation of ESI and class-based delta encoding." *Web Content Caching and Distribution*, 323–343.

[237]. Kotz, D., and Ellis, C. S. (1993). "Practical prefetching techniques for multiprocessor file systems." *Distributed and Parallel Databases*, 1(1), 33–51.

[238]. Lei, H., and Duchamp, D. (1997, January). "An analytical approach to file prefetching." *USENIX Annual Technical Conference* (pp. 275–288).

[239]. Lee, H. K., An, B. S., and Kim, E. J. (2009, July). "Adaptive prefetching scheme using web log mining in Cluster-based web systems." *Web Services, 2009. ICWS 2009. IEEE International Conference* (pp. 903–910). IEEE.

[240]. Yang, Q., Zhang, H. H., and Li, T. (2001, August). "Mining web logs for prediction models in WWW caching and prefetching." *Proceedings of the seventh ACM SIGKDD international conference on Knowledge discovery and data mining* (pp. 473–478). ACM.

[241]. Shailesh, K. S., and Suresh, P. V. (2017). "An analysis of techniques and quality assessment for Web performance optimization." *Indian Journal of Computer Science and Engineering (IJCSE)*, 8, 61–69.

[242]. Shailesh, K. S., and P. V. Suresh. "Performance driven development framework for web applications." *Global Journal of Enterprise Information System* 9.1 (2017): 75–84.

[243]. Shivakumar, Shailesh, and Venkata Suresh Pachigolla. "MCWDF: Micro Chunk Based Web Delivery Framework." *International Journal of Information Technology and Web Engineering (IJITWE)* 13.1 (2018): 1–19.

[244]. Shailesh, K. S., and Suresh Pachigolla Venkata. "Personalized Chunk Framework for High Performance Personalized Web." *International Journal of Web Portals (IJWP)* 9.1 (2017): 52–63.

Index

A

Amazon CloudWatch, 342
Amazon Simple Queue Service, 312
Angular-based solution architecture, 265
Apache Server Log Files, 188
Application performance
    monitoring (APM), 192
Application performance testing
    (APT), 390, 391
Application server configuration checklist
    cache settings, 367
    container thread pool, 367
    data source connection pool, 367
    JVM heap size, 367
    server infrastructure, 367
    server monitoring, 367
Application under test (AUT), 398
App shell, 281, 282
AWS microservice architecture, 340, 341

B

Business components performance
    analysis, 249
Business process, 398

C

Cache-aside pattern, 286, 290
    advantages, 290
    considerations, 288
    context, 286
    drivers, 286
    high-level flow, 287
    solution, 287
    tools and technologies, 290
    variations, 289, 290
Cache configuration analysis, 251
Cache warming, 311
Change data capture (CDC)
    pattern, 304, 324
Client-side caching, 251
Client-side rendering (CSR), 280, 286
    app shell, 281, 282
    service worker, 280, 281
Cloud-first approach, 275
CloudFront CDN, 341
Column store pattern, 320
Compensating transaction pattern, 310
Content delivery network (CDN), 18, 251
Content management server (CMS)
    Layer, 22
Content optimization, 65
Continuous integration and continuous
    development (CICD) setup, 209, 340
Couchbase, 320
CPU usage guidelines, 384
CQRS pattern, 308, 313, 314, 325, 338
    advantages, 313
    components, 309
    drivers, 308, 309
    solution description, 310, 311

INDEX

D

Database performance analysis, 250
Database performance optimization
    DB2 performance tuning
        checklist, 375–377
    Oracle performance-tuning
        checklist, 369–374
Database per service, 337
Data lake design pattern, 314, 316–318
    advantages, 317
    applications, 316
    considerations, 316, 317
    data ingestion, 315
    data processing, 316
    data sources, 315
    drivers, 314
    sample data lake architecture, 315
    tools and technologies, 318
Data partitioning, 304
Data-related antipatterns, 302
DB2 performance tuning checklist
    DB2 monitoring configurations, 376, 377
    key DB2 performance-tuning
        parameters, 375, 376
    performance-tuning
        considerations, 375
Decomposition patterns
    business capabilities, 337
    business subdomains, 337
    business transactions, 337
    resources, 337
    services needed by UI components, 337
DevOps
    agile delivery steps, 130, 131
    CICD setup, 128, 129
    cloud-native DevOps platform, 127
DevOps layer, 340

Disaster Recovery (DR) Strategy, 204
    preparation phase, 204
    recovery phase, 204
Distributed enterprise systems, 323
Domain-driven design (DDD), 330, 356

E

Early warning system (EWS)
    implementation
        applications monitoring, 236
        health check/heartbeat
            monitoring, 235
        Splunk-based Error Reporting, 236
        synthetic monitoring, 236
        System and Service Availability
            Monitoring, 235
E-commerce order management, 322
Endurance testing, 71
Event-driven architecture (EDA), 347, 351
    advantages, 351
    considerations, 350
    context, 347
    event broker, 350
    event consumers, 350
    event mesh architecture, 349
    event producers, 350
    tools and frameworks, 352
    vs. SOA, 348
Event mesh architecture, 349
Event sourcing pattern, 309, 310,
        313, 314, 338
    advantages, 313
    components, 310, 311

F

Functions as a service (FaaS), 332

INDEX

G

Generic performance optimizations, 374
Google Web Analytics (GWA), 248
GraphQL, 352, 353, 357
    advantages, 353
    considerations, 353
    drivers, 352
    solution, 352
    tools and frameworks, 353
Graph store pattern, 320

H

Higher-order components (HOCs), 87

I

Index table pattern, 304
Infrastructure analysis
    cache configuration analysis, 251
    capacity and network analysis, 250
    infrastructure recommendations, 251, 252
    server configuration analysis, 251
Infrastructure layer
    hardware servers, 24
    load balance, 24
    network optimization, 24
    protocol optimization, 24
Infrastructure planning
    DR strategy, 204
        preparation phase, 204
        recovery phase, 204
    initial infrastructure sizing process
        define, 202
        Generic n-tier enterprise infrastructure, 202
    NFRs
        application growth rate, 197
        archival requirements, 199
        auditing and logging, 198
        availability, 196
        data security, 197
        define, 196
        internalization requirements, 200
        multitenancy requirements, 200
        performance requirements, 200
        scalability requirements, 200
    process of, 201
Infrastructure testing, 71
In-memory database (IMDB), 305
Isomorphic pattern, 294, 297
    advantages, 297
    considerations, 296
    context, 294
    drivers, 295
    solution, 295, 296
    tools and technologies, 297

J

Java performance checklist, 363–365
JavaScript framework, 247
Java Server Pages (JSP), 246, 247
Java virtual memory (JVM) parameters, 181
JDBC performance checklist, 366
JSP-based web page performance optimization, 365

K

Key-value store pattern, 320

423

INDEX

L

Layer-wise building blocks
    enterprise platforms layer, 113
    middleware layer, 113
    presentation layer, 112
Load testing, 70, 249, 252–256, 269, 388
Log aggregation, 338

M

Marketing and customer data
        management, 323
Materialized view pattern, 303
Medium-term performance plan, 264
Memory leak analysis
    checklist, 366, 367
Microservice patterns, 332, 344
    access token, 337
    advantages, 343
    API gateway pattern, 336
    application metrics, 338
    blue-green deployment model, 339
    circuit breaker, 335
    considerations, 342, 343
    context, 333
    database patterns, 337, 338
    decomposition patterns, 337
    drivers, 334
    exception tracking pattern, 338
    externalized configuration, 338
    health check API pattern, 338
    log aggregation, 338
    microservice ecosystem, 339–342
    saga pattern, 338
    server-side page fragment composition
        pattern, 339
    service discovery pattern, 334, 335
    service integration contract test, 339
    service monitoring, 338
    technology choices, 344–347
    tools and frameworks, 344
    user experience layer, 340
    variations, 343
Microservices architecture, 10
Microservices model, 265, 266
Microsoft Active Directory (AD), 247
Minimalistic design, 276
Mobile-first approach, 276
Mobile web framework
    Angular framework
        ahead-of-time (AoT) compilation, 82
        async attribute, 83
        remove unused code, 82
        service workers, 82
        UI thread, 83
        unit testing, 82
    Angular, React, and Vue, 80
    design phase
        atomic design pattern, 87
        CommonsChunkPlugins, 89
        container components, 88
        HOCs, 87
        immutable objects, 89
        lint command, 88
        React UI frameworks, 86
        remove unused code, 88
        run build command, 88
        throttling and debouncing, 89
        Using React fragment, 89
    HTML5
        element attributes, 101
        hardware acceleration, 101
        initialization, 101
        localStorage and
            sessionStorage, 101
        multimedia files, 101

INDEX

JavaScript frameworks
    compression algorithm, 91
    critical rendering path, 96
    data stream, 95
    domain sharding, 92
    font optimizations, 94
    HTTP/2, 95
    HTTP cache, 93
    image optimizations, 93
    links and images, 94
    profiling tools, 96
    progressive web apps (PWA), 93
    SEO, 95
    server-side rendering, 92
    SSG, 97
    video optimizations, 94
    web worker model, 92
Network performance optimizations
    Browser Rendering Stages, 98
    bundle size, 83
    implementation, 99
    key resources, 97
    lazily load, 84, 90
    middleware, 90
    minification, 83
    Network Timing, 100
    prefetch application, 84
    remove unnecessary methods, 84
Runtime performance optimizations
    AoT compilation, 85
    cache function, 91
    change detection, 85
    enableProdMode, 85
    production mode, 91
    Pure attribute, 86
    shell architecture, 85
    shouldComponentUpdate() method, 90

Model-view-controller (MVC) architecture, 9
Modern web data patterns
    common data patterns
        CDC pattern, 304
        data partitioning, 304
        data streaming pattern, 304
        eventual consistency pattern, 304
        idempotent transactions, 304
        IMDB, 305
        index table pattern, 304
        materialized view pattern, 303
    CQRS pattern and event sourcing pattern, 308–314
    data lake design pattern, 314–318
    data-related antipatterns, 302
    data-related best practices, 302, 303
    modern web scenarios, 322–324
    NoSQL pattern, 318–322
    saga pattern, 305–308
Modern web design
    Angular-based modern web application, 118
    Angular framework
        Angular app modules, 120
        Async services, 121
        components, 120
        interface, 120
        payload, 121
        Request processing, 119
        state management, 120
    applications
        extensibility, 136
        integration modules, 139
        maintainability, 136
        principles, 136
        responsive design, 135
        single code base, 135

INDEX

Modern web design (*cont.*)
    SRP principle, 134
    testability, 135
  business imperative
    DevOps, 114
    enterprise integrations, 114
    methods of, 115
    omnichannel user experience, 114
  core capability, 110
  digital delivery channel, 105
  implementation
    DevOps, 127
    Key Governance Metrics, 132
    tools, 125, 126
  key drivers, 107
  layer-wise building blocks, 112
    enterprise platforms layer, 113
    middleware layer, 113
    presentation layer, 112
  modern web architecture, 116
  principles of, 122
  PWAs, 134
  request processing, 117
  vs. Traditional Web, 106
Modern web integration patterns
  EDA, 347–351
  GraphQL, 352, 353
  integration-related antipatterns, 328, 329
  integration-related best practices and common patterns
    API first approach, 331
    asynchronous invocation, 330
    back end for front end, 331
    canonical data model, 329
    contract-first approach, 332
    data load on demand, 331
    DDD, 330
    façade pattern, 330
    lazy loading, 330
    mini service design, 331
    multispeed services, 332
    offline-first approach, 332
    retry pattern, 329
    serverless functions, 332
    WebRTC, 331
    WebSockets, 330
  microservice patterns, 332–347
  modern web scenarios, 354, 355
  network-related antipatterns, 328
Modern web performance patterns
  cache-aside pattern, 286–290
  common performance antipatterns, 274, 275
    resource-related antipatterns, 274
    testing-related antipatterns, 274
  common presentation patterns
    cloud-first approach, 275
    micro frontends, 277
    minimalistic design, 276
    mobile-first approach, 276
    network independent design, 276
    page templates, 275
    resource prefetching, 275
    separation of concerns, 276
    SPA, 276
    UI composition pattern, 275
  isomorphic pattern, 294–297
  modern web scenarios, 298
  presentation layer best practices, 277, 278
  PRPL pattern, 290–294
  PWA, 278–286
MongoDB, 320
Multispeed services, 332
MVC and model–view–view model (MVVM), 10

N

Network-related antipatterns, 328
Non-functional requirements (NFR), 187, 244
NoSQL pattern, 318, 321, 325
　advantages, 321
　column store pattern, 320
　considerations, 321
　document store pattern, 320
　drivers, 319
　features, 319
　graph store pattern, 320
　key-value store pattern, 320
　tools and frameworks, 322

O

Oracle performance-tuning checklist, 369
　delete statement optimization, 373
　generic performance optimizations, 374
　insert statement optimization, 372
　optimization of joins, 373
　select query optimization, 369–371
　update statement optimization, 372

P, Q

Page load time (PLT), 14
Page response time (PRT), 14
Page templates, 275
Performance engineering, 243, 269
　availability analysis, 257
　bottleneck analysis, 257
　common performance problem pattern
　　application, 257
　　suboptimal deployment architecture, 258, 259
　high-level flow, 246
　infrastructure analysis
　　cache configuration analysis, 251
　　capacity and network analysis, 250
　　infrastructure recommendations, 251, 252
　　server configuration analysis, 251
　iterative performance test execution, 245
　long-term plan
　　angular platform, 264, 265
　　architecture principles, for modern solution, 266–268
　　microservices model, 265, 266
　medium-term performance plan, 264
　performance analysis and recommendation, 245
　performance optimization recommendations
　　server-side, 260–262
　　web, 259, 260
　performance testing, 252–256
　performance test strategy and design, 244, 245
　process, 244
　report, 245
　requirements and KPI definition, 244
　short-term plan, 263
　technology eco system
　　database components, 247
　　infrastructure components, 247
　　presentation components, 246
　　security components, 247
　　service components, 247
　web performance analysis, 247

427

INDEX

Performance engineering (*cont.*)
    business components performance analysis, 249
    database performance analysis, 250
    page load times and page size analysis for key pages, 247
    presentation component analysis, 248
    service performance analysis, 249
    web analytics report analysis, 248
    web frameworks and JavaScript framework, 247

Performance monitoring metrics
  APM
    health-check monitor, 193
    monitoring setup, 193
    real-time performance monitoring, 194
  business metrics, 181
  monitoring
    API and Service monitoring, 190
    application topology, 190
    cloud monitoring, 191
    containers monitoring, 192
    continuous monitoring, 187
    database monitoring, 190
    dependent system monitoring, 190
    error monitoring, 189
    heartbeat monitoring, 188
    log monitoring, 188
    mobile monitoring, 190
    real time notification, 188
    security monitoring, 192
    SLAs, 187
    synthetic topology, 191
    virtual machine monitoring, 191
  RUM, 195
  server metrics
    Cache Parameters, 181
    connection pool size, 181
    JVM, 181
    number of sessions, 180
    thread pool size, 180
  service metrics, 176
    error-handling, 178
    latency, 176
    throughput, 178
  system metrics
    network metrics, 180
    resource metrics, 179
  Tools and Frameworks, 184
  web metrics, 183

Performance optimization checklist
  application server configuration, 367
  Java performance checklist, 363–365
  JDBC performance checklist, 366
  memory leak analysis checklist, 366, 367
  performance testing checklist, 359–363

Performance optimization recommendations
  server-side, 260–262
  web, 259, 260

Performance testing, 252, 269, 389, 391, 398
  concurrent user testing, 256
  design, 253
  execution, 253, 254
  isolated load test, 255
  load testing and stress testing, 254–256
  mixed load distribution, 255
  response time report, 256
  risk mitigation plan, 397
  sample mixed load testing results, 256
  sample ramp-up test, 254
  tools, 252

INDEX

Performance testing checklist
    execution, 362
    pre-execution, 361, 362
    reporting, 362, 363
    scripting batch transactions, 360
    scripting web transactions, 360
Performance test report template, 383
    application design tuning opportunities, 382
    architectural model, 381
    automation tools, 381
    database/SQL tuning, 382
    objectives, 380
    performance monitoring tools, 381
    performance testing dependencies assumptions, 381
    performance test results and observations, 382
    recommendations and benefits, 383
    scope, 380
Performance test strategy template
    application monitoring parameters, 393, 394
    application monitoring tools, 393
    database tuning support, 389
    data setup, 389
    design, 392
    enterprise applications, 388
    entry criteria, 388, 396, 397
    environment setup, 389
    execution cycles, 394, 395
    exit criterion, 388
    infrastructure setup, 389
    integration tested code, 389
    objectives, 385–387
    performance data capture and performance report generation support, 389
    post execution performance tuning, 396
    requirement gathering
        batch application, 392
        online application, 391
    test data set, 389
    test execution contingency planning, 397
    test result capture guidelines, 396
    tools, 392, 393
Presentation component analysis, 248
Presentation layer best practices, 277, 278
Proactive monitoring and alerting setup
    alert manager, 209
    application monitoring, 209
    components, 207
    container pod monitoring, 208
    database monitoring, 209
    features, 206
    log monitoring, 209
Product data management, 322
Progressive web architecture (PWA) patterns, 134
    advantages, 284, 285
    considerations, 283, 284
    context, 279
    CSR, 280
        app shell, 281, 282
        service worker, 280, 281
    drivers, 279
    features, 278
    high-level flow, 282, 283
    SSR, 279, 280
    tools and technologies, 286
    variations, 284
Push, render, precache, and lazy load (PRPL) pattern, 290, 292–294, 300
    advantages, 293, 294

429

INDEX

Push, render, precache, and lazy load
        (PRPL) pattern (*cont.*)
    considerations, 293
    context, 291
    drivers, 291
    solution, 291, 292
    tools and technologies, 294
    variations, 293

R

Real user monitoring (RUM), 195
Resource prefetching, 275
Resource-related antipatterns, 274
Responsive web applications (RWA), 278
Responsive web design (RWD), 276

S

Saga pattern, 308, 324, 338
    advantages, 307
    choreography, 306, 307
    considerations, 307
    drivers, 305
    orchestration, 306
    solution, 306
    tools and frameworks, 308
Scripting batch transactions, 360
Scripting web transactions, 360
Search engine optimization (SEO), 95
Select query optimization, 369–371
Server configuration analysis, 251
Server-side caching, 251
Server-side performance optimization,
        260–262
Server-side rendering (SSR), 279, 280, 286
Service discovery pattern, 334, 335
Service-oriented architecture (SOA), 348

Service performance analysis, 249
Service worker, 280, 281
Shared database, 338
Short-term performance plan, 263
Single-page application (SPA), 276, 277
Social media content
        management, 322
Spike testing, 71
Spring Boot, 342, 344
Static site generators (SSG), 97
Stress testing, 70, 254, 269
Systems of record (SORs), 305

T

Testing-related antipatterns, 274
Time to first byte (TTFB)
        optimization, 44
Top-down performance optimization
        steps, 62
Transaction, 398

U

UI composition pattern, 275

V

Virtual user, 398

W, X, Y, Z

Web analytics report analysis, 248
Web-oriented architecture (WOA), 10
Web performance analysis, 247
    business components performance
        analysis, 249
    database performance analysis, 250

INDEX

page load times and page size analysis for key pages, 247
presentation component analysis, 248
service performance analysis, 249
web analytics report analysis, 248
web frameworks and JavaScript framework, 247
Web performance maturity model, 76
Web performance optimization recommendations, 259, 260
Web performance optimization (WPO)
  architecture
    lean architecture, 238–240
    performance-by-design, 241
  categories of, 5
  components, 3
  early warning system (EWS), 234
  high-level architecture, 216
  impact of, 5
  key challenges, 218
  key components, 218
  key page, 221
  key parameters, 225
  layers
    application server layer, 20
    CDN layer, 18
    CMS layer, 22
    database server layer, 21
    end-to-end flow, 16
    enterprise interface layer, 21
    file storage server layer, 22
    infrastructure layer, 23
    user-agent layer, 18
    web server layer, 19
  layer-wise performance assessment, 223, 224
  lifecycle stages
    design of, server calls, 12

    development phase, 12
    performance design patterns, 11
    performance monitoring, 13
    performance testing, 13
    web architecture patterns, 9
    web performance patterns, 8
  Page Metrics, 225
  performance assessment checklist, 221, 222
  performance assessment scope, 219
  presentation layer
    AJAX calls, 231
    Cache static assets, 231
    components, 227
    CSS file, 227
    duplicate calls, 230
    duplicate files loaded, 230
    duplicate functions, 230
    errors, 229
    Height and Width of Images, 229
    HTML compression, 228
    JS files, 228
    Minimize HTTP Calls, 226
    multiple domains, 229
    scripts, 227
  server layer, 226
    database optimizations, 231
    infrastructure optimizations, 233
    server code optimizations, 233
    service optimizations, 232
  server-side components, 238
  taxonomy of, 7
  Tools to Improve Performance, 234
  top-down approach, 220
  web performance governance
    KPIs, 13
    monitoring, 16

431

INDEX

Web performance optimization
(WPO) (*cont.*)
    page load times, 16
    SLAs, 13
    web page metrics, 14
Web performance optimization (WPO)
    framework
    Bottleneck and Antipatterns, 63
        asset optimization
           techniques, 67
        content optimization, 65
        impact of, assets, 66
        performance matrix, 64
    design phase
        principles, 57
        rules, 55
        tools, 59
        web performance principles, 58
    lifecycle stages, 53
    reference architecture, 50, 51
    UI optimizations, 59, 60
    Web performance governance
        define, 73, 74
        dimensions, 74
        reference solution
           implementing, 75
    web performance maturity
        model, 76
    web performance monitoring
        multi-geo monitoring, 72
        performance tracking, 72
        process, 72
        real-time monitoring, 72
    web performance testing
        dimensions of, 70
        infrastructure testing, 71
        load testing, 70
        transactions and processes, 71

Web performance optimization
(WPO) methods
    Bottlenecks and Performance
        Patterns, 37
    cache architecture, 39
    caching and prefetching, 39
    cloud-based web applications, 45
    content chunking method, 43
    end-to-end tool, 45
    mobile devices, 44
    network and request processing
        DNS records, 44
        TTFB, 44
    prefetching techniques, 41
    techniques, 35
    tools, 29
    troubleshooting and
        analyzing, 45
Web Performance Validation
    activities and deliverables, 157
    data details, 155
    define, 147
    generic requirements, 154
    goals, 155
    infrastructure, 154
    issues, 152
    key performance metrics, 151
    mobile apps, 161
        hybrid mobile apps, 163
        mobile web application, 162
        native mobile apps, 163
        non-functional testing, 163
    performance testing maturity
        model, 171
    phases of, 156
    solution ecosystem, 154
    tools, 160, 161
    trends, 149

types of, 150
user profile, 154
web performance prediction
    model, 159
web performance test
    methodology, 167
  continuous performance
    testing, 169, 170
workload modeling
  application and load analysis, 165

key business scenarios, 166
Load Distribution, 166
needs, 164
process of, 165
user and data load
    analysis, 165
workload template, 167
Web real-time communication
    (WebRTC), 331
WebSockets, 330

Printed in the United States
By Bookmasters